SEE

THE GOLDEN THREADS

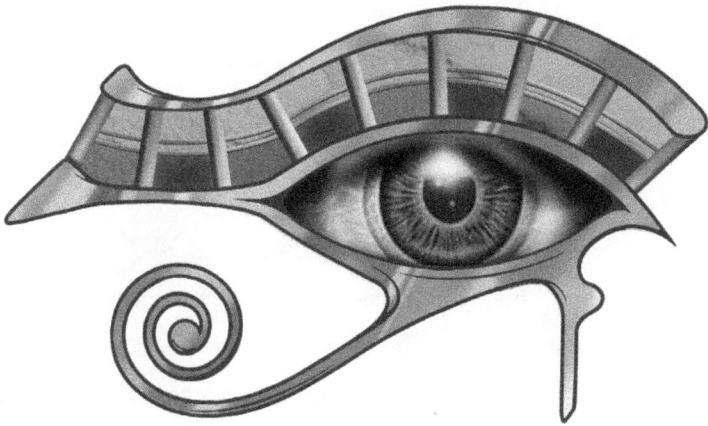

KEVIN WESTRICH

RT
PUBLISHING

RTH Publishing

Red Tailed Hawk Publishing

PO Box 2023, Sedona, Arizona 86340

SEE the GOLDEN THREADS

Copyright 2024 by Kevin Westrich

Cover & Interior Design: Peggy Sands, Indigo Designo

Cover Head Shot: Barbra Noh

Interior Photos: Kevin Westrich

This book is a work of nonfiction.
Only names of the people within this book have
been changed, as a courtesy for their privacy.

ISBN: 978-0-9892954-2-0

DEDICATION

To my reader I hope you enjoy what I have written.

And

To those who have accompanied me along my journey.

*For it is those shared experiences, that brought into my
life a tapestry of lessons and joys.*

I am most grateful!

Also

*I thank SPIRIT that animates my very existence and I
look forward to our deepening connection.*

*I have the greatest of Gratitude and Thanks for those
who are also to enter my story.*

Love and Light

ALSO BY KEVIN WESTRICH:

TRUST, PATIENCE, SURRENDER
Moments of Illumination and Grace

CONTENTS

version 2

Contents, cont'd

THANK YOU

To Barbara and Charles S. for seeing that I was to live in the
beautiful hacienda in Sedona.

To Linda for holding space for me unconditionally.

Laura, for our final dance.

To the many others, who are to many to name,
my deepest gratitude.

Joseph Grey Wolf, my deceased friend and brother
on the Red Road.

Grandfather Morning Owl, who allowed me to fly.

Jodi N., for Rocky and Buck. They were just what I needed.

Lorraine R., who has shown me light along the way.

To the women who have been my teachers and lovers.

Peter and Lynn M., Founders of the Pyramids of Chi in Bali.

Day S., Who pulled me from the disaster in Jakarta.

Judy B., who challenged me beyond reason.

Peggy, as always your design skills and your talents bring me joy!

Editor., who wishes to remain anonymous.

Barbra N., for the photos at the pyramids.

SEE

THE GOLDEN THREADS

*The pineal gland has a romantic history, from pharaonic Egypt,
where it was equated with the eye of Horus, through various religious
traditions, where it was considered the seat of the soul or the third eye.
[https://pubmed.ncbi.nlm.nih.gov/29095071/]*

"The Unexamined Life is not worth Living." Socrates

Introduction

"There is no Secret truth, only truths we refuse to acknowledge. Truth undermines the self to which we so desperately cling. The Truth is not hidden from us. We are hiding from it."
    ~REB YERACHMIEL BEN YISREAL

There is so much I wish to share with my readers. This book is a continuation of the ideas I presented in my previous book, *Trust Patience Surrender: Moments of Illumination and Grace* (although you do not have to have read *Trust Patience Surrender* to read this book). The upcoming chapters are filled with my life's synchronicities, new awareness of the Divine Mother, Mother Nature (Gaia), soul contracts, past life encounters, pyramids in Bali, and divine guidance and grace. This book will reveal a deeper connection to my son, my deceased brother, and my mother. These experiences are a continuation of moments where the divine touched my life while opening me to an ever expanding awareness of the world of experiences.

My hope is that the words I've placed on the page give you a sense of truth. A truth that is inside each of us. Rather than take what I am about to share as *your* truth, I suggest you allow the words, feelings, and experiences to percolate within you so that you can see how they fit into your own life.

I trust one thing, and it is this: An individual truth. As you enter your own journey of learning and self-discovery, you will know your own connection to your truth. This I know, and I am ecstatic to be a part of it. I ask that you measure the content of this book against your own experiences. They will bear out your truth of understanding. It is also my hope that the stories and experiences I've shared will give you insights into your own life. If you are someone of total disbelief, my hope is that these words open a window of opportunity to seeing within your world. An opportunity to make deeper, more exploratory queries. I wish for you to open your heart and your feeling state. Because I'm still exploring this concept, as of today my understanding of the heart is that it is the window to our soul, our connection to source and all that is. I know of two ways of arriving there. One is through a moment of grace. The other is through our emotional body and feeling state.

My experiences have continually proven to be quite fruitful and purposeful in giving me a greater understanding into my own life and my relation to this world and beyond. They have guided me into a deeper, fuller understanding of Life's gifts and joys and the ability to see— even with pain present, at times—all is part of Love and the great Mystery. It is Love asking us to see it from many different viewpoints, such as kindness and compassion, universal love, redemptive love, hot sweaty love, and much more. Seeing all is a gift given.

Along the way, I have consulted AstroCartography and astrology charts, along with seers and psychics. In thirty-plus years of experience, what I have come to learn is that some seers and psychics are connected and gifted, and others are not so gifted. Listen to your intuition to see if what they are sharing resonates with you. With time and experience, you will be able to discern quickly whether or not the person comes across as legitimate.

Another awareness that dawned on me through the course of my life is that what seers and psychics have to share should be viewed with a sense of discernment and openness toward viewing the information they are sharing, what I call guideposts and signs. Use them as a guide but not as 100% truth for your life. Allowing what they have shared gives you a framework. Otherwise, you might try to literally follow their recommendations and potentially miss or postpone something vital to you.

Opening myself to the deeper sense of self and my connection to others has given me a glimpse of the "Love and Light" that is always present if we choose to be open to it. Having lived a good many years has helped me to understand my relationship to the divine and my relationship of co-creation within myself, others, and God source.

All of the stories you're about to read are my truth of understanding. All are as factual as my notes and memories bear out over this period of my life. I have tried to recreate the experience, feelings, and wisdom that I extracted. Know that these are mine, and mine alone. You may find a similarity with my journey in your own life, or this book may begin to activate the opening of a pathway of self-discovery and your connection to all that is. My final hope is that your life becomes a fuller, more open authentic version and expression of you and your relation to all that is.

A couple of caveats:

- My whole world could change at 2:00 tomorrow. In other words, everything that I know could, at any moment, become completely and radically different from what I currently know and understand.

- "The more I know, the less I know." This leaves me with an openness that always holds me in an expansive space of exploration and discovery. I have a sense of the beauty in all of this, a sense that my life is a journey from the unknown into the known. It's a remembering, of sorts. Seeing it is an ever-expanding gift given.

I hold several other truths. One is that fear of the unknown will, at times, try to drive you back to an old understanding of beliefs and to old patterns you held. Once you have tasted the sweetness of new understandings, I urge you not to go back to your old beliefs. The most important thing to remember is to check into your intuition and feeling state, ensuring that energies between you and others seem to flow effortlessly, and then step into the fear. After some time of developing your intuition and feeling in your body, particularly in your heart and gut, you will have a sense of feeling heard and safe.

The reality is, some people's energies are quite argumentative and crass. You must develop an inner knowing of safety that comes with experiences. From there, you can step into the fear, as long as you are safe. Simply meet it, no matter how big or small the fear appears to be. Some of the greatest understandings come when the fear is the greatest. It is my belief that you will come into discovering that fear, simply wanting to see beyond your current level of awareness and see a greater wisdom within yourself.

This is not for the weak of heart, for it takes courage and strength. Trust that the journey gets easier with time. Over time, you'll find that you don't need to try so hard. It's a surrender or a softening, if you will.

Another truth I hold is that when the frequency of Love, or vibration of Love, is present, you are invited to meet it. This too can be a bit tenuous and frightening. You are being asked to meet it, for it is the core of all that exists. Love, that vibratory force, simply wishes to meet itself. Co-creation is at the very core and fabric of our lives. You will come to understand that these experiences are of both the "Light" and the "Dark." Each having their own purpose reveals a greater wholeness of this world of duality, which ultimately leads to a new wisdom.

I am also reminded of a good friend of mine and psychic who shared another piece of wisdom that I hold as truth today. After a long period of time off, she shared that she had stopped doing readings with people for two reasons. One was that people wanted answers but didn't want to do the work. The other is that people being read changed their trajectory—that is, their direction and desire. Wrapping it with their heart's longing and emotions, they would be lead onto that new path. It was simply another trajectory. As a result, some clients would return to my friend, saying that what she read about them didn't come true. They would be slightly agitated. Her first question was, "Have your desires or feelings changed?"

I invite you to read the following stories and experiences from a place of curiosity and openness, and see where the journey takes you. Most importantly, enjoy this life as much as possible, allowing the idea or belief that everything given is from Love. Love in expression. Love of learning, Love of remembering, and Love of Joy!

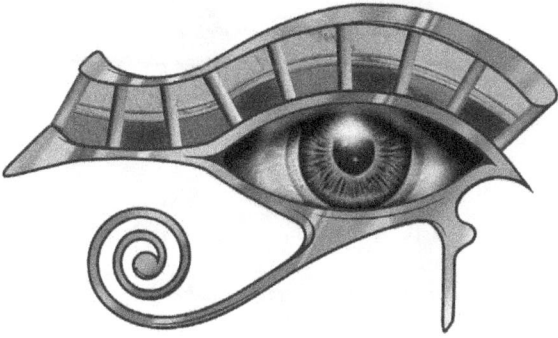

CHAPTER 1

Chapter 1: The Time is Now

"As you start the walk on the way, the way appears." ~Rumi

A Brief Recap

I was set on writing this book after I completed *Trust Patience Surrender*, but daily life took over. It has been a few years, and it seems the time is now. To give you a sense of how this will provide a bit of completion to some areas and a whole new start to others, I want to give a recap of what was going on at the end of my last writing.

For one year I lamented and suffered at the ending of my relationship with Sarah, a woman with whom I'd been deeply involved on both a spiritual and physical level—but it had to be. Oftentimes I beat myself up, asking the question, "What have I done?" Our love was that of fairy tales. As well, I'd had a near-death experience, and when I came out of it, I remember quite clearly God saying, "Do not become attached to her; she has her own journey."

This decision pained me for a full year; oftentimes, I fell asleep with tears welling up. At the end of that twelve months, I simply found it so hard to let go that I pleaded with spirit, "Please let me see what there is to see, learn what it is to learn, but I can't do this anymore."

As I lay there, ready to fall asleep, I heard this voice, an inner knowing, saying with clarity, "How do you love yourself that much? She was your teacher. For you both asked of me to give you incarnate love, and that's what you received, so you would know its power."

God was asking me, "How does one care and nurture oneself in a loving manner, caring for the body, mind, emotions, and spirit?" This was an internal knowing, an inner counselor who told me that Sarah had been reflecting back to myself, in order to see how I can place such care and attention upon myself.

So many people try to please others, trying to make the world around them happy and safe for all. There is virtue in that, but sometimes we give far too much of ourselves. We need to ask ourselves if we are giving to and nurturing ourselves equally.

In that moment, my breath deepened and a wave of truth flowed through my body. I could feel the presence of truth running through me. I sighed with relief, as though all of the past lives Sarah and I had shared simply lifted from my shoulders and dissolved.

As I allowed this to happen, I also realized that I wanted to share this newfound wisdom with Sarah. So, I called her and asked to meet for lunch.

Somehow, when Sarah arrived, she intuited my newfound realization, just like she always had in the past. As soon as we sat down at the table, she looked deep within my eyes, as though she was looking into my soul.

"You don't need me anymore. Do you?" she asked.

"No," I replied. "I don't, but I love you with all of my being, knowing that you and I are walking on planet earth once more."

I was filled with joy and release. We both sighed a great release. It felt as though all karma between us had been completed, leaving me with a sense of unconditional love.

Another powerful experience resulted from me sharing nine pages of channeling I'd written sometime earlier. This occurred on a flight. I'd been in Santa Monica to look for a place to establish a retreat center. To return home to Sedona, I had to fly from Los Angeles to Phoenix.

As I walked to the boarding gate to catch my flight, I noticed I was being followed by a middle-aged woman. From time to time, she moved through the area as I did. I wasn't quite sure how to take it, so I simply acknowledged the situation and kept it in the back of my mind. I also caught her sneaking an occasional glance at me. It seemed as though she had something to share, and it felt like more than a glimpse of potential affection. But several times when I saw her gazing at me for an extended period of time, I began to wonder what her story was.

When it came time to board, I noticed she had disappeared, only to see her reappear on my flight. If that wasn't enough of a coincidence, she ended up seated across the aisle from me (on a flight with assigned seating). I took a deep breath and released it with a sigh. The woman exclaimed, "I knew that I needed to talk with you. There was something about your shoes that caught my attention." She shared that she wanted to talk with me but hadn't known how to approach me. She went on to say, "I have many questions, and I believe you can answer them."

Mildly relieved, I smiled, exhaled again, and said, "Please share your story."

She wanted to know: Why was she experiencing so much chaos in her life? Why was her throat continually bothering her? How could she connect to her higher self? I was happy to give her my thoughts on these issues.

As our conversation went on, I noticed the man sitting on the other side of me, in the window seat, was leaning into our conversation with notable interest. Finally, the woman said to me, "Thank you; you have answered all of my questions, and then some, and more. I just knew you were the one."

At that point, the man spoke up. He introduced himself as Mark James Christian. He revealed that he worked in the medical field as a cardiac care nurse, a field in which he'd been practicing for a very long time. During the flight, he also shared thoughts and ideas that were of an esoteric bent. We discussed numerology, astrology, chakras, and the world of spirit. As our conversation progressed, I found it refreshing that a well-seasoned medical professional could simultaneously hold both views. He began asking me questions, and I shared with him passages from my recently-completed book, *Trust Patience Surrender,* as well as nine pages of channeling I'd written while writing the book.

I never saw the woman again, but Mark James Christian and I stayed in touch. I'll share more about that later in this book.

This new wisdom and these insights seemed to come and go as

I continued my landscaping business, workshops, and counseling practice. What seemed to come was both profound and subtle. Over the next few years, I released aspects of myself that no longer served me. I also had a number of women enter my life to teach and reflect back to me certain aspects of myself, aspects or characteristics that I had either given away or that had been taken from me over past lifetimes, including this lifetime. Some of those qualities and characteristics included self love, innocence, beauty, and passion. (It should also be noted that all encounters and exchanges were available to each person involved, whether or not they wished to see them and their purpose. Some individuals were still being driven by their subconscious. It was not in their awareness.)

THE MEANING OF "SEE"

I want to share another event, as well as a poem I wrote while my "Dark Night of the Soul" was occurring, shortly after my near-death experience. This event occurred when I drove up Oak Creek Canyon and stopped at the infamous Garlands Trading Post. It has to do with the song "Amazing Grace."

I'd always loved driving the winding curves among the beautiful juniper and oak trees that lined Oak Creek Canyon. The canyon features a beautiful flowing stream on one side of the road and majestic sheer cliffs on the other. Every Sunday, I hopped in my car with several three-gallon glass bottles to fetch my weekly drinking water. The water spout was on the west side of Highway 89A. The aquifer was nestled among one of the largest Ponderosa pine forests in the world, with a couple of campgrounds at the road's edge. From time to time, I stopped, wrapping my arms around a pine while sticking my nose in the crevices of the bark, enjoying the sweet butterscotch-vanilla scent.

Oak Creek's water flowed continuously, day and night, 365 days a year, and I had the good fortune to drink this pure mountain water for some twenty years. The icy cold water's source flowed from the mountain range referred to as the San Francisco peaks, located in the northern section of Flagstaff, Arizona. I so loved the purity of the water and the slick feeling as I drank.

The night before, I'd been trying to help my graphic designer for this book. I wanted her to understand where the title and its meaning come from. Also, for several days prior, I had been talking to a friend who worked at the trading post. She and I spoke quite a lot about the spirits of the Native American Elders that inhabited the interior walls of Garland's restaurant. She shared her times of seeing them, and I told her about the sense that I also had of them being present.

But something began to happen that Sunday morning. I greeted many friends, ordered my food, and sat down at the counter. As I waited, a field of energy surrounded me, and I could feel it as a gentle buzzing within my body. It felt as though I had entered a field of energy that was holding a place for me of understanding.

Simultaneously, I entered a field of synchronicity that allowed me to see several perspectives at one time, each flowing into the other in my state of expanded awareness. When multiple events or beliefs merge into one, creating a greater sense of awareness of the experiences, I refer to this as an expanded state, while holding multiple moments of awareness as "Fragments" or "Shards of God"(SHEKINAH: in Jewish and Christian theology, the glory of the divine presence, represented as light or interpreted symbolically. In Kabbalism, as a Divine Feminine aspect. I will discuss a bit later in more detail) It is in a moment of Grace that they all flowed together into a new greater understanding.

The evening before I had explored some old boxes and paperwork. In them I discovered a poem I had written several years earlier when I was experiencing my "Dark Night of the Soul." Titled "SEE," it was a poem written when I was in a full blown depression, but the words seemed to flow through me despite my pain. "SEE" was a poem about my connection to my mother and her deeper role that had and was playing out in my life. Most of my adolescent life was spent visiting my mother in a psychiatric ward, thus leaving me with "mother issues," shall we say.

But now, something different was happening. I seemed to return to the time when I'd experienced intense suffering and the beginning of a deep depression. In this moment of an altered conscious state, I remembered conversations that a friend and I had been having about the Elders in the trading post. As this awareness took hold, I could see the energetic forms of the Elders in one of the corners of the restaurant. They felt so *present*. In another flash, the presence of my elder brother, Kurt, who had long been deceased, was made known to me. His suffering and his life represented another brief flash that entered my thoughts. And then, in a moment of illumination, I understood what the title "SEE" really meant to me.

My memory raced back in time, to when my eighteen-month-old son spoke his first word. It was the word *SEE*. Each time he spoke the word, he either looked at a very bright light or pointed upward toward the Sun.

In this highly energized moment, I began to understand the meaning of *SEE*. I also realized why I'd written the poem. All of these fragments came flooding together in my consciousness. It was a moment of grace, and I began to decipher *SEE's* deeper meaning.

In that moment of illumination, I realized several things. The first was how Kurt gave up his body for me. His leukemia diagnosis and death at the age of twelve devastated me, and I never processed it fully. Simultaneously, I realized my mother's role in my life, allowing me to see the wisdom of *her* life experiences as well.

I use the word *wisdom* because that was what the Elders were representing to me. The wisdom of this experience, theirs and mine...all at once. My mother lived and died to show me a greater understanding. Many of my life experiences were learned and developed based upon my mother's and Kurt's level of understanding.

Comprehending this, I wrote these words:

"Wisdom is when the head and heart gather as one, understanding the experience."

For the first time, I saw how each of the experiences in my childhood and adolescence made sense from a greater perspective. I also realized that, despite the heartaches, my brother's presence and even his leukemia had been a gift to my family. I saw that both Kurt and my mother gave me a part of their experiences so I would understand love's deeper meaning.

I saw this in a whole new light. Through their suffering, I understood that mine was also connected to theirs. Theirs was mine, mine theirs. In a flash, as it began, I understood, with deep insight, my connection to this love. I was being asked to see the greater meaning.

In another flash of insight, I was reminded of my son's first spoken word: *SEE.* I began to realize the magnitude, and that there was a higher purpose to all that was happening.

Seeing God, the Light of creation, the Elders as wisdom, and my brother asking us to experience his presence as a deep and abiding loves — these pieces swirled around in my mind for a few mere moments, while at the same time I felt as though lifetimes were finding a final resting place within me. I also realized the gift of grace enveloping me and within me. And then, in a final moment of awareness, I had a realization of the song playing in the background. It was "Amazing Grace."

> Amazing grace, how sweet the sound
> That saved a wretch like me
> I once was lost, but now I'm found
> Was blind but now I see
>
> 'Twas grace that taught my heart to fear
> And grace my fears relieved
> How precious did the grace appear
> The hour I first believed
>
> Through many dangers, toils, and snares
> I have already come
> This grace that brought me safe thus far
> And grace will lead me home
> When we've been here ten thousand years
> Bright, shining as the sun
> We've no less days to sing God's praise
> Than when we first begun

Amazing grace how sweet the sound
That saved a wretch like me
I once was lost, but now I'm found
Was blind but now I see

I took a deep exhalation, understanding another layer of my connection to God, my mother, my brother, my son, myself and all that is.

<u>SEE</u>
Brother
You gave up your body
for me

Mother
You gave up your life
for me

In all my life
I struggled yet to see

Through broken marriages
and relationships
that failed
to be

and after my long search
I began to see All you've given up
for me
A road of love and compassion
You've laid in front of (before) me

A SENSE OF CONSISTENCY

After this, my life returned to some sense of normality and flow, following my typical routine of landscaping and counseling sessions with clients. This normality was the thread that kept everything together. It represented a sense of consistency.

From time to time, guests came to stay in my home. Some I knew, and others I were acquaintances only through friends. All were fellow travelers in search of their own truth and the beauty of Sedona. Occasionally, events would present themselves in order for me to open to a more expansive look into my relationship to life.

A NEW ASPECT OF INTIMACY

One of these experiences was when I traveled to Santa Monica to attend a surprise birthday party for one of the alumni from the university where I'd completed a Masters in Spiritual Psychology.

In Los Angeles, I stayed with a friend from school, Linda. She was from England, currently working in Hollywood. Linda was a linguist who helped actors master proper use of the English language. She was also in the theater. She was a good friend, and at times a confidant.

We arrived at the birthday party, and I settled in quickly, connecting with friends and greeting Habib, the husband of the birthday girl. But after some time of mingling, a feeling of unease and discomfort started to well up inside me, for no apparent reason I could summarize.

The guest of honor soon arrived, expressing great surprise, which was received with lots of cheer. The party continued; dancing commenced. As I watched Habib dancing with abandon, I grew more and more uncomfortable.

But the worst was when Linda reached out her hand, asking me to dance. By then, I was nearly shaking. Nonetheless, with great hesitancy, I took her hand, and we stepped onto the dance floor. I did my best impression of moving my feet and arms, awkwardly fluid. With each move, I became increasingly uncomfortable.

Linda gave me a look of concern. "Wow, you really don't like to dance!"

"I would love to know how," I said. "But I can't seem to get past my self awareness of not being a good enough dancer."

It was truly a painful experience. At the end of the evening, when we returned to Linda's apartment, I took the bedroll she'd given me, placing it on the floor at the foot of her bed. At that point, something began to take hold of me. I started trembling, then felt an intense shaking. It was the kind of frigid shaking when your body's survival mode kicks in, trying to regulate and create heat.

"Good night," I said to Linda, my voice wobbling.

She must have realized something wasn't right. She came down to the bedroll and wrapped me in her arms. This went on for some time. Then she invited me to lie next to her in her bed. Only then did I feel some release.

During this shaking and release, I became acutely aware of a thought racing through my mind. It was fleeting but very present, sparked by the closeness we were sharing.

This could very easily turn sexual, I thought.

Perplexed by what my mind presented to me, I heard a loud, internal *NO*. This *NO* pronounced itself quickly, with great clarity.

To be clear, this wasn't because I was not attracted to Linda. But as we lay there holding one another for the next several hours, I recognized a pattern of behavior. I began to understand that my past behavior would be to turn such innocent intimacy into something sexual, providing me with a sense of power over the woman.

But I didn't want that. Instead, I realized how grateful I was for Linda to just hold me, while I allowed myself to simply receive her kindness.

That evening, I learned a new aspect of intimacy. It was a pivotal moment.

Not a Coincidence

Linda, her partner Paul, Sarah, and myself met several years later at my place of business in Sedona, a cigar shop. Once again, I need to digress a little in order to set the scene.

Outside of the cigar shop's side doors stood a large, freestanding chair designed with an artistic flair, by the late sculptor John Soderberg. Titled, "Merlin's Chair," it was ornate and shaped in the form of a shell. It perched on a small bridge overlooking a trickling waterfall and pond, within a common area where many musical gatherings took place.

Some hundred feet away, toward the central parking circular driveway, stood the chair's counterpart: a majestic, twelve-foot tall bronze statue of Merlin the Wizard. It drew a lot of interest from strolling pedestrians. Rumor had it that the sculpture was anatomically correct in many ways. Women were often determined to peer under Merlin's kilt to see if a true replica of a man's anatomy could be found there. Many emerged with blushing faces after they peered underneath.

Many powerful occurrences seemed to happen in proximity to Merlin and his chair. This location was featured in the Hollywood movie *Sedona*, which captured a number of these extraordinary events.

But back to Linda and Paul. I'd received a call from Linda saying she and her partner were driving from Los Angeles to Phoenix via Flagstaff, and they were contemplating a stop in Sedona. Since it wasn't too far out their way, they decided it would be nice to stop and see both myself and Sarah, my former partner. Linda seemed authentically excited to come, but in the background of the conversation, I could hear and sense Paul's hesitancy.

I said to Linda, "If you'll be that close to Sedona, why wouldn't you stop?" Then, once again, I listened closely and heard Paul's hesitation. But I continued. "I would love to see you and your new partner. So would Sarah."

Linda finally gave in after I told her, "I feel there's a reason why you're coming. It goes beyond reminiscing over old times."

Still, I wasn't really sure of the reason. Nonetheless, they arrived that afternoon at my cigar shop, where both Sarah and I warmly welcomed them.

As we caught up about our lives, Linda said she thought it was important that Paul and I should meet, but she really wasn't sure why. "But I should mention," she said, "that Paul has been working on a documentary about Merlin and his connections to archeological excavations of mounds that he discovered in Ireland."

Paul seemed reluctant to talk about his project, but eventually he opened up and shared about his discoveries. His enthusiasm gained momentum as he told of the artifacts he'd unearthed. Linda interjected several times, saying that Paul needed to talk with me. She kept encouraging him to share his findings. It was interesting to learn that Linda grew up only a few kilometers from the archaeological site.

I sat patiently while Paul shared his insights. Then I said, with great enthusiasm, "Turn around and look at the chair behind you." As they turned, I went on. "It's a sculpture of Merlin's Chair. And a massive sculpture of Merlin is in the circular driveway."

As I pointed toward Merlin, both Linda and Paul looked astonished, while sporting big grins on their faces. I could see that it was a moment of inspiration for both of them.

"It's no coincidence that Merlin's Chair and Merlin were only a few feet away from you, Paul," I said.

Linda smiled gleefully, seeing Paul's newfound enthusiasm. It turned out that his motivation for completing the documentary had been fading.

"I didn't think anyone would believe what I want to share in my documentary—that Merlin wasn't a fictional character, and my excavations can prove that to the world," Paul said.

Linda thanked me, giving me a look filled with such gratitude and hope. She went on to say, "I knew we had to come and see you for some reason—and now I know why."

It never ceases to amaze me how synchronicities abound when we're open to the flow of life. So often, we dismiss such feelings and urges. I'm glad Linda listened to hers. An hour or so later, with Paul again energized about his new project, they continued their trip to Phoenix.

But before they left, Paul sat in Merlin's Chair and we snapped a photo of the four of us. What a magical moment it was. We then returned to the table, and Sarah realized there was a number on our table, and it was the number 11. I'll continue this part of the story a bit later in the book, with an understanding of numerology, 11:11, and the process of awakening and an indication that one is on their divine path.

Before their departure, Linda and Paul approached the twelve-foot statue to peek underneath and learn if the artist really made the statue in a lifelike image, capturing all parts of a male's anatomy. Reaching up Merlin's kilt, blushing, Linda looked back at us with a big smile and loudly yelled, "Oh yah, it's lifelike."

TRANSITION AND TRANSFORMATION

Ten years have passed since the afternoon when Linda and Paul sat in Merlin's Chair. Since then, I've closed my cigar shop and made a major move, leaving Sedona and choosing to experience life in Bali.

During the interim years, a series of relationships, movies, and songs reinforced my newfound belief that we're always guided in the direction of our highest good when we're open to it. Many other realizations began to flow, too. They arose after considerable contemplation. I began to understand their deeper meanings and their relevance in my life.

As an example, just now, after I stopped typing on the keyboard and arose to get some tea, I observed a tree frog stuck to the surface of my glass door, facing indoors directly into my eyes. It was peering directly at me, at eye level. This was the first time I'd seen one since moving to Bali five years ago. So, I picked up Ted Andrews book, *Animal Spirits*, and here is what I read:

"The frog as Spirit animal or totem reminds us of the transient nature of our lives. As a symbol of transition and transformation, this spirit animal supports us in times of change. Strongly associated with the water element, it connects us with the world of emotions and feminine energies, as well as the process of cleansing, whether it's physical, emotional, or more spiritual or energetic."

Animal Spirits went on to read, "Frog symbolism of the frog appears in many traditions around the globe. This animal is generally associated with the water element and its cleansing attributes. The frog is symbolic for:
- Cleansing
- Renewal, rebirth
- Fertility, abundance
- Transformation, metamorphosis
- Life Mysteries and ancient wisdom"

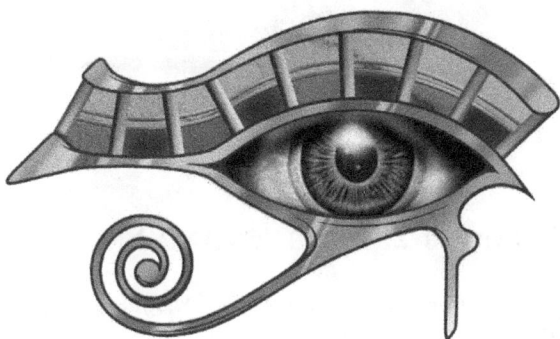

CHAPTER 2

Chapter 2: Psychics and Seers

"I promise if you keep searching for everything beautiful in this world, you will eventually become it." ~Tyler Kent White

I feel it's appropriate, for what I am about to share, to include definitions of various Psychic mediums. This is a good place to start, providing an overview of the various talents.

Below is a list of alleged psychic abilities that have been attributed to real-world people. Many of these abilities are also known as extrasensory perception, or the sixth sense. Superhuman abilities from fiction are not included.

This is a dynamic list. It may never be able to satisfy particular standards for completeness. The list below is from Wikipedia, but you can make your own list—or you can help by adding missing items with reliable sources. (You can send them to me here: https://www.kevinwestrich.com/contact.)

Psychic Abilities

- **Apportation.** The disappearance, or teleportation of an article from one place to another, or an appearance of an article from an unknown source.
- **Astral projection or mental projection.** The ability to voluntarily project an astral body or mental body, being associated with the out-of-body experience, in which one's consciousness is

felt to temporarily separate from the physical body.

•**Automatic writing.** The ability to draw or write without conscious intent.

•**Divination.** The ability to gain insight into a situation using occult lists.

•**Dowsing.** The ability to locate water, sometimes using a tool called a dowsing rod.

•**Energy medicine.** The ability to heal with one's own empathic, etheric, astral, mental or spiritual energy.

•**Levitation or transvection.** The ability to float or fly by mystical means.

•**Materialization.** The creation or appearance of matter from unknown sources.

•**Medium-ship or channeling.** The ability to communicate with spirits.

•**Precognition or premonition.** The ability to perceive future events

•**Psychic surgery.** The ability to remove disease or disorder within or over the body tissue via an "energetic" incision that heals immediately afterwards.

•**Psychokinesis or telekinesis.** The ability to influence a physical system without physical interaction. This typically manifests being able to exert force, control objects and move matter with one's mind.

•**Psychometry or psychoscopy.** The ability to obtain information about a person or an object by touch.

•**Pyrokinesis.** The ability to control flames, fire, or heat using one's mind.

Rddhi. The enhanced state of being through Buddhist meditation.

•**Remote viewing, telesthesia or remote sensing.** The ability to see a distant or unseen target using extrasensory perception.

•**Retrocognition or postcognition.** The ability to supernaturally perceive past events.

•**Telepathy.** The ability to transmit or receive thoughts supernaturally.

[https://en.wikipedia.org/wiki/List_of_psychic_abilities]

"IT'S IN THE STARS" — BOB

As I entered the definitions above, I was reminded of an experience I had some twenty years ago, when I was in the corporate world of investments and retirement plans. The memory involves a man named Robert Franklin, called Bob by those who knew him.

Bob was a fixed-fund manager at my workplace, Boatman's Trust Company in St. Louis, Missouri. His responsibility was to buy and sell fixed-fund investments such as bonds and U.S. Treasury bills. He was known throughout investment circles as the only man alive who could outperform the market with record returns over long periods of time. He was viewed by many as an investment guru, because no one knew what his strategies were. I, too, had always wondered how Bob achieved such high, consistent rates of return over many years.

At the company Christmas party one year, someone asked him, "Bob, how do you do it? How do you consistently outperform the market rates of return—and over such a long period of time?"

Grinning, Bob quipped, "It's in the Stars."

So he used astrology charts, planetary movements, and other celestial indicators to predict the market's movements? We were all flabbergasted, hearing this response from such an accredited fixed-funds manager.

That was many years ago. I don't know if Bob really meant it or not, but since then, my comprehension has evolved, and in my own life, I've come to understand how to use information given by gifted individuals as a guidepost, considering it useful for insights and confirmation regarding what's going on in my own head. Sometimes, such information brings a subtle cognizance. This is something I wasn't aware of back then.

As a result of what Bob said, I became more curious about seers and psychics. But back then, if I ventured to talk with friends and family about such topics, I didn't know what kind of response I'd receive. It generally brought forth a mixed bag. Sometimes, people scoffed at the idea or even ridiculed me for even suggesting this sort of thing. Other times, they showed great interest, with a confirming smile and an acknowledgment that there is some truth to it.

I never did talk with Bob about it. He was a bit of a recluse, not allowing many to visit him. So I was never able to follow up with him.

HOW DID SHE KNOW? — PSYCHIC IN NEW YORK

During those years when I was administering corporate retirement plans, shortly after the Christmas party where Bob said his market predictions were "in the Stars," I made a business trip to New York City to meet a client and his company, Keystone Foods. Keystone was the meat processing plant and distributor for McDonald's. I was lucky to have my brother Keith (who is fourteen months older than me) accompany me on this trip, and we spent time together in between my meetings.

One evening, strolling through downtown Manhattan, we stumbled across a sign that said, "Readings," with the picture of a genie wearing a turban. It was beneath the street level, so Keith and I stepped down into the lower level apartment.

When it was my turn, I listened as the woman told me things about myself and relayed certain incidents in my life. These were things no one who didn't know me could have known. She began by talking about a business meeting I'd had before leaving Chicago. She went on to say that a meeting with a man whose name began with the letter "J" went terribly wrong. I was a bit stunned hearing this, since my colleague, John, had just pummeled me in front of the client—to the point of my embarrassment. John's job was to provide a clean transition of his current book of accounts to me, due to his mishandling and the customer's dissatisfaction. It had not gone well.

To say the least, I was quite surprised that she knew that. She opened my eyes to the possibility that some people could see into the lives of others, and it began me on my journey of consulting and learning more about them. This began my contemplation and understanding of readers, psychics, and seers.

Following this incident, over the years, I would indulge myself with the opportunity to visit seers to help give me a sense of what was going on in my life. As with that first visit, often their information proved to be quite fruitful.

Spot-On Predictions — Tierza

Tierza was another gifted psychic and friend I often visited. I have vivid memories of several powerful, accurate visits with Tierza.

On one of those occasions, Tierza predicted that my wife and I would get divorced. About a year later, we went through a tumultuous divorce. Some time after that, I was trying to buy the wine bar adjacent to my cigar shop because I wanted to expand my business. Although the funding was on track, the purchase of the wine bar fell through.

Soon afterward, I went through my near-death experience. Suddenly, it felt like everything was falling apart. I decided to sell the cigar shop, but the process moved slowly. I was facing bankruptcy, but after my near-death experience, nothing else mattered.

I decided to go see Tierza. I was truly mystified by what was about to happen. In our reading, Tierza mentioned that a man with blonde hair, someone I knew who smoked cigars and was from Texas, would buy the shop.

I didn't think much of it. But then a friend talked to me about my condition. He said I was in a "Purple Haze," and that he couldn't figure out what was going on with me.

Then he made me an offer on the cigar business, including all of the inventory, furniture, and other assets, with the offer that he'd give it back to me for the purchase price of one dollar. He called this offer a "Willie Nelson."

My friend's name was Keith (not to be confused with my brother Keith), and he was—you guessed it—from Texas. He didn't want me to lose everything due to my "Purple Haze."

I didn't take him up on the offer. I was in a mental state of disarray and couldn't make a rational decision if my life depended upon it. I didn't know it yet, but that was the beginning of my mind rewiring from my old way of understanding the world to a new state of being.

I eventually lost the shop and entered a new and painful chapter of my life, what I refer to as my "Dark Night of the Soul." (I shared extensively about this in *Trust Patience Surrender*.) After I'd eventually brought my life back into some sort of semblance, I recalled what Tierza had said in her reading—that a man I knew with blonde hair, who smoked cigars and was from Texas, would buy the shop. She'd also mentioned that I would begin a new chapter of my life, and it would be painful, but with the support of friends, I'd get through it.

As I went through the experiences she foresaw, I gained a more expansive understanding of trust and surrender. Tiera was spot on with her predictions. Funny, I didn't make the connections as I started my new chapter. It wasn't until later that I remembered her predictions and accuracy with greater clarity.

"RETURNING TO MY INNOCENCE" — CHAYA

Another woman I encountered with the gift of seeing was named Chaya. She was of German descent and living in Sedona. Tarot cards and other decks of cards were her specialty, and I visited her from time to time. Chaya always provided some level of clarity about what was going on in my life. I would see her when I couldn't make heads or tails of ideas that were running through my mind.

Chaya gave me some card readings that seemed fairly accurate regarding what was going on with me. Other times, her readings weren't as relevant as I'd have hoped. There was one reading, however, that touched some cord within me. During this reading, she said I was "returning to a time of Innocence within me." I left the reading slightly perplexed about "returning to my Innocence." However, this notion of innocence soon led me into a new friendship with a young woman named Colleen, as described below.

HOLDING SPACE FOR ME — COLLEEN

I met Colleen through friends. Our first encounter was at the Unity Spiritual Center. Colleen was an attractive young blonde who seemed to fill the room with joy. Her bubbly nature quickly revealed another quality, what I'd call a bit scattered. On occasion, it required patience on my part.

Being in her early 30s, Colleen was trying to figure out the direction of her life. She desired marriage, children, and a loving relationship. Leaving her Midwestern town in Ohio months earlier, she'd been trying to navigate her new location, living accommodations, and relationships with men. I think she simply found life to be too much, at times.

During the next several weeks, we spent time together over lunches, phone calls, and social media, generating a mutual fondness and openness that seemed to flourish. One of our first times rendezvousing over lunch was in the garden of Chocolatree, a health food cafe in Sedona. There was a light breeze blowing. Colleen was wearing a French style, blue-and-white striped seersucker blouse that clung tightly to her, accentuating her fullness. A small ribbon was tied around her neck. Her blonde hair flowed in the breeze, and her youthful, soft white skin soaked up the morning sunlight.

I felt as though I was in Paris at a cafe, listening as she shared stories of her broken heart and life's journeys. I drank in the moment and her vulnerability, all the while comforting her with wisdom from my own years of life experiences and relationships. It was a beautiful time enjoying her company, innocence, presence, and conversation.

Over the span of the next year, I would help her purchase a vehicle, putting a recycled motor in it, since it had an immaculate interior and the body's exterior and paint work were pristine. Colleen and I would go on to share our thoughts about anything and everything that came to mind. Oftentimes we were both searching for answers and not holding back any thoughts or topics. Each thought was spoken and shared with a sense of awareness, caring, and attention. I could feel our friendship blossoming. Frequently, I believe she viewed me as a wisdom figure and a counselor when she was in need.

One day, a mutual friend phoned me. "I promised Colleen a place to stay," she said. "But the accommodations I'd offered were filled with family, so there's no room for her. Can you help out?"

I lived on the west side of town, in a two bedroom apartment with two levels. I was happy to accommodate Colleen for the couple of nights needed. When she arrived, I showed her the bedroom and private bath on the first floor. As she settled in, I prepared dinner, then we watched a movie. Afterwards, we lounged on the couch talking.

I noticed that there was a subtle tension in the air. Not a *bad* tension, but something was stirring. It wasn't long before our lounging turned to something more intimate.

Holding one another was welcomed by both of us. We were enjoying the moment, and when it escalated, I took her hand, leading her upstairs to my bedroom. But as we lay there, a feeling of discomfort came over me.

Initially, I fought it back. But as the next few moments became more heated, I said, "This can't happen between us, as much as I would love to enjoy it."

I was certain it was the right thing to do. I didn't want Colleen to feel obligated because she was staying in my home. We rose from the bed and returned downstairs.

Unfortunately, Colleen became emotional, storming into her room. I experienced feelings of regret and sadness, but I simply didn't want to take advantage of the situation.

The next day, we talked about what had happened. Colleen shared that she was angry that I'd refused her, and my refusal brought up a lot of past traumas for her.

"I'm sorry," I said. "I understand."

She nodded. "It's a good thing for me to face what had happened," she said. "And you had the right to not go forward with where last night was heading."

I shared that I had mixed feelings. On one hand, I wanted intimacy with her. On the other hand, given that I was considerably older, I didn't want to take advantage of her. And yet another part of me was simply confused.

As we talked about the experience, I began to realize, on a deeper level, why older men enjoy the company of younger women. I felt a strong desire to experience that, to feel the youth within myself. Colleen represented that to me. In all honesty, however, I didn't come to a full understanding of why older men are attracted to youthful women until some time later, when I spoke with another friend who had been dumped by her husband for a much younger woman.

Fortunately, Colleen's and my friendship remained intact and continued to grow. As a result of this misunderstanding and challenge,

I began to see that she, too, had a wisdom and a sense of openness about her that I enjoyed.

We kept in contact, sharing our lives and understandings, all the while entering into another level of friendship. Some time later, she relocated to Northern California. When I went on a book tour there with my PR representative to sell and distribute my first book, *Trust Patience Surrender*, I ended up visiting Colleen.

She was living in a studio apartment that was nestled under the main house, with a side entrance and a small yard. The yard bordered on a wooded area with lots of trees and dense vegetation. Being so close to trees and wooded areas is always a comfort for me, reminding me of bathing in the sun after school, on the hill at the edge of the woods where I grew up.

We went to lunch at a local restaurant. As our meals arrived, Colleen said, "It doesn't seem to be happening. No relationship, no children, and the guys I've met via an internet dating website aren't working out as I'd expected." She sighed. "I feel so hopeless!"

I gently reminded her to be easy on herself. "It will happen at the right moment," I said. "Just be patient, although I know that's sometimes easier said than done."

When we returned to her studio, we observed a small deer entering the woods. We traversed the walkway and entered Colleen's place, passing her large picture window.

And wow! There it was, a beautiful young doe lying in the yard facing us, just a few feet away. It didn't even move, just watched us.

"See," I said. "It's a beautiful reminder to be gentle with yourself, and what you desire will come." We both giggled, knowing *she* was her answer to her desires.

Over time, my conversations with Colleen became less frequent, but occasionally we'd spend a good amount of time on the phone. In particular, one of our last conversations opened my eyes to a whole new world.

At the time, I was bored with work and life, so I decided a movie was in order. Nothing on the movie marque seemed too exciting, but out of boredom, I popped into a movie titled *Populaire*. An excerpt about *Populaire* from RogerEbert.com is as follows:

A candy-colored, feather-light voyage back to the styles and mores of France in the 1950s, Régis Roinsard's "Populaire" inserts the conventions of romantic comedy into the context of a now little-known and long-bygone sport: competitive speed typing. While the melding of two genres produces a rather odd amalgam—imagine a Doris Day-Rock Hudson vehicle imbued with the spirit of "Rocky"—deft execution by Roinsard and his appealing cast make the film a solid, genially retro entertainment.

The film doesn't announce its sports theme immediately. When it opens, provincial lass Rose Pamphyle (Déborah François), impatient with the limited options of small-town Normandy, goes to the town of Lisieux and bids for a secretarial job with insurance executive Louis Echard (Romain Duris), who's skeptical until she impetuously demonstrates her self-taught but impressive typing skills.

Not only does she get the job, but Louis asks her to move in with him. She explodes at this, but misunderstands: he doesn't want her as his mistress. He wants to oversee the development of her manual gifts. In short order, he transforms himself into her coach, and begins to wean her away from her frenetic two-finger method.

Before long, their office work is seldom mentioned as Louis and Rose together begin aiming her more polished skills toward the arena of typing competitions. (Apparently these were quite popular some decades back, even if they didn't leave much of an impression on popular culture. Maybe they'll have a revival, now that typewriters are enjoying a certain return to vogue.)

[https://www.rogerebert.com/reviews/populaire-2012]

As I watched the movie, I observed a parallel to mine and Colleen's world over the past few years, and I began to extract a deeper understanding. It was a reflection of my own life in relation to Colleen's on the big screen. After the movie finished, I returned home in a state of emotional flux, knowing that something was truly on the verge of happening—but I wasn't quite sure what it was.

31

I felt a strong urge to pick up the phone and call Colleen. When she answered, I began to share what the movie was about, what I was feeling, and what the movie represented to me. As she explored this with me, deep insights began to flow, and we continued exploring what was happening within me.

I could feel that Colleen was holding a safe space for me to express my thoughts and emotions. She had become a good friend and confidante over the years, allowing each of us to receive the other's calls. We often talked at great lengths.

Coming to the realization that she was holding the space for me and my growth, I felt tears roll down my cheeks. I shared what I understood about who she was to me, reflecting back to me her own innocence and beauty, which I had seen over the years.

At that moment, I realized the magnitude of what was happening. She had held, by her mere presence, a reflection of Innocence, and that innocence was returning into my own being. It felt so real, it was palpable.

This new sense of innocence within me blew my heart wide open. Even as I write this, I feel the emotions percolating to the surface once again.

With great gratitude and joy, I began to understand why I had never responded to her when she told me, "I love you." She said it a number of times, and my response was always a soft, "and I you." Never before had I realized that this stemmed from a sense that if I said the words "I love you" to her, it would come with a level of commitment that I wasn't ready for.

This realization was so profound, I could feel my heart pounding with love that was opening my heart to her—and simultaneously, for myself. With each breath, the realization grew.

I then spoke the words with such meaning and joy. "I love you," I said.

It felt as though my whole world opened within me. We had shared such deep-seated and simple joy. "Love" meant each holding a space for the other. And it was nourished and given the time and space to be realized, expressed, and received—all at once.

As I thanked her for her love, we both understood the magnitude of what had just happened.

Now, lifting my hands and fingers from the keyboard, I push my chair away from my writing desk and lay on my bed, remembering this beautiful experience. I remember it as much as my mind can muster. And then, with the next few breaths, I allowed it to softly fade into the memories of my heart and mind.

"People are waiting!" — Nicole

Nicole was a seer/psychic who blew my world open. It was during the time when I was trying to write my last book. At the time when we met, I was stuck in procrastination. My procrastination needed a jumpstart from my guides and spirit. Nicole had had her gift of seeing since she was a young girl, and she lived a life filled with sex, drugs, and alcohol. (I share this because she herself shares it publicly.)

Nicole had denied her gifts for many years, until a traumatic life-and-death situation left her with the question: "Do I want to stay in my body and live, or do I want to leave this world?"

I'm grateful that she stayed on the planet. I'm sharing these thoughts and remembrances because most of us who have had challenging situations such as this, moments that presented us with the potentially earth-shattering question "Do I want to live or die?" having a gift hidden just below the surface.

Nicole came along at the right time in my life, along with archangels Gabrielle and Michael and a few friends who guided and nudged me into writing *Trust Patience Surrender*. This occurred shortly after my near-death experience. By then, I'd had enough time to move through my "Dark Night of my Soul," going through a year-long, excruciating period, one that was so difficult, I didn't know whether or not I'd be able to move through it.

This wasn't the first time I'd contemplated suicide—but I did contemplate it, as I often did during rough patches. And yet, somewhere inside of me there was a knowing that wouldn't allow me to do it. I sensed in my understanding that it was my soul, that part or energy that I believe gives us life and its experiences. I am extraordinarily grateful to have this hindsight now!

When I was trying to write about the Archangels who visited me and other guidance I had received, I found it challenging. Where to start? So many pages, so many words and chapters flowed through my mind. But I needed inspiration and guidance. I needed a graphic designer to lay out the book, and an editor to smooth out the edges and syntax. The thought of it overwhelmed me.

I had gone into uptown Sedona, where I sometimes visited the local psychic, Chaya, whom I mentioned earlier. But I was told Chaya was on vacation, and I would instead be introduced to Nicole. I was skeptical at first, but the sales associate was a friend, and she convinced me that Nicole had had the gift of seeing since an early age. So I decided to stay.

Still, when Nicole entered the room, I was a bit leery. She seemed a little rough around the edges, with tattoos all over her body. One arm was completely covered in designs and color. She called it a sleeve.

I took a deep breath and listened to what she had to say. Strangely, she started to whip her head around, whirling it from side to side. I took another deep breath, and then her first few words hit me like a ton of bricks. She belted out, "Archangel Michael wants to know why you haven't written your book. People are waiting!" As she said these words, even her demeanor and facial expression changed dramatically, as though Archangel Michael was present through her...fierce and demanding with a discerning look, wondering if I'd heard her or not..

Her next statement was equally earth-shattering to me. She told me, "You will have a retreat center between Santa Barbara and Big Sur."

I found this disorienting, because I had just returned from traveling to the exact locations she mentioned. I was certainly caught by surprise. Again, a deep breath was in order, helping me feel more grounded in myself.

Her voice became agitated. "It's time to get on with doing your work and stop procrastinating." She went on to say that if you don't do what you are asked to do, you may be taken out in order to allow someone else to come in and do what you're unable to do.

"A walk-in, perhaps," she suggested.

I was unnerved to my core, but in a good way. To ground myself from the experience, I went to dinner at Troias Italian restaurant, something I did to come back into my body. The waitress, Cindy, was a friend, and I talked with her about what had just happened.

"You better write the book," Cindy exclaimed.

As I began to leave after my meal, I opened my cell phone to the social media page for my alumni of the university where I completed my masters in Transpersonal Psychology. The background screen was a soft aquamarine, and these words leaped off the screen:

Archangel Michael wants to know, are you listening and are you going to do as you are asked?

I gasped for air and turned the phone toward Cindy. As she read the screen, I said, "I'll start tonight."

This was the third and final major event of guidance that motivated me to write *Trust Patience Surrender.*

My Etheric World — Lorraine

The most recent seer/psychic reader in my life is Lorraine. She resides in the town of Torquay, a seaside town in Devon, England. Torquay is south of Exeter and east-north-east of Plymouth, and it sits on the north side of Tor Bay. I was referred to Lorraine through a woman I know named Amara, who does similar trauma and healing work.

Lorraine's and my friendship has covered a span of more than eight years. Her ability to see into other worlds has been instrumental in guiding me to different parts of the world, as well as into deeper knowledge of my own psyche and etheric world. Lorraine has helped me learn how I interact and understand myself within the context of my life.

If I were to share all the insights and guidance that she has tapped into over the years, it would probably be a book in and of itself. However, later in this book, I will share a couple of her predictions and sessions of her seeing. When I talk further about Bali, Indonesia, I'll discuss how Lorraine guided me with so much clarity and precision, the events she saw unfolded literally. I've been so moved by her insights and her accuracy over the years that I have made it a habit to share her contact information with many others around the world.

But I'll save these descriptions for subsequent sections of this book. Suffice to say here, one of Lorraine's predictions was that I would receive three keys moving toward enlightenment and power—and she was absolutely correct.

GUIDEPOSTS

I've often wondered about the influences around all of these predictions and guidance. Were some of these predictions actually premonitions that I'd had? Were they precognition, manifestation, or a self-fulfilled prophecy? Which one played the largest role? Or was it a mixture of all of them?

I've given this a bit of thought and have determined that it doesn't really matter. I've adopted a more laissez-faire attitude about it. I'm not discounting their gifts of seeing, but instead allowing this conscious awareness to flow within myself. I'm allowing my strong desire to seek answers from another, while trusting and reconnecting with the guidance and intuition that flows through me.

I view their insights as guideposts. If we take everything said to us literally, my sense is that we might miss something along the way, because of the constant seeking out of the seers' readings.

This isn't to say that I will never speak to another seer, psychic, or reader. But I view it as a dynamic process. Each experience takes on a whole new flavor. This deepening has required me to surrender and trust a little more, knowing, ultimately, all that is—it's as it should be.

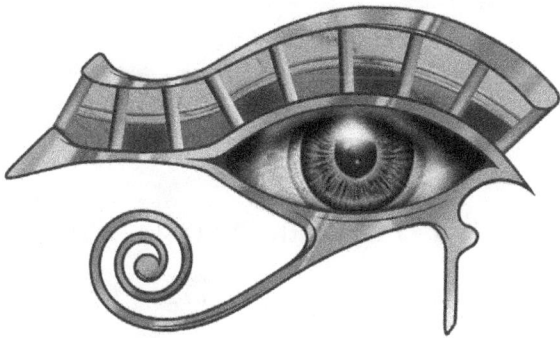

CHAPTER 3

CHAPTER 3: TEACHERS AND TEACHING

"Pain travels through families until someone is ready to feel it."
~Stephi Wagner

LIFE'S COLORFUL TAPESTRY

Allow me to bring you back to a few others who have entered my life via rather serendipitous encounters, weaving my life's colorful tapestry. I have continued to stitch these experiences, understandings, perceptions, and insights together to create and discover a truth of my own. This process has truly enhanced and benefited my life in so many ways.

Sophia de logos, Gnosis, are concepts I oftentimes refer to as "The Word of God." At times, I also refer to this concept as the Divine Feminine wisdom. To me, based on my experiences, they all share similar stature, form, and features.

I realized how each word, each experience and each woman who entered my life was divinely orchestrated to help me see something greater than myself, and to see a divine wisdom that I refer to as the Divine Feminine. To see her in her wounding, her glory, her fierceness, and her wisdom. It is the feminine aspect of God or of the creator. God has both masculine and feminine energies on a simpler level of consciousness, and then eventually transcends into the neither masculine or feminine. It transcends into a field of consciousness. It is no longer about duality. But I believe we are able to see and describe these aspects in the 3D world.

The Divine Feminine is also represented by Mother Mary, Quan Yin, White Buffalo Calf woman, Saraswati, and White Tara, just to name a few. It is the Divine Feminine that has been guiding me with a strength and tenderness that I believe my father also felt and understood. As he understood her, and I, too—at first.

My teacher, Swami Buddhananda, from time to time would share a particular concept, which he believes was written in the Vedas, where God was known to say, "I created all of this and its beauty." He was referring to all of creation. In the background, Mother can be heard to say, "And yes, and I created you."

My recent understanding of what this means is that the Mother comes not from a place of power *over*, but from a place of *empowerment*. I perceive the Mother's energy as the Divine Feminine that gives life, nurtures, and supports each of us into ourselves. It is a strength of knowing that comes from a place of balance. It's not a power that wishes to subordinate, control, or harm another. Rather, it is a power that is gentle, receptive, creative, and in union with all that is. It's also a power that can cut through all of the deception. In Hinduism, it's signified by the goddess of Cali.

Even as I use the word Feminine, I am not referring to the female per se, but rather to the energies. Those energies have many attributes. These include softness, communication, kindness, and receptivity that finds balance within. The feminine energies are found in each of us, as are the masculine. Even beyond this, I hold a belief that neither is to be adorned more than the other, but rather they should be seen in their combined wholeness, thus transcending the idea of polar opposites. Good versus bad, light versus darkness are not part of the combined wholeness. Instead, it is a time of transcending this patriarchal nature that we have co-created for many generations. It is now a time to live in harmony and balance.

"When the power of love overcomes the love of power in the world, we will know peace." – Jimi Hendrix

I wrote in a free-form manner, "There are those ready to transcend duality." As I continued to type, newfound energy was flowing through me and onto the keyboard. It was all quite spontaneous, and the flowing thoughts and words came through:

I have been given a glimpse into her essence...
"The Giver of Life"
The DIVINE MOTHER
you have given to me
you have received me
you have guided me
you have held me
you have....
Also shown me that this is
the end of the Kali Yuga and the time of Aquarius.
[https://en.wikipedia.org/wiki/Kali_Yuga]

You are the very breath of life, the very breath of existence within me, within us all

THANK YOURSELF

For the longest time, I didn't know where writing this book would lead me, but I am now beginning to understand. During this free-form writing of the ho'oponopono prayer (below), the verse seemed to complete itself. As I wrote the stanza *I love you*, auto-correct added *self*, thus completing the verse as *love you self*. At this time while writing, I was experiencing a powerful energy of the Divine Feminine. I could feel her presence.

My free-form writing continued:

I needed all of these experiences to know you... to know myself
I fully gave myself to you, to this, to me....
Understanding aspects of myself as you, as me....
All have been in preparation of my (this) awakening of awareness...

And then the Ho'Oponopono prayer entered my thoughts within this flow... all have prepared me for this knowing, this remembering.

I'm sorry

Please forgive me

Thank you

I love you...yourself.... (This seemed strange since it was not a part of the prayer)

There is where you will know me...

Please be gentle with yourself...with each other, for you are walking each other home. Home to your very existence and to your heart...

I always felt inside of me that My final piece was somehow connected to the female and to the feminine. Always wanting to be loved, to be held, to be forgiven. I now realize I have and always will.

The Divine....the essence and to all that exists

I now realize that all of these experiences are me...reflected back to me so I may know thyself and the connection to the divine. And then this poem, The Pond, wished to be placed on paper. Taking me deeper into the experience.

THE POND

You have been trying to reach me

Through my brother and my mother

Through each cleanse of my body

And Through each woman and experience that has moved through me and entered me – bringing me into a new state of awareness (and I through them) each of us recognizing it in the other....)

recognizing the beauty of all that is.... Within as without

All but a mere reflection (on the pond) of Love

My father tried to reach out to the divine mother, Mother Mary.... She was his safe haven

My Marriage to Muffy.... Our Dedication to the Virgin Mary

Again at Lourdes Virgin Mary came to me

And all of the women and experiences

and to my sense of self - as you -looking through me.

Remembering the many times reciting in my sacred fire circle ceremony while gathered around the fire. That too, the circle, which contains no beginning or end...simply creation

You needed us to see the masculine, the patriarchal, the female, and the feminine in order to understand the wholeness....

For it was always a transcendence to the masculine and to the feminine—and once again from the male to the female....

TO WHOLENESS

The mother has held us through the masculine and the feminine in order for us to see the wholeness

To see beyond (the) duality... into ONENESS

It's not about doing but of presence...

How would you know the masculine if not for the feminine or the feminine without the masculine?

In order to know the Wholeness

and to that of the Light and to that of Darkness

Each holding its own place, it's own wisdom

For we may recognize once more the life lived in a world of duality.

[end of free-form writing]

As I finished the free-form writing that generated the thoughts above, something inside of me, an inner knowing, was blossoming. A knowing of the next and final piece of

my journey and of my life's understanding.

A NEW EXPANSE OF KNOWING

As I entered into this new expanse of knowing, I began to understand why, what, and where this book was leading me. As I typed my thoughts onto the keyboard, the words flowed from my hands effortlessly onto the screen. I simply began to melt into the words as though they were poetry in the making. I began to understand how the Divine Feminine energies and its wisdom were anchoring themselves within me and how this experience allowed me to peer deeper into the soul connection and wisdom. This inner awareness went beyond my sense of self, finally settling comfortably within me.

I also began to be aware that this book was about the feminine and its power that resided in me, as well as my newfound level of gratitude and integration.

As I continued processing what I had written just moments earlier, the beautiful Hawaiian teaching above called the Ho'oponopono prayer took on further meaning in my mind. *"It's very touching, especially given how simple and universal these words are. With regular practice, reciting these four simple phrases helps develop self-love and self-esteem at the time when we need it most."*

At the time, the prayer and energy surrounding the experience appeared to be taking on a life of its own. The energy of the words was flowing through me in a new way. I felt my newfound awareness expanding, then suddenly I sensed it was opening me to a greater Source of understanding.

And then another thought followed: "Everything and Nothing." This new awareness was penetrating all of my current beliefs of understanding. Even as I typed the end of the teaching's line ("I love you") something unexpected happened! Auto spell had completed the word "you" for me, at the end of the stanza, "you" became "yourself." The word "self" was even highlighted in yellow. This was miraculous because this was the first time, in five hours of writing, that auto spell hadn't added any additional word, let alone a word highlighted in yellow. A warm fuzzy feeling of completion washed over me.

I'm Sorry, Please forgive me, Thank you, I Love yourself!

In this moment of grace, I was transfixed to a new understanding: "I am that which I seek." My connection to all that is, my very existence, is merely a piece of the whole.

This rocked my world, and it became my new understanding. This was the first time I allowed this simple truth in, and I allowed its energies to embrace me. And in a flash, I envisioned myself peering into a pond at the water's edge, once more seeing my reflection. This gentle wisdom was so expansive that in the moment, my ego simply melted away, leaving me with a sense of calm.

As I sat in that moment of silence and awareness, another mantra immediately entered my mind, giving me a sense of permission to receive it.

I am

Love

I am

I took a deep breath, then stood up from my desk. Feeling invigorated, I opened the curtains and allowed the warmth of the morning sunlight to bathe me and fill the expanse of my bedroom.

NO MORE SHARDS OF GLASS — LILITH

Some months later another, young lady entered my life. Her name was Lilith. This was a time when I was receiving many energies and insights, along with experiences around ArchAngel Gabrielle. The song titled "Gabrielle's Song" from the movie *As It is in Heaven* continued to set me up for further learning. At that time, Mark James Christian (whom, as mentioned earlier, I met on a plane) used chakras (energy centers in the body) to help me understand, from a Hindu perspective, what I had been experiencing and where I was on my journey.

Let me share a bit more. I was enjoying a beautiful spring day. From my vantage point, sitting at a table in front of New Frontiers Health Food store enjoying my lunch, I began to notice the sun's warmth upon my body and how the sky was filled with light, luminous, white fluffy clouds gently moving through the noon sky. I was transfixed with the peacefulness of the moment.

Then a young woman with light golden hair falling down onto her shoulders, a warm smile, and bright azure eyes that could pierce through any man's armor walked through the sliding doors and onto the patio, accompanied by a woman I knew, Jamie (known as the harp lady). Something struck me about the golden-haired woman. Yes, she was attractive. But I noticed something else in her eyes: a certain shyness and sadness. When we introduced ourselves, I learned her name was Lilith.

The three of us started conversing. Jamie mentioned that Lilith was leaving the day after next because the workshop she wanted to attend had been canceled.

Suddenly, both Lilith and I spoke simultaneously. We both said something like, "Somehow, you look really familiar to me. Like I know you somehow."

We both grinned, shook our heads, and nodded with a smile. We made plans to meet later that evening.

We ended up spending that afternoon and most of the evening getting to know one another. In the evening, Lilith told me she had decided to stay another day because she wanted to share more of her intimate life experiences with me. She said that she and I had something to further investigate.

As the words came out of her mouth, we exchanged knowing smiles. We both knew it wasn't the first time we'd met—at least, not in this lifetime. We had known one another somehow; we both felt the familiarity. And at the end of the evening, we made plans to meet the following morning and spend the day together.

Later, at home, I meditated on this energetic connection and the possibility of a newfound friendship or the rekindling of a relationship from a past life. I also felt I knew somehow, in the recesses of my mind, that she was severely traumatized and had been sexually abused. It even felt ritualistic and sadistic to me. A powerful and unsettling feeling came over me.

In the morning when we met, Lilith seemed hesitant. I could feel her discomfort. Based on what my meditation had revealed, I could understand how she felt. Before leaving home, intuitively, I'd picked up a petite, intricately carved crystal goblet that I knew I was to give to her. This goblet was one of my favorite pieces of stemware. I often used it to enjoy a small pour of tawny port wine, along with a good Cuban cigar. It had a sacredness to it, sort of a holy grail. But somehow, it was connected to our conversation the night before. We had talked, at length, about a sacred chalice and what it meant to the both of us.

The next morning, when I presented the goblet to her, she began to shake. Catching her breath, she told me some of her deepest, darkest secrets of the horrific and sadistic things that had been done to her from early childhood. She then shared that whenever she felt an attraction to a man, she would experience a painful feeling in her uterus. She described it as though there were glass shards ripping her yoni to shreds.

As my body tensed and my emotions came to the surface, I was filled with such anger at hearing her descriptions and knowing that close family members perpetrated such atrocities on this innocent young woman. Then in a flash, a profound sense of compassion filled my heart. This compassion and warmth connected her with me, and me with her. There wasn't any judgment on my part, just a heart overflowing with kindness and compassion.

Sensing this, Lilith began sharing more of her traumas. Eventually, in her most fragile moment, she glanced up at me and whispered, "Would you hold me?"

I felt her little girl's presence. I wrapped my arms around her, and compassion engulfed us both. As my eyes began to tear, I felt the energy of a loving father cradling her as she cried from the depths of her soul.

Moments later, she entered a state of absolute silence. Eventually, I offered that we go to Oak Creek Canyon and sit next to the water's edge, so I could guide Lilith through a ceremony to help her finally release these old traumas into Oak Creek River and begin anew. What my mind immediately envisioned was placing her gently into the flowing waters of the river while she cleansed the last remnants of her tormented past and, at long last, released the broken glass shards and trauma that had plagued her life from such an early age.

Minutes later, we were driving up Oak Creek Canyon. We gently climbed down its steep short embankment and I supported her body down the short descent to the water's edge. As she began to place her feet into the water, I again supported and guided her steps over the slippery, moss-covered rocks. While placing her gently into the stream, I asked that she squat down into the icy water, using her own hands to wash herself and release all these memories.

In that moment it felt as though we had traveled back in time, to the moment when St. John the Baptist anoints Jesus and others in the River Jordan. This feeling generated thoughts of the phenomenon that some refer to as "born again." The vibratory and emotional effects were swirling through me and around the both of us. It was a moment that felt as though not only Lilith but I too was somehow being "born again."

I helped her exhausted trembling body out of the river and over the rocks to a seated place on the riverbank. She was shaking from the chill of the water and her psychological and energetic release. I unfolded the blanket I'd brought and gently wrapped it around her. I then wrapped my arms around her, as a loving father would, sealing her with my love. She softly gazed upward, meeting my eyes, and in them I saw her renewed innocence.

I will remember that moment for the rest of my life. Those few second's glance allowed me to see the little girl in her, peering at me to see her beautiful azure glow. This glow seemed to permeate and envelope her whole body, and before my very eyes she transformed into a little girl. Right before my eyes! I felt a wave of Love and compassion, once more, and as that breath-filled me, I let out a sigh. I knew a new chapter of her life was just beginning.

Looking up at me, Lilith softly asked, "Would you hold my hand?" There was a tenderness that melted us both when our hands folded into each other's. We ascended the riverbank, hand in hand while being bathed in the summer sun's warmth. Upon reaching my truck, I opened the passenger door for Lilith and helped her into the seat.

We drove to town and ended up spending the rest of the day together, with hearts so filled as I watched her go in and out of retail shops, one after another, in uptown Sedona. I was forever grateful to see her in such a happy state of childhood. Her beaming smile filled my heart. After our walk along the creek and her joyful shopping spree, I took her back to her friend's home. She was leaving early the following morning.

In our final moments together, I asked her, "How do you feel about the affection and sense of love that we shared?"

With a gentle resolve she replied, "I don't feel the glass shards in my womb anymore."

The affection she had for a man (or men in general) would no longer be accompanied by the sensation of broken glass that she'd always felt in the past. We hugged one another for quite some time, then parted with a smile, our hearts filled with such gratitude knowing that something wonderful and profound had just been shared.

A moment of tenderness and release. Another moment of Grace.

AURIC FIELDS AND AKASHIC RECORDS

I'd like to take a moment to share a little of my understanding about auric fields (aura readings) and the meaning of Akashic records. For some this may be a little too much to grasp. I have encountered those who believe wholeheartedly in such concepts and others who thought it was, as they'd say, "Hogwash." Such individuals discount any potential that something might exist beyond the 9-5 job, movies, and meals.

For many years, I, too, did not really understand such concepts. For a number of years, I had a knowing that my life wouldn't just consist of simple routines and simple comforts. I would experience them from time to time but something else always would disrupt their flow. Then came a powerful day that took me into another world of experience and understanding. I'll talk about that day later in this book, but for now, explanations about auric fields and the Akashic records are below.

AURAS AND AURA PHOTOGRAPHY

Auras/aura photography is another phenomenon that I would dabble in from time to time, and I would like to give you a taste of what it is and what my belief system is in relation to this concept.

First, I will explain what auras are, and then aura photography. I know this might sound a little New Age-ish for some of my readers, but please read on.

The aura is an electromagnetic energy field that surrounds the body. This field and several other auric fields are also related to colors. Colors hold a particular frequency. On an energetic level, auras are said to correspond with our chakras and our overall state of consciousness.

Dating back to the Christian Mystics of the Middle Ages, painters and artists haven't portrayed the aura as a light surrounding the human body.

Over the years, scientists and researchers have attempted to capture the aura through photography. One of the earliest photos was taken by engineer Nikola Tesla in 1891.

According to New Age philosophy, auras are a colored emanation said to enclose all living things. It is a manifestation of mental, physical and spiritual health.

From time to time, I have had these aura photos taken. At first, it was out of simple curiosity and then, later on in years, I used them as an additional tool to see if what I was feeling overall corresponded with the auric field and the colors it displayed. Quite often, the aura photo reflected back to me a similarity to what I was feeling in my physical and energetic bodies.

AKASHIC RECORDS

The last concept I'd like to share, with you, is the concept of Akashic records and a couple of descriptions. My understanding and belief of this concept lie in the esoteric and celestial realms.

In the religion of theosophy and the philosophical school called anthroposophy, the Akashic records are a compendium of all universal events, thoughts, words, emotions and intent ever to have occurred in the past, present, or future in terms of all entities and life forms, not just humans.

[https://en.wikipedia.org/wiki/Akashic_records]

A well-known expert on the Akashic Records was clairvoyant Edgar Cayce (1877 – 1945). Cayce's many insights are in a book titled, *Edgar Cayce on the Akashic Records* by Kevin J. Todeschi, who worked for forty years as Executive Director and CEO at the Association for Research and Enlightenment (A.R.E.), which Cayce founded in 1931. The description of the book is as follows:

This book describes the Akashic Records, the source from which Edgar Cayce received many of his remarkable insights. Also known as the Book of Life, the Akashic Records is the storehouse of all information — every word, deed, feeling, thought, and intent — for every individual who has ever lived upon the earth. "

[https://www.amazon.com/Edgar-Cayce-Akashic-Records-Book/dp/0876044011]

Anna Bel Laura's song lyrics feel appropriate here, as they are particularly poignant. As I remember it, her song title was, "What About" on the CD *ibu pertiwi,* which translates to *Motherland.* It was regarding an often-used phrase where she rearranges the lyrics of the song to create a new thought or way of seeing things.

Many people say, "I'll believe it when I see it" when they're having a hard time believing something to be true. In her song lyrics, Anna Bel flipped the words around to create the new idea: "What if Seeing is believing, they'd say?"

I will share a bit more, later in the book, about her presence, music, and a card representing the Divine Mother.

You may be thinking that I had experience after experience that were esoteric, and that my life was full-on. I want to remind you that these experiences happened over the course of several years. My daily life consisted of running the cigar shop, then later a landscaping company and a counseling business.

Quite often I held two contrasting and complimentary thoughts: *I live in this world but I am not of it.* I was merely open to such new experiences. Living my daily life, I had my ups and downs, emotional highs and lows that seemed to soften over time. But I was still human and living in the world.

A GOLDEN BUBBLE — EMMA

Another young blonde entered my life, by the name of Emma, whom I felt had similar energies to Sophia de Logos (referred to earlier). Emma, too, was from Los Angeles—the City of Angels. She came into my life sharing her wisdom about the mystery school she had been attending in LA, and after spending a bit of time together, we discovered that we knew a number of the same people.

What stuck with me about Emma was her ability to see things and elaborate about different energies that she could see, including auras. Often, we talked at great length about initiations and lost worlds, such as Egypt, Lemuria, and Atlantis. We were both of the mindset that these places were real and not fiction. We had a profound belief that we'd known each other, but we couldn't pinpoint the time or place. Again, it was simply a pervasive, intuitive knowing. Perhaps it was in another lifetime.

As we got to know one another, something else popped into my awareness. I felt intuitively that Emma had other powers and gifts. For example, I felt she could sense or see into others' energetic/psyche or auric fields.

One particular afternoon when Emma and I were spending time together, it became evident that she could see something within me, something one's normal perception or awareness couldn't have picked up on. We were talking about the Akashic records, then Emma looked directly into my eyes and, with an exhalation, shared her understanding.

Speaking in a soft voice, she said, "You have a golden bubble around you. Be careful you don't keep yourself too protected. You might miss something or not allow what you'll need."

This both startled and encouraged me. I told her something that I very rarely shared with anyone. "I do invoke a golden bubble," I said. "I visualize it encircling my body as a form of protection. I've done that for years."

How could she have picked that up by simply looking at me? She also shared a few other insights about my aura and my general state of being. Once more, I felt a stronger connection growing to her gifts as we spent the afternoon together. During the next few months, I made several trips to LA, where we connected over lunch or spent the afternoon together.

MARK JAMES CHRISTIAN AND THE ACARDIAC TWIN

You will recall that I mentioned Mark James Christian (whom I met on a flight from LA to Phoenix) earlier in this book. I want to follow up here about Mark. We talked for most of the flight, and upon landing, he asked where he could buy a copy of *Trust Patience Surrender*. As luck would have it, I had one with me, which I gave to him. He said he would read it and share his thoughts via email.

Some days later, he emailed me the following. These are his actual emails:

July 22, 2014

"I'm finishing the book in the next day +/- I'll let you know when I'm done. I think it's great your owning the origins of your names. No coincidences right. Incidentally, your first name Kevin origin Gaelic Irish "Caoimhin" or Caoimhghin, meaning "gentle child, nobly born". Also English origin "Little Comely "Loved One" K E V I N 2 + 5 + 4 + 9 + 5 = 25. The 25 is then further reduced to a single digit number by adding the 2 and the 5 together so 2 + 5 = 7. Your number is:7. The characteristics of Number 7 are: Analysis, understanding, knowledge, awareness, studious and meditating. The name Kevin creates an overly-sensitive nature which causes you to sense and feel far more than you can understand or put into words. You have a deep, artistic and creative side which shows through a love for music and literature. Writing is a more natural mode of expression for your deeper thoughts and feelings than the spoken word. You have an ability to concentrate and work intently on anything which holds your interest. However, you prefer to avoid routine, monotony and menial tasks. You enjoy the out-of-doors and find your greatest peace and relaxation from the beauty and harmony of nature. You prefer to limit your friendships and associations to those who share your interests and appreciate your quiet, refined ways. Others often find it difficult to understand you. Your feelings tend to build up within you and, if you cannot release them through a creative, constructive channel, you could suffer with frustration, moods, and much inner turmoil This causes tension in the region of the solar plexus, as well as the heart and lungs. Health problems would center in those areas of the body. Best wishes, I'll keep in touch. Mark Christian.""

July 24, 2014

"Hi Kevin. I finished the book and found it to be an interesting fast read. The important parts were clearly keeping one's heart open and feeling each message that's given to us. Even from our dreams every moment is important to one's spirit. I also picked up on some interesting points that you went through. It's very common to have turmoil from chakra to higher chakra and it's messy in the spaces in between. It's very clear you're in between heart and throat chakra, if I was to guess. But also you have moments of enlightenment which is third eye and crown chakra. I imagine that's where Jesus, your best friend was when he witnessed, and blessed the meek with miracles. Which is kind of what you're doing in a way, Spreading the spirit from heart to heart. I'm glad mine was open the day I met you. Also I can't stop thinking about where you said must call "Trisoflobian" remember I studied medicine and work in pulmonary critical care, well it immediately made me think of an article I read on triso fallopian "the acardiac twin." I don't know if you had a birth twin or soul twin or could even be soul mate. But it was one of the more profound moments of your story. I felt a pleasure to share your events and discovery, at times I was right there in your story witnessing your soul journey. Thank you friend, bless your heart. Mark Christian"

He ended by saying, "One more thing the green aura you see is, in my opinion, the other soul twin to the right of the physical heart. Interesting huh..."

This last statement implied that my soul twin was with me. Let me explain what the acardiac twin is. When I wrote the words *Trisoflopian* within those nine pages of channeling, I immediately looked it up on the internet. To my surprise, I found nothing at all about its meaning. Each research attempt came up blank.

Arcadiac Twin or "Twin-twin transfusion syndrome (TTTS) is a rare disorder that sometimes occurs when women are pregnant with identical (monozygotic) twins. It is a rare disease of the placenta, the organ that joins the mother to her offspring and provides nourishment to the developing fetuses. During the development of identical twins, there are always blood vessels in the fetuses' shared placenta that connect their blood circulations (placental anastomoses). In most cases, the blood flows properly through these vessels. However, in twin-twin transfusion syndrome, the blood begins to flow unevenly, with one fetal twin receiving too much blood (recipient) and one receiving too little (donor). The recipient twin may experience heart failure due to continual strain on its heart and blood vessels (cardiovascular system). The donor twin, on the other hand, may experience life-threatening anemia, insufficient nutrition and oxygen due to its inadequate supply of blood. Such an imbalance in blood flow (i.e., twin-twin transfusion) can occur at any time during the pregnancy, including during delivery."

[https://rarediseases.org/rare-diseases/twin-twin-transfusion-syndrome/]

As I re-read his emails a few years later, while writing this book, I began to realize that an expanded, more meaningful version was emerging. Initially when the emails arrived, I interpreted that moving up the chakras from the heart to the third eye and crown and in between them could be quite messy. It made perfect, logical sense. *Chakra* is a Sanskrit word that means spinning wheel, and it is believed by some that we have seven of these spinning wheels, or energy centers, in our bodies. One located at the top of the head (crown), the third eye (center of the forehead), throat, heart, solar plex (area of large intestines), sacral (approximately 4-5 finger width below) and the root chakra (located at the base of the spine). These energies may lie dormant for periods of time and then become activated by chi (life force, energy, or source) entering into them. When these energies become active, they're often referred to as an opening and/or realigning of these energy centers.

As I re-read the emails again, today while writing, the green aura to the right of my heart is something I, too, now interpret in a more thoughtful, expansive way. I have begun to be open to Mark's interpretation of referring to the twin acardiac/twin soul that has been with me all along, just to the right of my heart. It's certainly food for thought.

I was quite happy to revisit his emails regarding the acardiac twin and its meaning. I began to interpret that this twin could very well be one of my internal acting sources of knowing (spirit guide), where I receive guidance. I was in such a state of relief when I read his emails because it helped me to see my life's journey in a more panoramic, peaceful way. I was eternally grateful that we'd crossed each other's path.

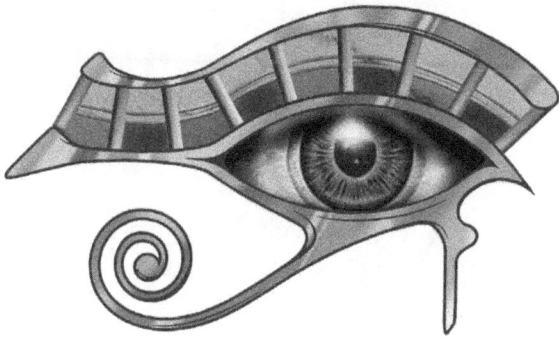

CHAPTER 4

Chapter 4: Sedona Experiences

"Be still and know that I am God." ~Psalm 46:10

Fragments

Keep in mind that my understandings are based upon my belief systems, and it is my interpretations through my own lens of experiences. There is a beauty in and of itself, because I now understand that even in the future, other experiences and insights have the potential to broaden the truth of my understanding in any given moment. There's a saying I often use: "The whole world could change tomorrow at two o'clock."

Although the initial experiences were quite powerful, it seemed they'd come back again and again in subtler ways, asking me to see their wisdom from a more intimate, broader perspective. A sort of layering effect that is closely tied to my emotional body, my mental state, and vibration.

Something else was occurring around this same time, and it was the word Shekhinah. This word kept rising in my thoughts throughout my daily life. I hadn't heard of this word or its meaning, let alone in a religious or spiritual context. But I began to understand, as I researched the word and its meaning, that it means the "Fragments of God." They were the bits and experiences that oftentimes swirled around in my mind but that I was unable to piece together.

This led me to further investigation of the word Shekhinah and its connection to the Divine Feminine. What follows is a bit of research I completed to help me understand other perspectives that I had on this similar theme of the "Divine Feminine and Masculine."

My research brought me to Rites of initiation, which often involve invocation of the hieros gamos, the Divine Feminine. Below is an interpretation by Cynthia and Robert Hicks. This goddess is in reality the sacred prostitute, which Cynthia and Robert Hicks borrowed from The Sacred Prostitute: Eternal Aspect of the Feminine for the Promise Keepers publication Masculine Journey.

[http://www.mat.auckland.ac.nz/~king/]

"Many Kabbalists conceive of God as embodying both male and female energies, which were divided during creation as part of the process of emanation. They speak of the shekhinah, which in traditional Judaism means the divine presence on earth, as the feminine aspect or mystical bride of God. And they often use language as a means to analyze such mysteries, as in this excerpt from a contemporary non-Jewish Kabbalists which offers an explanation for the mysterious use of the plural form for God early in the Bible:

"The Hebrew word used to denominate God in Genesis is Elohim. This word is a plural formed from the feminine singular ALH (Eloh) by adding IM to it. Since IM is the termination of the masculine plural, added to a feminine noun it makes ELOHIM a female potency united to a male principle, and thus capable of having an offspring. The same intended misconception is given in the Christian idea of the Holy Trinity: Father, Son, and the Holy Ghost. In the Kabbalah the Deity manifests simultaneously as Mother and Father and thus begets the Son. We are told that the Holy Spirit is essentially masculine, but the Hebrew word used in the Scriptures to denote spirit is Ruach, a feminine noun. The Holy Spirit is really the Mother, and thus the Christian Trinity properly translated should be Father, Son and Mother.

~ Migne Gonzalez-Wippler, A Kabbalah for the Modern World

The website of Hebrew scholar Eliezer Segal of the University of Calgary explains the function of the Ten Sefirot of the Kabbalah as

the pathway to divinity. The union of the Shekhinah with the upper sefirot consummates the marriage of male and female elements:
    [http://acs6.acs.ucalgary.ca/~elsegal/Sefirot/Shekhinah.html]

"The Ten Sefirot of the Kabbalah: This Sefirah unites all the upper nine powers....Tif'eret is the offspring of Hokhmah and Binah. It is often symbolized as a bridegroom or prince who strives to be united with the Shekhinah. Their union produces the human soul."
    [http://watch.pair.com/HRintitiation.html]

The reason I included the above text and interpretation is not to come from a specific religious interpretation but from one of my own. It's based on a number of other experiences that pointed very directly to my perceived understanding that Shekinah is the feminine aspect of God being revealed. And the above quotes seemed appropriate, at the time of the writing.

I also had a knowing that I would personally refer to the "shards" as fragments. Additionally, my vedic teacher of fifteen years, Swami Buddhananda would occasionally share his teaching of understanding that connected to the shekhinah, shards or fragmenting. He confirmed this knowing. Often I took his words to heart, since his teachings not only came from his Vedic traditional studies, his knowledge he drew on came from his studies, over thirty years, of comparative religions. During these thirty years, he was fostering Vedanta centers throughout central California. Swami Buddhananda teachings, I felt, were giving me a broader breadth and scope, which was an inclusive view of world religions.

One of his teachings in particular stuck with me, and I will do my best in remembrance and interpretation of it. He would share with me that in the Vedas there is a story in which God was sharing and saying how he had created all of this, as if in admiration of the cosmos, but in the background a voice appeared, a knowing that quipped in response, "And yes, I created you."

He often referred to it as the Divine Mother. This stuck with me, because a truth rang in it. As a result, I have expanded that belief with a knowing that beyond the sacred Mother aspect of creation is yet another stopping point. I now realized even with that concept, one must go beyond, leaving behind the world of duality.

My belief now is there is no gender relation at all. It is simply an aspect of "Creation" or "Consciousness." I often refer to it as, "Source." These are interchangeable.

Now, this made more sense to me, with regards to what I had written in *Trust Patience Surrender* and what I described in a separate writing of nine pages, my free-form writing or channeling. The very root of free-form writing is to write without thinking about what you are going to put on paper. You simply allowed the writing to flow without conscious thought. The mind isn't actively involved during the writing.

What I'm referring to was a passage that I wrote at the end of those nine pages of channeling I jotted down while writing my book, Trust Patience Surrender. In this passage, my inner guidance or Source said:

"I am hear with you, you are me. (not a misspelling of hear. It is what I wrote.) Learning to heal and love myself. Yes, me one who is all powerful so you believe that all the answers are in me or elsewhere. Stop looking elsewhere, look hear not there, for your life is endless without beginning or end we are the alpha & omega. Creating the moment you accept me. You create me..."

All of these experiences, what I refer to as fragments, seemed to fill my thoughts and began, creating a more expansive world of understanding for me.

BEE SEASON

If these experiences weren't enough, a Hollywood movie that I felt called to watch revealed a shining light of truth and understanding which added another level of confirmation to my then-burgeoning beliefs. It was the movie *Bee Season*.

Bee Season is an American drama film adaptation of the 2000 novel of the same name by Myla Goldberg. Written by Naomi Foner Gyllenhall. It stars Richard Gere and Juliette Binoche.

Saul Naumann (Gere) is a somewhat controlling Jewish husband and father. A Religious Studies professor at UC Berkeley, Saul wrote his graduate thesis on the Kabbalah. Because he was a devout Jew, his wife Miriam (Binoche) converted to Judaism when they married, and he nurtured his son Aaron (Max Minghella) into a traditional studious Jew like himself. When Eliza (Flora Cross) wins her class spelling bee they go on a course of Kabbalah study to help her win. The film follows the family and the spiritual quests upon which they journey, in large part because of Saul: Miriam's attempt to make her life whole, Aaron's religious uncertainty, and Eliza's desire to be closer to her father." "Miriam lives a secret life throughout her entire marriage to Saul, trying to fulfill the religious idea she learned from him, tikkun olam, or "repairing the world" and "reuniting its shards. "She takes this meaning literally and slowly collects trinkets she finds beautiful (sometimes breaking into people's houses and stealing them) and storing them in a warehouse, trying to hold the light of God in them."
[https://en.wikipedia.org/wiki/Bee_Season_(film)]

The story continues with the son seeking a young blonde woman (Chali) who brings him into the Hare Krishna group. It goes on to spelling bees that Eliza wins, seeing the letters of the words swirling in the air before her. All of these fragments or subplots really drove home the point of my understanding. In a moment of Grace, Eliza misspelled the word "origami." A Japanese word that Dictionary. com refers to as, "the Japanese art or process of folding squares of paper into representational shapes." Ori meaning "folding," and gami meaning "paper."

It was so powerful for me on so many levels. It had to do with the character Miriam, played by Juliette Binoche. I felt a strong connection and familiarity with her. This connection was about having a mother who had suffered from an apparent mental disorder. Miriam's appearance and features were similar to those of my own mother at a younger age. Seeing her character on the big screen was mesmerizing. It wasn't until my mother's death that I realized, while standing at the foot of her hospital bed and seeing the look she gave me, speaking to my soul's knowing, that her eyes revealed something with great clarity. It was deeply profound and yet, in a way, funny. Her eyes and expression seemed to say, "Ha ha I got you!"

I won't reveal what I initially thought. But a smile of understanding soon filled my consciousness. It's as though Shakespeare was in the hospital room, reminding all of us, me in particular, of his words: "All the worlds a stage; we merely actors."

I then said my final goodbyes to my mother. She passed a short time later.

On a side note, Swami Buddhananda, not knowing what had happened with me and the movie, presented me with a small, plain paperback book titled *OPEN SECRETS, The letter of Reb Yerachmiel ben Ysreal.* Swami said, with a sense of reverence, "This book is out of print and this is my only copy, and I want to give this to you."

After reading it multiple times, I felt it took me even further into these concepts and an understanding of tikkun olam. It is a book that I have read many times over, extracting the subtle nuances of tikkun olam.

Countenance

To this day, I can't remember if I saw *Bee Season* before or after what I am about to share occurred. But listening to my intuition, it feels as though it was before seeing the movie.

I began to experience such a phenomenon around the word *countenance.* This word had intrigued me for some time. Not really knowing what it meant, I would meditate upon it quite often, asking to know the meaning behind the word itself. I wanted to know the vibratory or energetic force that animated the word, the very energy that gave it life.

One day, I was meditating, sitting in my cigar store office and staring at the word *countenance,* which I had written on a sticky note and placed in the center of my cork work board. I began to understand the meaning, and a powerful, palpable vibration filled my body.

After several minutes sitting in this energy, I decided to go out onto the patio of my shop to get some fresh air. Exiting my shop, I felt the warmth of the sun. As I walked through the open door onto the patio the energy was getting quite strong, and in that moment, I encountered my friend Tierza (a psychic seer mentioned earlier).

She looked directly into my eyes, inquisitively scanned my body, and said, "Wow, you have countenance all over and around you. You seem to exude countenance."

At that moment, I knew something profound had just happened. I began to understand what I was trying to comprehend. I saw that this word, through this experience, did have a vibratory expression to its meaning.

I have come to believe that the vibration actually creates the word through resonance. I began to know it on an energetic or vibratory level. Tierza and I both smiled, then I went on to explain what had happened just prior to our encounter. Her knowing smile returned once more.

Out of curiosity, I looked up the word on the internet. Here is what the Cambridge dictionary said:

"The appearance or expression of someone's face:

He was of noble countenance.

So God's "shards" or "fragments" oftentimes in my life seemed to be swirling around in the atmosphere. And then, all of the sudden, in a moment of Grace, the pieces would fit together into a divine puzzle, revealing an ever-expanding knowing. Over time, I have had the pleasure of looking back, and in hindsight, I have begun to have a fuller understanding and a desire to anchor this new belief.

A PASSIONATE ANGEL — CORRINA

I'd like to share a couple of experiences. The first is about a woman named Corrina, someone I met briefly who turned into a kindred spirit and a teacher, but not in the way I'd first expected.

One hot, sultry summer afternoon (I believe it was 105 – 110 degrees Fahrenheit), I needed to go to the local cell phone company to address an issue with my phone. It was so scorching hot out, when I grabbed the store's metal handle, it burned my hand.

As I sat waiting in the queue for service, an attractive, mature woman with dark hair beyond her shoulders and bronzed skin seemed to be peeking around a six foot high glass display in the center of the store. Her beautifully pressed white blouse was slightly opened. She wore jean shorts and an infectious, innocent smile. Amidst the heat and sweat that was rolling down my neck, she exuded a freshness.

Several times, she peered around the display and we exchanged glances. The first couple of times, it wasn't acknowledged by either of us. But after pacing the floor for several minutes, she seated herself on the comfy cloth recliner next to mine.

We struck up a conversation, exchanging names and where we were from. She told me that her name was Corrina and she was from Portugal.

Was I excited to hear that! I explained a humanitarian medical mission I'd participated in in Havana, Cuba, and how it touched my heart. I then shared more about the experience I'd had on the flight from Jose Marti International Airport back to Miami, en route to Phoenix (to be followed by a two-hour drive to Sedona). The Havana-to-Miami flight was fairly empty. I'll always remember this flight because I witnessed two couples a few rows ahead of me speaking in a language that sounded quite melodic and beautiful. After observing and listening to them converse over the flight's duration, sometime toward the end of the flight, I asked them, "Where are all of you from?"

"Portugal," they responded.

I thanked them and returned to my seat. It wasn't simply the Portuguese language being spoken. It was also the manner in which they addressed one another, and the way they listened to one another. It was filled with such care and attention, I found it mesmerizing. At that moment, I quietly said to myself, "I will travel, one day, to experience Portugal and its people." It made a lasting impression on me. Over the years, the genre of Portuguese vocalists and music forever entered my world, as well.

Around the time I met Corrina, there was a song I heard repeatedly playing in my head. It was on the soundtrack on a CD from the movie *Phenomenon*, with John Travolta, Kyra Sedgwick, and Forest Whitaker, which was in theaters in 1994. It had entered my thoughts so many times over several weeks before meeting Corrina, I would find myself humming the melody and singing the words, "Corrina, Corrina." I was so intrigued by what was happening, I dug out my old CD player, dusted it off, found the CD, and popped it into the player so I could listen to the sound track. It gave me curiosity and exhilarating wonder about what was about to come.

Corrina and I ended up having lunch, flirting with one another, and chatting. As the afternoon went on, we both began to feel a fondness building toward one another.

During our lunch, I shared about the song "Corrina" and how it was a melody that I just couldn't get out of my head. Corrina simply smiled in acknowledgment.

It's true that a strong chemistry or sexual connection was present for both of us, but something was happening even beyond my current level of understanding. I sensed that her name, and the song being repeated in my head, meant that something far greater than a simple affection for each other was about to be revealed, an inner wisdom.

In the next few days, we spent more time together. During those dates, I began to believe that she was another angel sent to help both of us understand something.

We decided to watch the movie *Phenomenon* together. Phenomenon's story-line description is this: "On his birthday, how a mechanic George Malley (John Travolta) sees a flash of light and proceeds to exhibit extraordinary mental abilities. He becomes a genius, even showing an ability to move objects with his mind. George wished to help people, but the government wanted to take him in for observation. Soon, George finds out from Dr. Bruder (Robert Duvall) that he has a massive brain tumor. With this new knowledge, George decides to spend his time with girlfriend Lace (Kyra Sedgwick)." [https://www.rottentomatoes.com/m/phenomenon]

I shared with her that I didn't know what was about to happen but I was certain we were together that evening for a reason. I didn't know if we somehow created the moment, calling each other in, or whether it was a premonition about what was to come. Either way I was ready.

We placed the DVD into the player, settled into the oversized, cushy sofa, and pressed Play on the remote.

Several scenes in the movie touched us both on a number of levels. One was the love between George and Lace. Another was George's connection to superhuman powers, especially in the scene when he's standing in front of his house and the wind begins blowing through the trees. It seems like a perfect moment of remembrance.

But the big "Aha!" The moment didn't come until the scene where farm workers are tending to the orchards when a Portuguese woman enters the scene; later, her son is pulled from the grips of death via food poisoning. The Portuguese woman had a striking resemblance to the woman sitting next to me! When another character referred to this woman as "his angel," it made perfect sense. While this was happening, guess what song was playing? Yes, the song titled "Corrina."

Corrina and I looked at each other in shock. Wow, I was blown away! We both were. Afterward, we shared our thoughts and feelings about the film and how it had impacted each of us. We each listened to the other with care and attention. At that moment, something opened between us. Our connection became so animated, it seemed otherworldly.

Embraced by so much familiarity, we began to embrace one another, allowing each other to move into this moment without any hesitation. The passion seemed full-on as we climbed the stairs, hand in hand, to my bedroom. The lovemaking and intimacy was powerful! Immediately afterward, as we lay together, both catching our breath, she said, "Let's do it again."

But something struck me like a ton of bricks. She completely missed the moment of magic and innocence, wanting to rush right back into wanting and feeling another orgasm.

I heard my inner voice say, "Passion burns out. You are seeking Love."

Feeling a sudden disconnect from her, I realized a new, profound truth: she was an angel—but an angel to teach me about passion and its ability to sustain itself, even if it wasn't love. During the next few moments, we held one another, but I suspected she wasn't too happy with me as I expressed my unwillingness to re-experience her desire so quickly.

As quickly as the wave of attraction had come, it now departed, leaving me with a wisdom that I needed. My puzzled look and lack of response to her request left us both feeling awkward. We parted the next morning with a cool farewell. But the lesson for me was crystal-clear: I wanted love and not just passionate sex.

THE "FEELING STATE OF GOD" — NANCY

Another powerful experience occurred with my friend Nancy, a dear friend. Again, the experience illuminated me, because Nancy, like Corrina, was a kindred spirit and a teacher.

Nancy worked at my cigar shop a few days a week. It was always a pleasure to have her there, and the customers loved her. I was extremely grateful for her friendship, our conversations, and Thai massages.

Often, each of us had communicated nonverbally with the other that our connection went deeper than friendship. At one point, Nancy and I admitted to one another that there was a strong intimacy and chemistry between us. But we never acted upon it. For me, our friendship was all that I needed. It was as if we'd known one another from another time or place.

One autumn afternoon while Nancy was away at a retreat center, I received a call from one of her friends. Frantically, she blurted, "Nancy is hurt!"

"What happened?" I asked, ready to drop the phone and go to her.

"She dove into a swimming pool and struck her head really hard on the bottom of the pool!" She was afraid Nancy had suffered some kind of paralysis. "She isn't moving."

In a flash, it brought me back to grade school, when a friend had a similar fate. It had caused him to be physically impaired for the rest of his life. I told Nancy's friend not to move her, and to give me the directions to their location. In the background, I could hear Nancy saying repeatedly, "I am alright. It was a minor accident, and I want to see Kevin."

My initial thought was *absolutely, I'm on my way*. But then it occurred to me to ask: had the friend called Nancy's husband?

"No," she said. "Nancy wants to see you."

It seemed odd that she wanted me there instead of her husband. It seemed that something else was going on, and I had a sense the friend thought so, too. She went on to say, "Nancy has been experiencing some really powerful energy during the retreat, and they weren't able to understand what was going on with her."

Upon hearing that, I sensed it was something to do with a Kundalini experience. I felt that a powerful life force energy, often referred to as *chi*, was activated within her body.

In the background, I could hear several of her friends talking. They sounded upset and puzzled about what to do next. Once again, I told them not to move her and to call an ambulance, but Nancy insisted she was alright. I was then told she was beginning to move her body after the initial shock.

One of the participants at the retreat center was a registered nurse. She got on the phone and assured me that everything seemed to be returning to some sense of normalcy, but Nancy still wanted to see me. The nurse began to understand more when Nancy clearly expressed that I'd had a similar experience a few years earlier. Nancy said, one last time, that I was the one she needed to help her.

After repeated attempts to convince Nancy to call her husband, and her repeated refusals, I agreed to meet with her. I said I could go to her location or meet her elsewhere. She said she was fine to drive (and the nurse agreed), so Nancy said she would meet me. We decided to drive up the Prescott Mountain Range to a particular place where there was a small lake. When I thought of where to go, it immediately entered my mind that this was the place. It came with such clarity.

But I had one condition: that I first speak with her brother Stephen to let him know that she was safe, and to tell him where she and I were meeting up. I knew Stephen well; over the years, he and I had spent many afternoons together, smoking cigars at my shop. Nancy agreed to this condition.

I called Stephen and told him what happened. I shared my concern that Nancy's husband hadn't been called. I encouraged him to let her meet me. I eventually convinced Stephen to call the husband, and I told him where she and I were going to meet.

Nancy and I both drove to the agreed-upon location. After we'd parked in the parking area on the grassy knoll, I recognized that she was in a highly elevated state of consciousness and sensitivity. I could see it in her eyes and the energies around her body. I refer to this state of being as the "Fifth Dimension" and the "Feeling State of God." This is a state of awareness where one is aware of other dimensions, and one's emotional state is extremely amplified and highly sensitive. It's a profound state, and I recalled the first time I experienced it, which had happened in Lourdes, France.

We sat near the lake for several hours, talking about her most private thoughts and what she was experiencing. Our conversation affirmed that her physical and emotional states were highly attuned to deep levels of conscious awareness. After her time of sharing, we noticed a significant temperature drop and realized the sun was going down. Our mountaintop perch had turned quite chilly. We returned to my car, where I retrieved several blankets and a jacket that I gave her, as well as a pair of clean white athletic socks to keep her feet warm. Then, settling down on the cold ground, I expressed that I was delighted she called me to help her through this experience, the "Feeling State of God."

So often, people try to remain in an intellectual state of reasoning. But in this feeling state of awareness, the mind has to simply yield. In due time, it will understand. This is a powerful time of simultaneous release and opening. This energy and feeling state has to come through the heart of the individual, and it's best received while being guided by someone who understands the energy and awareness of the awakening process. Otherwise, it can remain a mental state of struggle and torture.

We continued to talk about many topics, but one in particular kept popping up: how structured religions and their perspectives on the world were skewed from original teachings. Nancy said she needed a deeper frame of reference for all that was happening through her. I explained as best I could, and it seemed to comfort her.

We realized it was getting extremely late, and we were getting quite cold. Then Nancy posed a very powerful question. It was about scriptures, and I don't remember the actual words but it referred to the passage that says something like, "When and how does the Lamb lie down with the Lion?"

In that moment, both of us were in an extremely heightened state of consciousness. She expressed her desire to understand this passage and asked once more, "How does the lion lie down with the lamb, and what does it mean? I can't resolve this conflict inside of my mind."

What happened next, as the words rolled off my lips, seemed to be that of something greater than I. When does the lion lie down with the lamb? In one breath, it came out of me: "It is when the two come together within you. Then you will truly understand."

A deep breath of the chilled mountain air escaped my lungs, and a long silence filled the air. With deep profundity, we both understood what this meant. In the next few moments, while holding one another, we began to open to its deeper meaning. Neither of us could speak. As our eyes met, there seemed to be a warmth that washed over us and we continued to hold one another other in this new awareness. I could see in her eyes that no other words needed to be spoken.

We shared a farewell and loving embrace, and we each drove down the Prescott Mountain Range's windy terrain, me following her to make sure she made it down safely. It was truly a time of intimacy, connection, and awareness that we shared. I felt deep within my heart that expression, "We are walking each other home." It was into that place of the heart's understanding. And as I drove home, a sweetness filled my mood.

FIFTH DIMENSION

I feel it is a good time to share about the fifth dimension. The fifth dimension, as I understand it, is about a deep, profound feeling state, not a mental one. It is a field of energy that requires an innocence of the ego's surrender. It's not a "how do I figure this out?" mindset, but rather a yielding or surrendering of one's will and ego. It is when one's being, an awareness, begins to transcend the mental. It is thoughts and feelings of a vast expansiveness. For me, the fifth dimension was best described by a mystic who said, "It is when the Center of one's Being touches its circumference."

Based on my experiences, the mind has a very difficult time trying to grasp such concepts and energies, leaving it frustrated and confused. This feeling state is essential to one's access to this new state of awareness, through surrender. And this surrender must be within the heart.

My perception is that the Heart is a gateway, or a portal, to this animating force many call God or Source within. I also use the term and concept of the "Soul." I believe the soul is our connection to all that is and our connection to Source. And most often, it is in a moment of Grace, when we are allowed to see, feel, and sense something so much greater than ourselves. I often refer to it as the Matrix of Love.

I was inspired some years ago to write these words, which came to mind during one of my experiences:

"True wisdom is when the Head and Heart gather as One understanding the Experience."

Around the time I wrote those words, I found an article that gave great explanations of the third, fourth, and fifth dimensions.

3D - 4D - 5D Perspective

In a nutshell:

3D is a level of perception/awareness in which the mind identifies the "outer reality" as the only reality. It perceives anything outside itself as other than itself through a lens of separation, and generally only receives input from the 5 physical senses. An identification with the "ego" is created/shaped over the course of a lifetime as a result of trauma and programming from the hijacked environment, and subconscious decisions are predominantly made out of fear in this state. It is a sort of masking or hiding of the true unlimited self which is always present, but is veiled behind this false identity.

5D is a dissolution of the ego identity in which the true nature of Self is uncovered/revealed (usually over time). As traumas are cleared and false beliefs are deprogrammed, the identification with this limited perspective weakens until it is seen as only one aspect—although no less valid—of a much greater awareness. The mind views experience more holistically and resolves the paradox of duality that is seen from the separation perspective of the ego. This is sometimes called unity consciousness and is representative of love, which is a connecting or convergent force. (Fear is a separating force.)

4D is the chaotic transition period through which the awareness moves from a state of separation (3D) to one of unity (5D). On an individual level, conflicts and emotions arise that catalyze the mind to seek different perspectives and become aware of subconscious programmed reactions and beliefs. Often the mind will bounce between 3D and 5D awareness until it is able to stabilize and maintain the unity perspective (while retaining the ability to view from the 3D). On a collective level, the individual belief systems combine to form the "chaos" of change that we see happening in our world, which in turn catalyzes the individual—it's actually one and the same. All of the issues we see arising in our societies are being presented to be evaluated and reconsidered just as needs to be done on the individual level. The best way to help the planet move through it is to move yourself through it and reflect the 5D unity perspective back into the world AKA shine your light! Hope this makes sense.

[From a Facebook post dated May 5, 2022 by Ariah Patricia Lovelight (https://www.facebook.com/pat.lovelight333)]

This process is happening in the world now and what I refer to as the "Dark Night of the Soul of the Collective Consciousness."

INSPIRATION AND WISDOM

I spent the next period of time (the years 2010 to 2011) continuing to build my landscaping business along with my counseling practice, both of which consumed much of my time. Of course, during this time, I was also writing my book *Trust Patience Surrender*, which took all of my free time.

I also had many dinners and meetings with Swami Buddhananda, discussing his wisdom and interpretations of the Vedas and life in general. Often, this involved me asking questions and listening intently to his many stories. Some of his stories were about his days in the military as a musician and composer/entertainer, his time as a dancer in a professional troupe, and time spent studying comparative religions. For twenty-five years, he established and operated Vedanta centers in Southern California. He was quite happy because he was the very first non-Indian (not being born in India) to have the privilege of opening the centers in the United States.

He is such a Renaissance man. I realize how blessed I have been to have him as my teacher. I view him as a friend, a mentor, and even a surrogate grandfather. He is ninety years old now, and our friendship has lasted more than twenty years.

I continued taking care of my Spanish Colonial house and quarter horses, but there was a thought that continuously popped into my head. It was about going to Bali, Indonesia. Years earlier, I'd torn a page out of a travel magazine, showing a native Balinese woman strolling through a misty jungle in a white muslin cloth dress. It seemed so quiet and serene, which intrigued me.

In Bali, there is a particular village called Ubud. As a result of the book *Eat Pray Love* by Elizabeth Gilbert, over the years I'd heard others talk about Ubud. Also, Max, the Balinese importer/exporter of Balinese art and sculptures who resided in Sedona, told me he traveled to Ubud several times a year. Over a few years, we popped in and out of each other's lives, and I even attended his wedding to a Balinese woman. The nuptials took place in the backyard of the house where I was living in a small studio apartment I referred to as the "Monastic Chamber." I lived there for one year. The studio apartment had been gifted to me when I was recuperating from my near death experience and the loss of everything I had owned. This was my individual dark night of the soul. My friend Sandy opened her home and the apartment to me.

At that time, I was unsure where life's path would lead me. I lived moment by moment, day by day. It was a time I found extremely challenging, more than enough for me to handle. I'd lost everything I thought was of value: my cigar shop, my house, my truck, my investments. I was blessed to have Sandy and her family's long-term friendship.

Max and his bride's wedding ceremony in Sandy's backyard seemed so magical, with colorful Balinese banners and umbrellas dotting the backyard. *Hmm*, I thought. *Bali could be an exotic vacation someday.*

As life went on, Grandfather's wisdom appeared to become part of my own, weighing his words within me to see if they fit in a way that felt like my truth as well. This reminded me of the little blue book by Rabi M. Shapiro titled *Open Secrets*, which Grandfather had given me some years earlier. It was a book that had such wisdom. The opening words touched me deeply:

My Dear Aaron Hershel,

Can it really be that you have moved so far away that we are reduced to speaking through paper and ink? It saddens me to think I may not see you again. Yet I am honoured that you have chosen to continue your studies with me. It will be a challenge, not simply because of the medium but because of the message. You ask difficult questions, seeking to open the secrets of the universe.

My teaching is not complex. Its difficulty lies only in its simplicity. There is nothing in what I will tell you that cannot be verified through your own experience. I will not ask for faith in my teaching nor trust in my person. On the contrary: I have faith in you that you will see what is so, and I trust you to judge my words against your own experience.

Write when you can and ask of me what you will. I will respond as clearly as I know how. I look forward to this venture. It is my charge to "raise up many students" (Pirke Avot 1:1). There is nothing a teacher desires more than a student hungry to learn. Let us "taste and see that God is good: (Psalms 34:8). Let us feast on the wisdom and take care not to grow too fat on illusion.

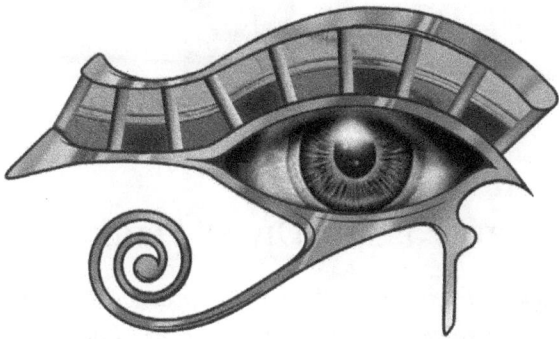

CHAPTER 5

CHAPTER 5: THE DIVINE FEMININE

"She is the Sophia of wisdom, the Maria of compassion, the Persephone of destruction, compelling Necessity and Fate, and the Muse." ~Unknown

I'd like to turn now to sharing some of the understandings that I learned based on certain experiences that occurred throughout my life. These are in no way the full extent of what has happened to me, but I want to share these experiences to assist you in following my thoughts, line of reasoning, and the impressions that have shaped my perspective of the world and what I call the Divine Feminine. During these experiences and moments of Grace, the Divine Mother, Mother Nature, Quan Yin, and Mother Mary entered my life. Grace seems to always come at a time when I need it most. Grace has carried me through some of my most challenging moments.

MY FATHER'S RELATIONSHIP WITH MOTHER MARY

My concept of the Divine Feminine, at the time known to me as Mother Mary, was formed at a very early age and continued throughout my years as a young Catholic. From ages nine to fourteen years I worked on a paper route with my father, my brother, and my three sisters, and on occasional Saturdays with my grandfather, who helped when my father couldn't be there.

I will never forget the extreme stress and hardship my father experienced when I was a child. He held a number of jobs, all of them needed to feed and clothe myself and my siblings. He was also struggling with an enormous amount of debt and pressure because of my oldest brother's hospital bills and his passing away of leukemia. Additionally, due to emotional strain and breakdowns, my mother was frequently in the hospital. Somewhere in all of the madness, my mother believed that God was punishing her. When she was hospitalized, my siblings and I would visit her in between working the paper route, school, and homework, leaving little to no time for enjoying childhood friendships.

One time, I witnessed my father beginning to break down from all of the stress. I will always remember what he said to me, while releasing his breath in a heavy sigh: "It's only through Mother Mary that I find any sense of peace and comfort." He also shared that Mother Mary was the only one who could hear him and understand what he was going through.

This really struck me! I could see in my father's facial expression how the Virgin Mary was a great comfort to him during his unbearable times. I even remember him holding back his tears as he exaggerated his next swallow. This, combined with my feelings that arose in that moment, an exaggerated awareness of how my own mother wasn't there for me, laid the groundwork for my connection to Mother Mary.

Some years later, as part of questions I was to ask while completing my Masters program in Santa Monica, California, Dad shared an elaboration on his concept of how the Divine Mother helped him through his most difficult times. This time he didn't hold back the tears as he began to share some of the experiences, which I will talk about later in this book.

MUFFY AND MOTHER MARY

Another encounter with the Divine Mother was on my wedding day at the Basilica of Saint Louis, King of France Cathedral, in St. Louis, Missouri (often referred to as the Old Cathedral). This historic cathedral was nestled under the St. Louis Gateway Arch and alongside the flowing banks of the Mississippi River. During the wedding ceremony, my bride, Mary (whom everyone, including me, called Muffy), and I went to the statue of the Virgin Mary, at the side altar, to lay red roses delicately at her feet.

Muffy also felt that her given name, Mary, was a dedication to her namesake, the Virgin Mary. She'd had numerous encounters with Mother Mary. She told a story about being a young girl riding her bicycle through the fog created by a mosquito fogging machine driving through her neighborhood; a milk truck ran over her, leaving her in critical condition. She believed that the Virgin Mary helped her survive.

Another event was shortly before she and I met in high school. Muffy was accredited in an English equestrian style known as "Hunters and Jumpers." At the age of sixteen, she was riding one of August Busch's horses (of the Busch Bavarian beer family). It weighed in around 2,200 pounds and stood seventeen hands tall. During Hunter and Jumpers, Muffy was entering and exiting what is known as an "in and out" jump pattern, where the rider is required to jump over a five-foot fence and then immediately jump over another five-foot fence. Only the horse's stride completes this "in and out" pattern.

While Muffy was riding the Busch horse, the horse came to a sudden stop between the two fences. The horse crashed into the second fence, causing Muffy to fall and crushing her beneath its body as it tried to find its footing. What saved her life was her mother's insistence that she wear her metal riding helmet. The size and depth of the dents in the metal helmet indicated she would have received serious skull and brain damage without it. Muffy felt it was Mother Mary's intervention that caused her to wear the helmet, saving her head and possibly her life.

As a result of the accident she needed serious surgery. The surgical team had to cut a large incision into her belly and remove her obliterated spleen. Once again, it was her strong faith in the Virgin Mary that brought her through yet another life-threatening experience.

MY DIVINE FEMININE EXPERIENCES

I, too, have had personal experiences with the Divine Feminine represented by Mother Mary, Quan Yin, and White Buffalo Calf woman. I have now come to the understanding that all are representations of the feminine aspect of God or Source. Some of this came through moments of extreme vulnerability and exhaustion, leaving me with an expanded understanding.

One summer afternoon, I was traveling down the winding road through the Prescott Mountain Range. I was feeling extremely frustrated, thinking of how my life and others were like blood caplets within the circulatory system, and how we collectively become so caught up in materialism and greed, we become clogged and stagnant, just as the circulatory system does. Simultaneously I visualized the veins in my body becoming clogged with plaque and debris. I could literally see the metaphor, and I wondered how to open this energetic field and release the stagnancy.

I felt what I was visualizing, and in that frantic moment I called out to Mother Mary, "Please help me!"

Seconds later, as I rounded the next mountain's winding curve, there she was, standing at the edge of a small overlook with the expanse of the beautiful Verde Valley behind her. The three-foot high statue of the Virgin Mary was right in front of me.

I could hear the melody, "Speaking words of wisdom, let it be, let it be." I immediately felt calmness, as the anxiety left my body. I pulled into the overlook, sat down before her, and shared my gratitude with her.

QUAN YIN

Another of these times occurred when Quan Yin came to comfort me during an uncomfortable time of indecision. Quan Yin is a popular deity or religious figure in the Buddhist faith and iconography. Quan Yin is known as the Bodhisattva of great compassion and a figure of mercy and compassion to those who are in need. She came to me during my time at the University of Santa Monica, when I was struggling with finances, primarily my university tuition payments and the monthly travel expenses to California for school. It was a time of deep internal shifts and a very uncomfortable new awareness of great confusion. I just couldn't seem to figure out how to make all these ends meet.

Other troubling questions were layered in my mind, as well. "Should I quit my university studies in Spiritual Psychology? Should I commit to full-time work and let it all go?" My mind and physical body were going through so much, I simply didn't think I could handle the stress. Tears even began to well up.

I took a deep cleansing breath, deciding to do my daily meditation to try and quiet my mind. As I knelt down, getting situated to lie on the floor, I glanced at the beautiful crème-colored porcelain statue of Quan Yin, asking her to comfort me and show me her compassion so I could navigate my current situation and find more balance with life.

As I lay there going deeper into the silence, I could feel tears rolling down my cheeks. I once more glanced at Quan Yin, closed my eyes, and began slowing my breath and entering a meditative state.

At first, I struggled a bit. As minutes passed, I began to feel a loving energy in the room. Suddenly, this loving energy was enveloping me. I could feel the presence of the Mother holding me with my head in her lap and her arms swaddled around me. I saw her in my mind's eye. As my tears flowed, I clearly saw the image of Quan Yin.

Resting in her comfort and meditation for several minutes, I fell into a deep meditative state, where all of my fears and tension simply melted away.

That wasn't the last time the Divine Feminine came into my life. She appeared several more times, appearing as White Buffalo calf woman and as the White Tara.

Still, in the recesses of my mind, Bali continued to pop up. Each time it did, I internally scoffed at the idea, pushing it aside to return to my everyday life.

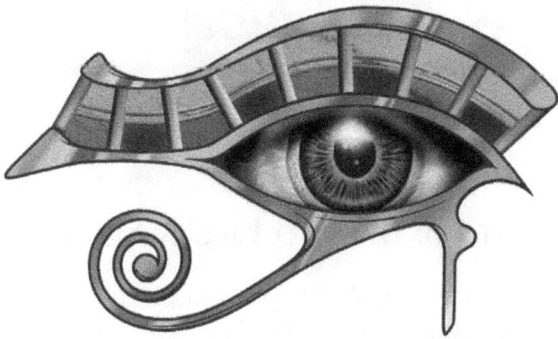

CHAPTER 6

Chapter 6: Blessed Life in Sedona

"The turnaround is the process by which the unconscious becomes conscious, often in a flash of deep emotional insight." ~*Richard Hidalgo*

Grandfather and the Three-Day Retreat

My daily life continued: landscaping, counseling, and guiding workshops with individuals and small groups. I remember the first Soulful Guidance workshop which I asked Grandfather Morning Owl to co-facilitate. I had contacted a few of my counseling clients and a few others, sharing with them the workshop's contents to gauge their level of interest. They appeared to be quite enthusiastic about participating, so I coordinated the scheduling with Grandfather. As I thought about our co-facilitation, my enthusiasm grew.

The inner guidance workshop that I now call "Soulful Guidance" began as "Spiritual Dimensions of the Healing Arts." It is a formal, three-to-five day intensive workshop that covers everything from emotional profiling to deep interrogative work around one's destructive or unhelpful patterns, kinesiology, and a number of other modalities. It was designed to help individuals see the powerful characteristics and qualities that they brought into the world and distinguish the patterns and beliefs which were learned and developed over one's lifetime. The intention is to bring a participant back into alignment with their true nature and authentic self.

Grandfather Morning Owl and I would be co-facilitating the

workshop. It felt as though that weekend arrived rather quickly, as I was excited to work with Grandfather and my clients. The clients were a bit apprehensive about delving deep within their life's context and having other participants listen to them, but their apprehensions seemed to fade away as soon as sharing began on the first day of the workshop. The group's work grew more and more powerful as it gained momentum. Each participant was exploring their psyche while unearthing quite a lot of interesting patterns and beliefs that they held. Some were not favorable but still insightful. The three-day, weekend workshop came to an end on Sunday. At its conclusion, I felt a real sense of completion with Grandfather.

As I said goodbye to the last client (who had been in therapy with me for a few months), something clicked as the client and I looked into each other's eyes while saying our goodbyes at the door. The way she looked at me, her knowing glance, spoke volumes. One thing in particular that I gleaned was that she didn't need my counseling or sessions any longer. It really struck a chord within me. Unbeknownst to me, and in this momentary state, I was unaware of what was about to happen.

The workshop was extremely gratifying on so many levels, but as soon as I closed the door after Grandfather's departure, overwhelming tears began flowing—slowly at first, then in a sudden burst of emotion exploding forth. I was taken by surprise at the magnitude of these feelings. I couldn't wrap my head around what was occurring. Was it because my client didn't need me anymore or was it something else?

For the next fifteen to twenty minutes, a floodgate of tears poured out of me. I simply paced around the house, then outside on my property, repeatedly making this plea: "Help me understand what is going on. Help me understand what is happening to me."

It seemed the intensity of the moment would consume my very being. I even went upstairs to ask a friend who was staying with me what could possibly be going on. She quipped a response that didn't make any sense, so I turned around as quickly as I'd entered her room and headed back downstairs, returning outside. This was the only thing that made any sense to me, to be out of doors.

Be in nature, I said to myself.

I continued for a half an hour or so walking around the grounds, pleading my requests. And then, in a flash, the answer appeared in my mind. I remembered what Grandfather had always told me: that it would be time for him to leave this world when he completed his work with me.

He shared this statement with me the first time we met. He repeated it regularly. He said he would teach me all he knew, and then it would be his time to die. Given his age, he pondered when he could leave the planet, since he had done so much work for humanity.

At that moment, feeling the weight of my emotions, I realized that the completion of our workshop was the culmination of all his work with me, and it was time for him to leave. In those moments in the yard, I came to the realization that for a very long time, I hadn't wanted to co-facilitate the workshop with him but I didn't know why. Pow—there it was, staring me right in the face.

As the tears flowed, I felt that he might die soon. Those were the thoughts connected to the emotions, and I realized in all of the years that I had known him and listened to his wisdom, I'd never really expressed my love for him. I often thanked him and always brought him an offering for our meetings and dinners. In that fleeting moment, it all made perfect sense and my tears began to slow to a trickle. This was it! I realized how much I would miss him. I continued walking the property as I let this newfound realization sink in.

I composed myself, allowing these truths to sink in. Then I decided to take him for dinner and express my deepest gratitude to him. The next day, I called him, and we set a time for dinner.

This pivotal moment made me aware of our friendship. I felt a sense of completion between us as well and a knowing that it was time to move on. I knew deep within me that his wisdom and knowledge was safely stored within the banks of my memories, and this wisdom would be shared with others in the future. His profound sense of guidance felt anchored within me.

The days following lead me once more into my daily routines. One of my greatest pleasures was saddling my horses and, with a friend, taking a long meandering ride along the cliffs, and experiencing the majestic sunsets of Sedona. Some days, I would just sit in the saddle mesmerized by her landscape and settings, knowing that life doesn't get any better than this.

Often, the vistas and breathtaking moments transported me to another place and time. How well I remember sitting on my front porch, legs fully stretched out, smoking a good Cuban cigar, breathing in both the waffling smoke and the visual panoramic landscapes and views. Memories of my missions to Cuba arose, and I had beautiful thoughts of the many friends and good times I'd had there.

Grandfather and I did have our dinner, a few nights later. I let him know how important he had been in my life and that I held love in my heart for him, as a friend and a spiritual figure. He seemed rather uncomfortable about my words, which I found a bit unusual, but I figured it was because not many others had expressed such gratitude to him. I'll talk more about Grandfather later, but I'm glad we had that time together.

CHARLES, GENII, AND RENEE

During this time, my landscaping company provided full-time employment and lots of enjoyment being in nature, as well as working with landscaping development, design, and maintenance. My evenings and weekends were often filled with counseling clients.

One scorchingly hot, 112-degrees Fahrenheit summer day I got a phone call from a man named Charles. He was in distress about water leaks in his backyard. He told me that several other landscaping companies and plumbers had tried to find the source but were unsuccessful. Usually, I stayed away from irrigation problems that others created, because they could become quite messy and not worth the time or money. But listening to his plea for help, I said I'd come have a look, even though it went against everything I knew.

When I arrived at Charles's house, he was appreciative that I'd come so quickly. He showed me his yard, where gallons of water were bubbling up from underneath the ground. I surveyed the yard and decided that this was going to be a big investigative process. I'd have to determine if there was one or multiple leaks on his property. I said I'd take it on, and both Charles and the two women of the house, Genii and Renee, were excited to see how I'd fix the leaks. I rolled up my sleeves and began digging in the soil.

After several hours of isolating the large lakes of water, I figured out what was happening. Covered in sweat and slippery mud, I dug up all the necessary piping and replaced several feet of irrigation PVC pipe, along with an irrigation valve that I determined was the root cause of the flooding. After being knee deep, my body covered in mud, for several hours in the hot summer sun, I completed the work.

As a result, I became friends with Charles, Genii, and Renee. This experience brought the four of us together on future occasions to discuss unique topics that excited my curiosity. Genii and Renee had their own kind of wisdom and experiences they wanted to share with me. Our conversations consisted of many topics but several in particular had me spellbound: the new earth, healing modalities, the Galactic Federation of Light, and the global reset of fiat currencies. Cities of Light, foreign Zimbabwe fiat currency, and an initiation were to come.

In turn, they were excited to learn more about my recently written book, *Trust Patience Surrender*. It started when Charles found out that I had written my spiritual autobiography. The three of them were intrigued to hear my stories. Charles was overcome with joy, saying that in the future, we could collaborate on a project. He pointed to a wall shelf full of books that he claimed he co-wrote and published with a number of authors.

I was intrigued but felt a little hesitant. Two more meetings took place, with some pretty interesting twists and turns. In one of our meetings, they asked if they could interview me. I shared about my near-death experience, non-extraterrestrial beings, Grandfather, and my experiences with angels and the realm of the spirit world.

I was filled with curiosity and excitement when Genii Townsend began talking about her visits to what she referred to as the "Cities of Light," and her desire to put me through an initiation process with her and her superior. It all seemed a little bit out there to me. I felt it had a subtle "woo-woo" factor to it.

But after several more conversations and remembering all of the previous experiences that had happened to me, I began to put this into a new perspective: the realm of possibility. *Why couldn't it be possible?* I asked myself. My own experiences over the previous few years had taught me to be less skeptical about such matters. I realized I was open to what Genii had to say.

Several days later, I arrived at Charles, Renee, and Genii's house for what Genii called an initiation and to give me the keys to the "Cities of Light." I'd thought she meant physical keys, but it was quite different than I 'd imagined. Genii and her counterpart, viewed by Genii as her Elder and higher in authority, began to talk about the Cities of Light that are stationed outside (i.e., running parallel) to planet earth.

The initiation was systematic. As they began to delve into their practices, I somehow knew what was going to be said next, and I ended up telling them many things regarding my own connections with the Galactic Federation of Light and what was to come in the upcoming years, especially the years 2020 through 2025. They seemed shocked that I knew as much as I did. I responded, "I am just the vehicle for this information." I went on to say, "This information was shared and shown to me just a few years ago, in a vision."

I was very pleased to hear about Genii's experiences being taken into the Cities of Light. She told me in great detail what the grounds looked like, the overall environment, the architecture, and the Light and Sound technologies that were being used for healing in the Cities of Light. She told numerous stories of her many visitations to the city. She said that she'd even written a book laying out the architecture, the grounds, and much more. She then shared how the technology has the abilities to heal every malady afflicting humans on earth. It was like something out of a sci-fi movie, but it made a lot of sense to me, almost as if I was revisiting a past life of sorts. Genii and her superior ended the initiation by giving me a certificate to the Cities of Light and saying, "You have now received the keys to the city."

Our early morning discussions and initiation blended into the afternoon. Our time together was exhilarating and expansive. After our time came to an end, as I headed toward the front door, their friend and housemate, Renee, called me over to where she was seated and began sharing what she'd been working on for the past several years. The discussion turned to the valuations and DE-valuing of all fiat currencies around the world. I stared at her computer screen for a good period of time as she explained what was happening in the world, and if and when things might happen. She said, "It is going to be a financial system reset."

Renee went on to talk about the catastrophic and cataclysmic events around the world that would occur, but her main mission was to follow world currencies. It wasn't like arbitrage, where one buys and sells currencies, but more of what was happening to them and what will come in the future. She explained it as a new monetary platform or system.

There was real efficiency to her voice as she spoke. She presented the information in a confident and structured way. Then she looked at me and said, "I have a currency that I am giving to you as a gift, along with this letter. Sometime in the future, someone will exchange it for whatever monetary needs that you have."

She went on to say that they would give me any amount of money, as long as what I was to build or create was in "Service to Others." She conveyed the idea that no monies that I requested would be too large or small, provided the work would be for the betterment of Humanity. She then exclaimed, "It is part of the global reset and the New World."

I was intrigued and quite interested in what this currency, along with the letter, might bring into my future. And yet, I still had a trepidation about the whole thing. Just a little healthy discernment, I thought. Our meeting ended with cordial farewells. The evening was falling fast upon me so I jumped into my truck and headed for home.

Over the next several weeks I mulled over what had happened that day with the three of them. Other thoughts too, would rise and fall about visiting Bali, Indonesia. These thoughts eventually got me seriously thinking of booking Max and Malati's villa in Ubud. But once more, it remained no more than a thought.

THE CHIMNEY ROCK HOUSE

I often reminisced about how blessed I was. It all started some twenty years earlier, when I left the corporate world and ventured off to Sedona by a combination of mystical chance and an internal calling. The corporate world came to a dramatic halt when I had one of my initial cathartic events that changed the trajectory of my life forever.

When I'd arrived in Sedona, I often drove by a two-story Spanish Colonial house flanked at each of its corners by 30-foot Italian cypress trees. I admired its majestic charm. The house was located on Dry Creek Road in West Sedona, and each time I passed by, I just knew that someday I would live there. Of course, I also thought it was a bit of a stretch, because it was nearly a million dollar property. I had no idea how I'd be able to come up with that kind of money. So I let it remain a dream and a desire in my heart. Still, from time to time when I drove by the house, I'd imagine myself living there.

Over the next twenty years, I owned several businesses, including a carpet cleaning business, a cigar shop, a therapy practice, and a landscaping company. One day, a potential landscaping client asked if I would come to their home and give them a quote on designing and mounting a large art installation in their front yard. I hadn't done that in the past but decided to accept the challenge.

Barbara, one of the owners of the home, was very polite, and we spoke for some time. "Could you start right away?" she asked.

"Sure," I replied. "I'd be happy to."

Barbara then asked if I'd like to do some work at their other house over on Dry Creek Road. I agreed and headed to the address she had given me to meet her husband, Charles. (A different Charles, it should be noted, than the Charles who had the irrigation problem in his yard.)

When I arrived at the house, I was surprised and shocked to find that it was the house I'd always known I would live in one day! What a coincidence! *No way*, I thought, *could this be the home I'd envisioned living in for so many years?*

I reminded myself to not get ahead of myself. I met Charles, and we assessed the work needed. We talked about the property's general cleanup and agreed on a monthly maintenance contract. I was just excited to be on the property.

Some time later, I shared with both Charles and Barbara my intuitive knowing that I would live in the house someday, but I didn't know how. I also told them about my love of horses, and how I missed having them. I grew up around horses, and when I was eleven years old, I would muck stalls in exchange for riding.

One of our conversations arose around the topic of my book *Trust Patience Surrender,* and Barbara asked if she could buy a copy. She was intrigued by the stories that I'd shared and by my other worldly experiences.

Then she said something extraordinary: "This house is meant to be yours." She named the rental price they'd want for the house.

I countered with an amount that made more sense for me. If I had accepted their offer, I knew I would be house rich but income poor, and I just didn't want to take that risk. They did not accept my counter, so I sadly declined their offer to rent the house.

Still, I was extremely appreciative to be working on the property, so I continued their maintenance contract and made a number of property upgrades. Soon afterward, they ended up renting the house to a client who didn't want a maintenance contract, and my time was no longer needed.

I told myself that they'd rented the home to someone else, and that was that. But I had not given up hope of living there.

A year or so passed, and I began to notice the new tenant was seriously neglecting the property. I saw the landscape and several mature cherry trees dying. I couldn't stand to see such decay of this beautiful property, so I left a message and sent photos to Barbara and Charles, telling them about the property and allowing the pictures to tell the full story. They were so touched by my care and attention, they eventually removed the tenant and offered me the house for what I had initially countered.

Wow, was I over the top with joy! I responded, "Yes, I'd love to!" A few days later, I moved into the house and began the property's massive cleanup.

"My Boys"

Shortly thereafter, a friend whom I hadn't seen in a while called and said that she had two AQHA registered quarter horses that she could no longer afford. She asked if I would like to take them off her hands and give them a good home.

Again, I got to say, "Yes, I'd love to!"

Of course, I had to make sure first that the horses checked out. I immediately called my friend Jay, an equestrian instructor and rider. I asked if he could look at them and make arrangements to have them trailer-ed to my house if everything checked out with them.

Jay went with me to inspect the horses and see if they were of a sound nature. Jay's visual inspection consisted of lifting their hooves and watching their every gate while moving around the paddock area. After his thorough inspection, he gave them the seal of approval. We loaded them up in the trailer and headed home.

Rocky was an eight-year-old, dark chestnut quarter horse with a small white blaze on his forehead and white stockings around three of his hooves. He was trained in the art of reining.

"Reigning is a western style and riding competition for horses where the rider guides the horse through a precise pattern of circles, spins, and heart pounding decelerated stops. Reining is also considered to be a lot like figure skating but with a 2,000 pound horse. All of the work is done at either a lope or gallop." [https://en.wikipedia.org/wiki/Reining]

Buck, on the other hand, was a bit cantankerous, given his age. He could be quite temperamental at times. Often, backing up on a trail, he nearly fell off a cliff face or into a thicket of chaparral and thorny brush. Buck was a buckskin horse with a golden-colored coat. I often imagined him being ridden in previous lifetimes among the First Peoples Nations. He had a stride and an attitude that seemed to show that he'd been down that road many times before.

Over the next twelve months, I endured many rides in the brutal heat of the summer months and the freezing temperatures of the winter months. But the horses and I enjoyed beautiful, colorful sunsets, and gorgeous days and evenings that we shared throughout the four seasons.

I thought this joy would be endless, but it only lasted until the summer of 2014.

A ROCKY ACCIDENT

I had a friend named Wolfie, a Swedish woman who loved everything Western (as in, jeans, cowgirl boots, cowgirl hat, and all western regalia). She often joined me for an afternoon or evening ride before the sun went down. She was a bit out there at times, I thought; she had an eccentric nature about her. But I enjoyed her company and her horsemanship. She knew a lot of the trails and she knew how to handle horses, which I appreciated and respected. She wasn't afraid of them; she had a deep respect for the equine. Whenever we went trail riding, she unloaded her two dogs out of her brick-red, 4-wheel drive Mitsubishi Montero. She actually lived in it for a while. She also lived by the seat of her pants, and I quite enjoyed that about her. Most often, she would say whatever was on her mind.

Over the period of about a year, we shared a good friendship and many rides with Rocky and Buck. We'd stop to take in the beautiful vistas, the chaparral, mesquite trees, agave, and the majestic scenery of the red rock formations. Each ride was a new experience as the sun's rays played with the mesas, spires, and cliffs.

One beautiful spring afternoon, Wolfie stopped by. We saddled up the boys and headed for the trails along with Wolfie's two canine companions. It was a usual ride of spectacular vistas and canyons along dry river beds, ending with another amazing crimson, blue, and pink sunset. We rode for about two hours, meandering our way back to the house from the winding trails.

Before it got dark, we arrived in front of my house. We were riding on the gravel shoulder alongside Dry Creek Road. As we passed in front of the property, I realized how grateful I was to be able to enjoy this moment. I remember looking up at the sunset. It took my breath away as I gazed at the reds, yellows, and gold radiating from the beautiful blue sky.

Then, all of the sudden, I heard a "twang" sound. In an instant, I realized Rocky had fallen on top of me with my legs straddled around his withers. I felt my cowboy boots being ripped out of the stirrup. I experienced a blackout lasting only a few seconds, followed by excruciating pain. I tried to orient myself, and as I began to focus on the roadway, I saw Rocky running and sliding down the asphalt pavement. My first thought was concern for Rocky's safety and that he might be hit by an oncoming car. But as I started to get up, I dropped back to the ground with a thud.

When I regained consciousness, I saw Wolfie holding Rocky's reins and riding toward me. I slowly stood up, quite confused and shaky, but I grabbed his reins in my left hand and began walking up the driveway. I used my left hand because of the excruciating pain I felt on the entire right side of my body, which had collided with the ground. My right side drooped with pain and lifelessness, and my head was throbbing severely.

Looking at me, Wolfie exclaimed, "Ah, you'll be just fine." But I didn't sense that would be the case, and I said so. So she suggested that she unsaddle and unbridled the horses. I agreed, and as I said goodbye to her, I was disoriented and in pain. I knew that I had at least a concussion, because I had experienced a number of them over the years. I went inside and got ice to put on my hand and wrist, alternating it to my neck, head, and shoulder.

Several hours passed, and I fought the urge to go to sleep. Around eleven or twelve, the pain was getting worse, and I knew I had to go to the emergency room. I drove the hour to the Prescott VA Hospital and checked into the emergency ward. The x-rays and CT-scan indicated that I had several broken bones, primarily in my right hand and foot, along with severe whiplash, a concussion, and brain trauma from the side impact. The nurse practitioner said that I was really lucky I didn't shatter my hip, given the force of the impact. Somehow, I sensed this was her way of comforting me.

I was kept in the ER ward for observation the rest of the night. The pain in my body and head was intense, despite the medication they had prescribed. But I knew there wasn't anything else that the doctor and nurses could do, so I rested till morning. Released from hospital observation, I drove home, crawled into my own bed, and tried to sleep—"tried" being the operative word. For a long time, sleep evaded me.

WHAT IS THIS PAIN TEACHING ME?

During the next seventy-two hours, I ended up having to go back to the ER a few more times. Then I spent the next two months mostly in bed, trying to recuperate. From time to time, friends came to tend to me, and most of them said something like, "Man, you look terrible. Are you going to make it?"

I remember a day that I thought could very well be the last of my life. I slowly rose from bed to walk down the two flights of stairs to the main floor, but I simply couldn't get beyond the stairwell landing between floors. My friend who came to check on me had to help me go back up to my bedroom. The pain in my brain was so intense, and it persisted for weeks on end.

When I came to the realization the pain was not going away any time soon, I decided to begin meditating into it. I asked the pain what it wanted from me and why did this strange and unexpected accident have to happen. I knew that I was careful when riding horses, and I practiced good horsemanship. But the question remained. "Why did this happen, and what is this pain teaching me or asking me to see that I haven't been ready to see".

I'd found several times before in my life that asking such questions could break me out of an old routine or help me see some other life path that I was either avoiding or refusing to acknowledge.

During this time of pain, my friend and neighbor, Karen, told me about an accident she'd experienced a few years earlier. While she was standing behind her horse in the stable, in a mere flash, the horse kicked backwards, striking her in the face. Tragically, it ended up crushing the left side of her face. She told me about the numerous reconstructive surgeries she'd had and the pain she'd endured. The results of her surgeries were evident; she still had some distortion in her left cheek and jaw.

Karen knew a bit about essential oils and their healing qualities. One of the remedies that helped reduce her pain significantly was a mixture of flower and essential oils that she'd combined, creating a special elixir. She claimed its ingredients were a combination of 'Young Living Oils' of RutaVaLa, Frankincense, Wintergreen, and

Panaway. This combination of oils, she said, reduced her pain by sixty percent.

At first, I was a bit skeptical but I remembered that I, too, had used tinctures and flower essences in the past that seemed to help certain discomforts and give me relief. So I asked if she had some to spare. Karen quickly produced the combination of oils and instructed me in their use. After a couple of applications on and around my head and neck areas, I was shocked by the effects. My pain lessened by fifty percent. I was amazed and quite thankful.

Still, the pain persisted, so I also decided to meditate again into it. Once more, I addressed the pain and asked it what it wanted from me and why did this fluke of an accident have to happen? Suddenly, a powerful thought arose: "Go to Bali."

In that moment of silence and realization, I decided not to hesitate. I took heed, listening to that internal voice. In that moment, I also took on a mantra to use whenever I experience a life-changing experience. When it happens, I now ask, "Please give it (the lesson) to me, with Ease and Grace."

This time of recovery also brought back thoughts about why the man who was going to buy my landscaping business the year prior, after completing his due diligence, had simply disappeared the day we were to sign the documents. I'd surmised that it was just the way it was to be.

After these challenging couple of months of slowly healing, I came to an acceptable level of pain. Armed with this new realization of "Go to Bali," I decided to make the necessary arrangements to visit Bali.

In the final stages of my recuperation, I scheduled a two-week vacation for what I called a "look see" of Bali. In other words, I wanted to see what Bali had in store for me.

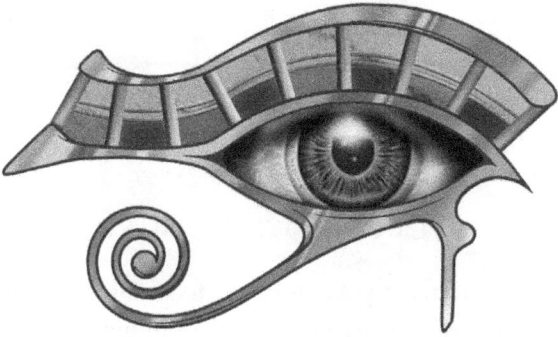

CHAPTER 7

CHAPTER 7: MOVING TO BALI

"When you start utilizing your third eye to seek truth, you will then learn to see that the divine is within you." ~Unknown

"I KNOW WHO YOU ARE"

The time had come to purchase airline tickets and reserve accommodations for my trip to Bali. Before long, I was headed to the Phoenix Sky Harbor to begin my trip to the tropical Island of the Gods.

Upon my arrival in Bali, I met the man who was picking me up from Ngurah Rai International Airport. His name was Agung, and he was the sponsor and ground coordinator for Max and Malati's Bali properties. When I sat down in the front seat of the van, something about him seemed familiar to me, but I scoffed it off, due to exhaustion from the long airline travel, as well as my feelings of excitement about being on vacation.

On the drive, we got to talking. Agung was an educated and well-traveled man. This was apparent by his diction, vocabulary, and references to many trips abroad during his employment history. For twenty-three years, he'd been a personal attache to VIPs at some of the most prestigious Four Season Resorts worldwide. In addition to English, he spoke four other languages: French, Japanese, Spanish, and Arabic.

I wondered why he would be driving my van. When I asked him

about it, he said he'd returned home due to his father's death; at his mother's request, he stayed.

At one point during the ride from the airport to the villa in Ubud, Agung turned and looked at me. A serious expression on his face, he said, "I know who you are, and you are going to be part of my family. And you are going to oversee my wealth, because I am going to die in five years."

Needless to say, I was dumbfounded by his statement. And yet, somewhere in the back of my mind, it seemed to make some sense, leaving me with a feeling of recognition. I responded, "You look familiar to me as well." I said these words without really knowing what was rolling out of my mouth. Still, it seemed right somehow.

Agung said he knew who I was not because I'd made my plans through his boss, Max, whom I'd known previously. Agung just knew me. Later in my two week stay, Agung shared that I was his big brother in a previous life. Being of the Hindu faith, I felt this made a lot of sense. I, too, believed that many of us have lived numerous lives.

WHAT CAN I MANIFEST?

One of the things that motivated me to go to Bali when I did was the Ubud Writers Festival, hosted by Janet DeNeefe. Before leaving Sedona, I did a little research on her and the festival. I learned what was necessary to apply, as the author of *Trust Patience Surrender*, to be in the author lineup for the festival. I knew this was a long shot, but I went ahead and sent a copy of my book and a letter of introduction. The festival was coming up soon, and I expected that on such short notice, nothing would come of it. *But why not?* I thought. I wanted to see what I could manifest. Unfortunately, I didn't receive a response from the festival submissions department. I wasn't surprised, given the short duration and my late submission. Still, I didn't regret giving it a try.

Agung drove an hour north to the area known as Ubud. Our chats were interwoven with moments of extended silence filling the van. I was trying to integrate what he'd just shared with recovering from twenty-six hours of international flights and layovers.

Ubud is situated slightly south of the center of the island. It sits among rice paddies and steep ravines in the central foothills of the

Gianyar Regency. It is said to be a place of spiritual inspiration, where you can seek the benefits of Balinese traditional medicine, yoga, massage, and retreats.

Agung and I arrived at the location where I was to stay for the next two weeks. Called Toko Toko, it was located just a few minutes from the center of Ubud. It featured a clean and simple Balinese style of architecture with a nice swimming pool at the back of the property and lush rice fields adjacent to the pool. Once settled into Toko Toko, I took the next day and a half to recuperate from my travels by lying poolside and getting a good tan. I also enjoyed the small restaurant, which they called a warung, where I sampled the country's cuisine, such as nasi goreng (fried rice), banana pancakes, and fresh fruit juices.

Agung spent the subsequent days driving me to Balinese temples and waterfalls. He took me to several Balinese ceremonies and introduced me to many foods, even some that were being sold on the side of the road. It was all quite colorful and festive. We'd spend eight hours a day traveling in the van, scouting his current and potential properties. It was exciting to see the sites and to experience Balinese ceremonies. My life felt full of possibilities.

TWO CHANCE ENCOUNTERS

Each time Agung and I left Toko Toko for our day's explorations, my attention was captured by a restaurant directly across the street. After much nudging from my internal voice prompting me to go inside, I decided to explore the restaurant, which was called Indus. The front of Indus had a steep, stone staircase that placed me at a good vantage point to view the surrounding scenery. The entry featured Balinese architecture: thatch roofing and vaulted teak wood ceiling beams. The walls were adorned with Kamasan paintings depicting male and female characters, as well as Batuan paintings displaying the incision of dark to bright colors, portraying mystical and traditional rituals.

The back of the restaurant opened up to an expansive balcony overlooking what is called the Campuhan Ridge. The edge of the balcony dropped off, appearing to fall a hundred feet or more. Rising up in the center of the jungle was the Campuhan Ridge Walk. I sat down at a table near the patio's edge and soaked up the panoramic view. I was mesmerized by the spectacular view of the Campuhan Ridge and the acres of lush tropical jungle. It seemed to go as far as the eye could see. I observed hikers traversing the trail, which rose several hundred feet from the ravine's floor. Graceful white heron birds dotted the crisp blue sky. It felt as exotic as if I were in a movie.

I opened Indus's menu and began browsing their Indonesian cuisines. Deciding on a light snack, I waved the young Balinese waitress over so I could place my order. Then, on the menu, I turned to the section about the restaurant's history and founder.

I couldn't believe my eyes. The founder was Janet DeNeefe, a native Australian from Melbourne—and the founder of the Ubud Writers Festival!

When the waitress arrived at my table, I asked if Janet might be around.

"Yes, she is downstairs working," came the reply.

This can't be happening, I thought. So I asked, "Would it be alright if I go downstairs and introduce myself?"

The young woman nodded. "Sure."

I headed down the stairwell to the lower level, holding onto the ornate wrought iron banister. As I reached the bottom of the stairs, there sat Janet, working on her computer.

I introduced myself and began to tell her one of the main reasons I came to Bali. I shared with her that I'd sent a copy of my recently published book to her submissions department some weeks earlier because I wanted to be considered being included in the lineup of authors. "But I haven't heard anything as of yet," I finished.

"Do you have a copy of the book with you, here in Ubud?" she asked.

Hearing the excitement in my voice, I replied, "I do, and I will bring it to you shortly."

I thanked her for her time and bid her farewell, then headed upstairs to my table. After finishing my lunch, I walked back across the street to my room and fetched one of my books that I'd brought for this purpose.

The following morning I shared this experience with Agung. As I told him about *Trust Patience Surrender*, he glowed with a smile from ear to ear, which left me a bit perplexed. He quipped, "I know who I am to give your book to."

I smiled. "Who?"

"Elizabeth Gilbert, the author of *Eat, Pray, Love*. The big Hollywood movie that takes place in Italy, India, and Bali."

The look on my face must have been that of amazement. Turned out that Agung had been a good friend of Elizabeth Gilbert's for quite some time. He asked if I had a copy he could give her. I cheerfully agreed and went back to the room to fetch a copy.

The following morning, after he gave her my book, she asked Agung for my phone number. So I gave it to him with a bit of excitement and a little skepticism.

So did Elizabeth Gilbert ever call me? No—but I was ecstatic knowing that my book was in the hands of esteemed creatives like Elizabeth Gilbert and Janet DeNeefe.

The two weeks in Bali simply flew by. I enjoyed cultural sites, villages, and the Balinese temples that dotted the island's landscapes. I even met with a Balinese healer.

When my visit came to an end, Agung took me to the airport. It was bittersweet. I deeply appreciated Agung's attentiveness, his family's kindness, and his extensive knowledge of Hindu/Balinese culture. I pondered the idea of potentially living in Bali one day—but I told myself that was just a passing thought.

READY FOR A NEW HOME

I returned to Sedona, but I only lasted for a brief stay of a few months. Since arriving in Bali for my first visit, I knew that it was the next place I'd call home.

With this idea firmly in my head, I told a few friends that I was leaving and that everything I owned, with the exception of one or two suitcases, would be up for sale.

The prospective owner for my landscaping business called and said he had cash and wanted to buy the business. I told him that I had priced it fairly and the price was firm. He said, "Yes, I know, that's okay. I want the business, and I will pay you cash."

I was quite relieved to hear this news. After that transaction was settled, it was time to advertise and sell the horses. I felt a lot of sadness about selling Rocky and Buck, but I knew it was meant to be.

A few weeks later, with my home furnishings, the horses, and the landscaping business all sold, I returned once more to the Island of the Gods.

HEALTH AND WELLNESS

Upon my return to Bali, once again, Agung and I traveled extensively around Bali. He showed me even more properties in Ubud and in the northern part of Bali on the ocean. I felt blessed to have seen all of these beautiful sights and ocean views.

When Agung had told me that I would oversee his wealth and his family, I felt concerned. I wasn't so sure this was meant to be a part of my life. On my second visit, he went on to tell me who his investors were in a number of his projects. They were some of the wealthiest people in the world.

There was a recurring theme that played out in my head, which I shared with him many times when we explored properties. I repeated this over the course of the first month or so of twelve-hour days exploring all of his and other investors' landholdings and future hotel developments. I told him, "I am not here to build hotels. If they want to develop retreat centers or places of healing for others, then I'm on board."

He found this amusing, but I held steadfast in my commitment and request. That's true to this day, eight and a half years later. In fact, the current-day classification for Bali is no longer simply *Tourism*. Instead, the Department of Tourism has reclassified *Tourism* as *Health and Wellness*. This is a big change for Indonesia.

When we met, Agung had said to me that he would be leaving this earthly plane in five years. That time is now upon us. Over the last couple of years, he has contracted malaria, as well as dengue fever twice. His immune system is pretty well under siege, and his white blood cell count is pretty much depleted. Thank goodness for one of his wealthy contributors/investors, who has flown blood transfusions and medications on his private jet in order to assist Agung through the maladies that he's been experiencing.

After three months of traveling around the island with Agung, I felt an exhaustion settling in my emotional and physical body. The twelve-hour days of driving on one-lane roads, some of them rustic and windy, became a bit too much. To regain my center and peace of mind, I realized I needed a rest from it all.

Over the course of several months, I asked myself, many times: *What is my purpose here on this magical island? What was I to learn? Why am I here?*

During this time, I moved into one of the Ubud royal family's villas in central Ubud. Ibu Rai's Villas were located on Jalan Raja Ubud. The villas were owned and operated by the first wife of the king of Ubud. I felt quite honored to be staying there. Agung's relationship to the royal family of Ubud was the result of his marriage to Ibu's daughter, the king's niece.

Agung and his family had shared so much of themselves and their culture with me over these several months, and I felt immensely blessed to have had such experiences with them. Even Agung's mother hand wove, for my personal use, several batik hand-painted sarongs that I'd wear while attending temples, ceremonies, and Balinese weddings. All of this seemed a bit too magical, at times.

THE LIGHT AND THE DARK

Despite the magic of Bali, not having a sense of why I was here still plagued me. One afternoon while I was lying in bed, my attention was captured by a couple of paintings hanging at the end of my bed. One was painted on a black velvet cloth, with a Balinese woman portrayed as seductive, sensual, and dark. The other painting was of a Balinese woman on a white canvas; that one, to me, held a purity. I was intrigued by this and felt something was signified by the light and the dark, by the idea of a sort of forbidden fruit and another of purity. The paintings represented the *Light* and *Dark* aspects of a woman.

Only later in my stay in Bali did I begin to realize that these paintings epitomized Bali in general.

I say this because over the years, as I've learned about Balinese culture, the more I see that their form of Hinduism gives worship to both the light and dark of existence. A good and evil, if you will. My understanding became clearer; it was another way of learning about *Balance*, and seeing that both the Dark and the Light exist within me and in this world.

In the first few months of extensive travel, exhaustion set in. As mentioned, I wasn't happy with the idea of building more hotels in Bali. I believed that Bali, as is true in most tourist destinations, had enough hotels and didn't need more. I became frustrated, and once again I posed the question aloud, "Why am I here?"

It got to the point where I was so frustrated with spirit (God) that I got quite angry, throwing my arms in the air and shouting out, "Either show me why I am here or take me home!"

At this point in my life, after my near-death experience, I felt that everything had to have a purpose. I wanted to know what was mine in Bali. Please don't misunderstand: I did have many times of enjoyment—appreciating the culture, learning some of the language, and visiting beautiful temples. I loved every moment of that, but the question of my purpose there continued to plague me.

A FORTUITOUS CONNECTION

The sale of my landscaping business had afforded me the opportunity to open this next chapter of my life. Then something amazing happened. When I was scouring Facebook for things to do and people to meet, I stumbled across a woman by the name of Amara who was also in Ubud and did workshops similar to some of the work that I did. Wanting to meet her to see if we could collaborate in the future, I sent her a message on social media, introducing myself and asking if she'd like to have dinner. She kindly replied that she would.

We met at Indus and enjoyed a wonderful conversation about our lives, our work, and some of the experiences each of us had had in Bali so far. During our dinner, Amara casually mentioned that I should talk to a seer/psychic she knew. I was intrigued to hear what this seer had to say about my purpose in Bali, or in life in general. I had recently come to the awareness that I was there to help people wake up, to come out of the 3D slumber and be especially awake to what was coming. I was interested to hear if the psychic had any thoughts about that.

Her name was Lorraine, and she lived in Torquay, England. Yes, this is the same Lorraine that I mentioned earlier, when I talked about the seers and psychics I've known in my life.

The next day, I sent Lorraine a text, inquiring about a reading. We set something up for a few days hence.

The Pyramids of Chi

During those couple of days, something else happened that gave me a bit of insight as to why I was here. It was a chance meeting with a man named Peter. It came about like this: My phone stopped working for no apparent reason, so I went to Bintang Market to have the phone looked at. While I was waiting, a tall, blonde man struck up a conversation with me. By his accent, I guessed he was Australian. We chuckled about how both our phones were broken, with no plausible reason. Then Peter asked me, "Why are you in Bali, mate?"

"To help people wake up," I told him. "And to do health and wellness retreat work."

He seemed rather delighted to hear that. He shared what had happened to him and what he was creating. Turned out he had a center under construction, called the Pyramids of Chi. He suggested that I visit the site, in part to check out the property but also to be a "food taster" for the menu his chef was putting together. I made plans to pop over the following day, in the early afternoon. I looked forward to tasting the new chef's food creations and experiencing sensations of Balinese and Indonesian flair.

The moment I entered the property, something blew me wide open. Only two other times in my life (once in Sedona, in my store's walk-in cigar humidor, and once in a European country) had this happened. It was such a strong and powerful awareness that it opened me into my mind's eye, to another etheric place that allowed me to see and intuit what this property was and what was going to happen in the future. I saw how it was a portal, a place of energetic opening into other dimensions. I had a clear knowing that this was a portal in between worlds. The energy and light that my senses detected was alive, even flurried.

Peter must have read my reaction, because he looked at me with a puzzled expression. I began to share that only two other times in my life had this massive heart opening occurred. He was delighted to hear that his project evoked this feeling in me.

I went on to talk about how when it was built, these pyramids would (as do many pyramids around the world) awaken to some strong field of energy. "Many people will come here for healing and awakening," I said.

"Fascinating," he said. "Let me tell you how the Pyramids of Chi project came to be."

"While my wife, Lynne, and I were living out our retirement days in Bali, after a long trip in the United States," Peter said, "In one of my meditations, I was shown and told to build two pyramids." He said he was puzzled by this, since he and Lynne were retired and living a comfortable life. "We didn't have the investment funds for such an undertaking," he said. "Neither of us knew how, what, when or where this would happen. But we decided it *must* happen."

Peter created a business plan, as he had done many times before in his professional career, and began to look for investors. But prior to this, he and Lynne went to a reader/seer to ask what they were to do and how the funds would manifest. The seer said not to worry; that there would be individuals waiting to contribute. So Peter placed a one-line ad on an Australian online ad website: "Building pyramids in Bali and looking for investors."

Within mere weeks, he had $750,000 US dollars to start his project. It was miraculous: several investors said that they didn't even want to look at his business plan; they just wanted to hand him the money. One of the investors said he was all in and ready to make the investment, but Peter was hesitant and wanted the investor to have his wife's approval as well. This happened in very short order.

Wow, I thought as I listened to his story. My head was taking in all of this wonderful information as quickly as it could.

Peter told me how the location was selected. He and Lynne did a channeling, or what I call freeform writing. This is an exercise in which you ask yourself a question, then write the answer with your non-dominant hand. When Lynn asked the question, "Where is the location?" her non-dominant hand wrote, "Ubud."

Now they knew where to look for a potential site. A short while later, when they found the property, they knew beyond a shadow of a doubt that it was right. "Here's what clinched it," Peter said. "Every home Lynne and I have ever owned was number 22. And this address was, you guessed it, number 22!"

As we looked out over the property and the concrete slabs where the two Pyramids would eventually rise, we enjoyed the chef's newly prepared cuisines and many of life's synchronicities. Peter shared that he wanted to include symbols or mandalas (those beautiful sand paintings by Buddhist monks) on the Pyramids, but he wasn't yet sure. We also talked about the symbology around the number 11:11 and what it meant. I told him what I believed its meaning to be: An alarm clock that we set before coming into our bodies this lifetime. It was a "wake-up call" designed to wake us to the knowing that we, too, are part of creation and all that is, and we need to remember why we came. The number 11:11 also signifies that we are in the divine flow of things. I believed it was to create a New World. It would be a world where Heaven on Earth would be realized.

All of this conversation and the time spent together expended a lot of energy for me, so I decided to head back to my villa before the sunset. Then, on the way home, something completely opened in me.

As I rode my scooter back home, my body began to shake so much, I had to pull off to the side of the road to absorb the information that was coming into my body and awareness. It was a clear and profound knowing that the number 22 divided by 2 (representing two pyramids) would result in the number 11. With the Pyramids each sharing the number 11, in an instant, 11:11 filled my consciousness. I felt an overwhelming truth flowing through me.

At that moment, I saw eleven mandalas being painted inside each of the Pyramids. I was blown away! I composed myself and headed for home. The number 22 would also come to me in a vision some time later, revealing a future event. But that's something to be talked about later in this book.

Exactly as She Said — Lorraine

A few days had passed, and it was time to meet with Lorraine, the seer/reader. I phoned her, and after a cordial and brief introduction, she began to channel information. I was shocked when the first sentence came out of her mouth and across the airwaves: "Have you seen the Pyramids?"

My mind was reeling with excitement. Lorraine went on to say, "They are building them for you and the others who will come. A soul family."

How did she know this? She lived in Torquay, England. She didn't know about the Pyramids being built in Ubud, Bali.

The next several sentences caused my head to spin even more. She went on to describe a woman I'd meet. Lorraine told me her age (42), her ethnicity (Hawaiian), and who she looked like (a singer by the name of Nicole Scherzinger).

"She will only be on the east coast of Australia for two weeks," Lorraine said. "You have to meet her. You and she have a soul contract with each other and the land of Australia."

Lorraine added that I would also meet a man and a woman who had what she described as "patents." Curious to know more and to get clarity, I asked her to describe what she meant by patents. After some querying on my part, we determined that she meant mandalas.

Man, I was trying my best to take all of this in. I had no idea who the singer Nicole Scherzinger was. But I knew intuitively where I was going in Australia: Byron Bay in New South Wales. This town's name had been stuck in my head for a number of years.

A recollection flooded into my memory banks. As an eighteen-year-old, during my U.S. Naval days, I'd served on board a ship called the *USS Hassayampa*, with the designation of AO145. Our task was to refuel other naval ships and task groups of all sizes while traveling on the open sea. My fascination with Australians came when the *USS Hassayampa* moored in Perth, Australia. I was completely mesmerized by the Australian families who lined up on the pier, inviting us sailors to their homes to enjoy home-cooked meals. Needless to say, as an eighteen-year-old, I found this just amazing!

Lorraine and I bid farewell, and I thought about everything she'd said. A day or so later, when the profile of a woman named Christabel flashed across my Facebook screen, I gasped. I began to read about her and the work that she guided. Each of the items ticked off the list of Lorraine's predictions: Christabel was of Hawaiian descent, her appearance and brown skin resembled Nicole Scherzinger's, and she would be on the east coast of Australia for only two weeks.

I nearly fell off of my chair. My heart was beating out of my chest. Everything was exactly as Lorraine had said. Now all I had to do was book a flight to Brisbane and take the shuttle to Byron Bay.

I felt again that I was in a synchronicity of flow that was undeniably open. I searched Airbnb and found a nice home in the coastal township of Lennox Head with a room available for my upcoming stay. After I spoke with the owner of the house, it seemed right in the flow of things.

I was ready for my next journey.

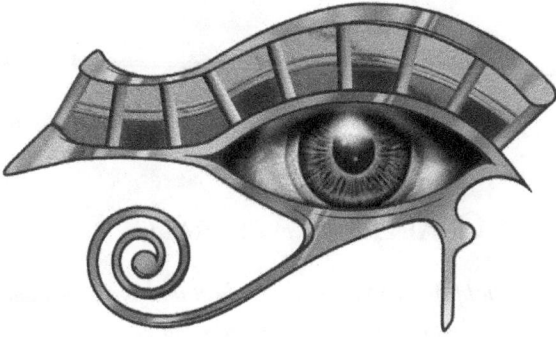

CHAPTER 8

CHAPTER 8: AUSTRALIA

"Everything will happen for you all of a sudden and you'll be thankful you didn't give up. Blessings are coming. Believe that."
~ *WeAreHumanAngelsTheBook*

"BLACKBIRD"

Two days later, I was on my way to Australia. Upon landing, I had a message from the owner of the house saying that she would be away from the house for the morning and that she would meet me at the Byron Visitor Centre. I went to the Visitor Centre to meet her, but did not see her. I texted her several times and received no reply. I thought that was rather strange, but I waited for another hour. No response, so I went into the Visitor Centre and inquired about lodging in town. The volunteer was all too quick to respond, "There are no rooms available, due to a big festival happening."

What was I going to do? After some searching, the volunteers at the Centre found a tent/structure that would cost me $100 Australian (around $75 US). *A tent for that price?* I thought. Nonetheless, I decided to take it, because I needed a roof over my head and a place to lie down.

As I walked from the Visitor Centre to the tent/structure, just before I crossed the railroad tracks, a large brown snake crossed my path a few feet in front of me. As I waited for it to cross, my mind went to the meaning of snake medicine: One of transformation. Later, I found out this type of snake was one of the more deadly snakes in Australia. *Wow*, I thought, *this a country of reptiles, spiders, and other creepy crawly things that are extremely dangerous and deadly.*

But I felt an extreme calmness as I passed the snake's path a few feet away. Then I entered the tent area.

One of the other things that Lorraine's reading had revealed was that I would no longer have to work with what she called "barley people." I asked her to explain that term, which turned out to be the same as what, in the U.S., we'd call "granola"—the tie-dyed, hippie type, usually with several seemingly malnourished dogs. It's not a term generally used with affection. In the tent area, I was surrounded by them. I took a deep breath, ignored my thoughts and feelings, and walked back into the Visitor Centre, wondering again, why my host wasn't available. Moreover, why was I here?

As I stood on the steps of the Centre, I heard music. At first it was faint, then it increased in volume. I looked to see where the tune was coming from. Across the street, a musician was playing a guitar and singing. And as I focused my attention on what I was hearing, I grinned from ear to ear, knowing I was being given another acknowledgment, from Spirit, that I was in the right place.

The musician was playing the song "Blackbird" by the Beatles. This song had first appeared to me years earlier in Lourdes, France, and it had continued to show up whenever I was in some sort of quandary, grappling with the unknown. Every time I hear "Blackbird," it's a confirmation to keep going on my journey, telling me that I'm right where I'm supposed to be.

Serendipity just at the right moment again, I thought. Tears welled up, and I thanked Spirit, with immense gratitude, for communicating with me once more.

MOVING THE ENERGIES

I ended up spending the night in a small concrete structure—better than a tent. I was relieved to have a shower and rest. The next morning I received a call from my host from Airbnb, Mimi. She apologized profusely about her neglect and forgetfulness, claiming she had put my arrival on her schedule incorrectly. Mimi arrived thirty minutes later and drove me to her home. I settled in, and in the next couple days, Mimi and I shared a lot of conversations about our life's experiences. I shared all of the intuitive thoughts and downloads, and what Lorraine had told me.

Then it was time to go to Christabel's breathwork class to see what was in store. We sat in a circle, about six or seven people, and each drew an animal card that was at the center of our circle. We read them aloud, observing in what part of the description we found some truth.

We then were asked to lie down, relax, and allow the breathwork session to start. At first, our inhalations and exhalations were slow and easy. As the session went on, our breath intensified to the point that, for me, a sense of lightheadedness began to occur. The music increased in tempo and in volume, as did our breathing.

The class ended with some people experiencing a cathartic release, while others felt a subtle euphoric presence. Each person then shared a bit about what the experience evoked in them. Then everyone hugged one another and left the studio.

Everyone except me, that is. I lingered, asking Christabel if she had a few minutes because I wanted to share something with her.

"Okay," she said. "But I only have a few minutes. I have another meeting soon."

Christabel and I went outside, sitting in a small grassy area beside the studio. I began to tell her about all that had happened to me and what Lorraine had told me. I shared with her that when I saw her picture on social media, I knew that she was the one that I had had the soul contract with, and I needed to pass this information on to her.

"I'm not a crazy person or a stalker," I said. "I just needed to share and move the energies."

Her expression seemed perplexed, but she listened intently. Then she said, "You are really looking for Love."

I responded, "That is all there is."

"I have a partner," she said.

"I'm not telling you this information to break you up with your partner," I replied. "I just needed to share the information with you."

Christabel stood. "I need to go."

I nodded. "Thank you for your time," I said. "And for the opportunity to share what I had come here for."

WHAT COMES NEXT?

The following day, I decided to sign up for Christbel's next class, which was only a few days later. When I arrived, I was once again seated in a circle with other participants, and we chatted about our lives.

When Christabel arrived, she looked at me with surprise. "I didn't know you were coming today."

"I signed up at the last minute," I said.

She sat down, tears welling in her eyes as she told our small group that she'd just broken up with her boyfriend because the relationship wasn't the love she was looking for. The thought that raced through my mind was, *damn, I broke them up.* I felt a little guilt, but it didn't last long, because I knew there was a greater purpose at hand.

The day-long session progressed, and we learned through a couple of exercises how to live in the world a bit more connected. I attended one more of her sessions before she left Byron Bay. At the end of the day's workshop, we tried to connect several times, but it didn't happen.

I decided to stay in Byron Bay for a month or so to see what else was in store for me. When I next spoke to Lorraine, she said I needed to start my work. I was puzzled about what she meant.

"Do my work, just start?" I asked. I was a bit overwhelmed by all that had happened.

My time in Byron was full of emotional ups and downs. When Lorraine said I should do my work there, I was concerned that I didn't have a work visa, and I wasn't sure what the legal consequences would be. The other thought continually moving within my mind was that I wanted a loving relationship, and I'd thought the connection that Christabel and I had would prove to be something more than a fleeting moment. For me, this desire became quite painful. Many days I walked along the beach at Suffolk Bay, asking why I was still alone and why I was struggling to figure out what was next.

My money was running low. I considered going back to Sedona, but

I knew it wasn't time yet, and that when it came to employment, I would be going back to what I had left off before. That just didn't feel right.

There were moments on the beach when I became quite tearful about Christbel and me not coming together. Over the next several months, Christabel and I kept in minimal contact and tried to connect for a retreat in the White Mountains, but I decided not to participate because there was plant medicine as a focal point for the retreat, and I just didn't feel it was appropriate for me at the time. During the next two years, I watched Christabel on YouTube as she shared her realizations and the pain they had caused her. I felt connected to that pain—but I'll share more about that later in the book.

STEPHEN AND ANNA'S MANDALAS

After my encounter with Christabel, I began wondering when and if the man and woman with the mandalas (whom Lorraine had mentioned) would show up before I left Australia. As it turned out, I met a woman named Vibhuti and got a reading from her. I shared with her all that had happened to me up until then. We became friends, and through Vibhuti, I was connected with a man and woman named Stephen and Anna. Vibhuti believed I needed to meet them, so I sent them a text and invited them to meet me for lunch.

Several days passed without a response. I wondered if we would actually meet, since I was scheduled to fly back to Bali soon. Then, out of the blue, I received a message from Stephen. He shared that his mother in England was really ill. He and Anna had visited her and just returned to Australia. They asked me to meet them at a local restaurant in Brunswick Heads.

Brunswick Heads is a small town on the north coast of New South Wales, in Byron Shire. It's a twenty-minute drive north from Byron Bay. Brunswick Heads is a friendly and relaxing little town, with a town square, situated next to Brunswick River that flows into the ocean nearby, as well as Torakina Beach.

I arrived early and had a seat. It wasn't long before they arrived. When we saw one another, it was like an old homecoming. All of us had the feeling that we knew each other and that this wasn't the

AUSTRALIA

first time we'd met. Our conversation enveloped us in our stories of a spiritual nature and of Anna's near-death experience. We talked for hours about so many things, and when I finally shared about the mandalas, they both smiled and said, "Yes, we have them."

Stephen went on to say that a very gifted Frenchman channeled the mandalas while Stephen was working with sound and vibrations through a synthesizer. Stephen said he didn't have the full rights to them, but he would share a few of them with me. He and Anna determined there were over one hundred of them that were channeled. Stephen suggested we meet the next day at their house to see his many gongs and his sound healing equipment.

Stephan and Anna lived in the beautiful Australian countryside. Their yard was lush and green, with a large wooden outbuilding with a car under repair inside. I was pretty excited about the opportunity for them to share the mandalas and his many gongs with me. Stephen said there were well over 125 different mandala geometric patterns.

We walked down the hallway into his studio where he stored his recording equipment. Once in the room, he pulled out a dozen or so of the mandalas that had been laminated. As he handed them to me, he looked at me with the eyes of someone giving away his children. I assured him that they were in good hands. I believe he felt that as well.

Anna was kind enough to do one of her healing sessions with me. We spent much of the afternoon continuing our conversations like long-lost friends. I shared that I was a bit torn as to whether or not I should stay in Australia to do my work, as well as to work with Stephen and his gongs. My savings were quickly dwindling.

Nonetheless, I stayed for several weeks, time spent praying and studying the mandalas with little happening other than discomfort looking at them for so long. Then, after a few weeks of visualizing them, something happened.

I entered one of the mandalas energetically. I could see myself in the center of the mandala, looking outward. It was simply amazing, and I found myself asking even more questions. What *does this mean?*

What will happen now? Will a greater knowing come soon, or would it be some years from now that the experience falls into place? Only time would tell.

Excited and puzzled by the experience, I made an appointment with Lorraine in Torquay. I told her there were 125 mandalas and I was meditating with twenty-five or so, but I wasn't sure how I could best utilize my energies with them.

"There are only twenty-two of the mandalas that you need to be concerned with," Lorraine told me. "They will reveal new information."

HEAVEN ON EARTH

Around this time, I met a travel agent named Jane. She and I became good friends, and she introduced me to several of her friends in Byron Bay. In one of our conversations she suggested that I go and see Nefrin, the owner of Crystal Castle in Mullumbimby, New South Wales, to ask if I could place my book in their retail shop.

The drive through the spectacularly green rolling hills, with an occasional peek at the ocean, took my breath away. I was so taken by it, I had to stop the car to soak in the scenery. It's one of the places in the world that I refer to as "Heaven on Earth."

When I arrived, I bee-lined to the retail shop to see if I could put my book on their shelves. During this visit, I had the opportunity to revisit something that I'd experienced in my travels a few years earlier during my trip to Europe, where I discovered for the first time how plants can communicate with us through the use of a synthesizer with electrodes attached.

At the shop, as I listened to a young woman doing a presentation on this topic, she exclaimed, "This is the first time the plants have been quiet. I'm not sure what's going on."

I knew exactly what was happening. Seated in the front row, I'd been asking the plants if they were here and to communicate about the "Light."

I felt deeply about what was happening. I sent a nonverbal thought to the plants, letting them know it was okay and that they were in no danger by my presence. Within seconds, melodic sounds started coming out of the speakers.

I also was able to talk with the Crystal Castle retail shop manager about my book, and as a result, the book was placed in the retail shop. Some days later, Jane invited me to a big event at Crystal Castle to meet with Nefrin, but so much was happening, I didn't think I could handle one more monumental event. So I declined the invitation, at the last minute.

TWO MORE KEYS

I was torn by the two experiences: wanting to see Christabel once more and learning sound healing with Stephen. In order to make sense out of all that was happening, I reached out to Lorraine for a reading, to see if she had any input that could help me. During our session, I shared with her my desire to be with Christabel. I also talked about the initiation and the keys given to me by Genii and her superior, and about Renee and the global currency reset.

Lorraine's response gave me a lot more information to digest. She predicted that I would receive two more keys. When I received the third key, the work I had truly come to do would proceed.

She went on to say that Christabel had the opportunity to connect with me, but she'd chosen another path. "You did your part," Lorraine said. "You let it unfold."

And as far as traveling back to the States, she indicated there would be several returns for various reasons. Overall, she suggested that I relax and follow the flow of my life.

THE LITTLE GREEN HOUSE

I heart-fully considered returning to Sedona. I remembered something that had happened right before I left Sedona, in those final days of living in the beautiful two-story Spanish style hacienda along with my horses. I had a memory of crossing the gravel road at the base of Chimney Rock Lane and exploring a little green house. It was a modest ranch style house, built in the 1950s or 1960's, with three small bedrooms and a kitchen with a wall heater in the main living area.

The amazing backyard view included the Chimney Rock formation peering over the property. It was peaceful and serene, with the Yavapai National Forest surrounding the house. As I walked the property, I'd envisioned building a sweat lodge in the backyard.

It all made sense to me. While in my host's home in Lennox Head, I began having flashbacks, remembering the little green house. But I was still laboring over two thoughts: how much I wanted to see Christabel, and whether or not I should stay to learn sound healing with Stephen. It happened that Stephen was a car buff like me, and he showed me his latest prized possession: an Aston Martin Db6 that he was restoring. One of my favorite hobbies and professions in my earlier days was restoration of antique and custom race cars. So that was tempting, too.

This was all going on in my head while I was doing a lot of meditation and prayer with the mandalas. It seemed a bit too much. So I reached (yelled) out to Spirit, with a deep breath, "If that little green house is available, I'm going back to Sedona."

This was a long shot. The little green house was owned by a family in Phoenix. They'd owned it for several generations and never rented it out. But I thought, *what the heck, I'll give it a shot.* So I sent an email to Sam, the owner, to see if he would rent me the house.

Low and behold, I received a quick response from him. I'd communicated with him in the past regarding other matters, and normally it would be days, even weeks sometimes, to get a response from him. And yet, within minutes, Sam called to say, "How did you know I was just finishing the house cleanup and light restoration? I was just about to put it on the rental market."

We both laughed about the irony of it. "I'm returning to Sedona," I said. "And I want to rent it."

"It's yours," Sam replied. "When are you returning?"

What were the chances of this occurring? This was my confirmation I needed to head back to Sedona. We worked out the logistics and payment for rent, and after we got off the phone, I booked a flight back to the United States to take up residence in the little green house on Chimney Rock Lane. I had no idea how long I would be there before my next adventure. But it seemed like the respite I needed.

Days later, I was at the airport, waiting to return to the United States and start over once again. While I was standing at the gate, I received a call from Anna to see what decision I'd made, as to whether or not I was staying in Oz. I told her about the green house and that I was returning home to the States for now.

I stood in line at the gate, waiting to get on board and relax into my seat. After about forty-five minutes of standing in line, I heard a faint voice down the hallway announcing my name. I thought that was odd, but I stepped out of the front of the line—and sure enough, the gate attendant was calling me to another flight that was held up because I had not boarded.

After realizing that there were two flights with similar departure times and I'd been about to board the wrong one, I ran down the long hallway to my new gate. I got on board and settled in for the long international flight back to the U.S.

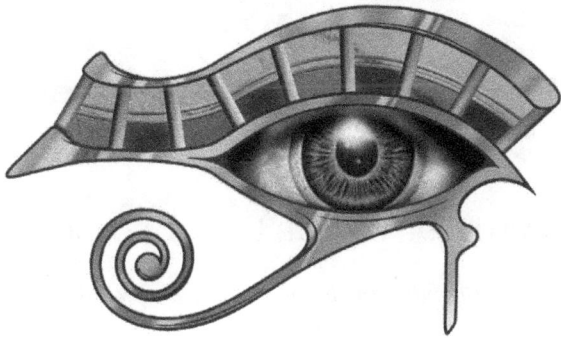

CHAPTER 9

CHAPTER 9: WHERE DO I BELONG?

"Be still, and the earth will speak to you." ~Navajo proverb

MORE WISDOM FIGURES

Back in Sedona, I resumed my previous life of landscaping and therapy work with clients. But something had changed—or perhaps I did. It just didn't feel right; I felt like a fish out of water. Still, I kept working. I ended up doing some home remodeling and construction work on the little green house, due to a large leak in the living room, and I visited Grandfather Morning Owl several times, enjoying our talks and his amazing home cooked meals. But the next couple of months, it seemed as though I was just biding my time. I didn't feel settled. I continued working with clients in both my landscaping business and counseling practice, but I felt I was simply going through the motions.

I felt empty inside. After a few months of this, I began to think I needed to return to Bali. It made me feel like a tennis ball being volleyed back and forth during a match. Still, I made arrangements to return to Bali. But before I left, I met one of my next wisdom figures. Her name was Mirtala, and she soon became my friend and mentor.

Grandfather introduced Mirtala and me, thinking our connection would be a good fit since she knew a bit about pyramids, energies, and sculpting. Her deceased husband, Itzhak "Ben" Bentov, was an Israeli American scientist, inventor, mystic, and author who, through his writing, would prove to be helpful in answering many of my questions. Itzhak had a way of taking complex theories and interpreting them in layman's terms. In his book *Stalking the Wild Pendulum*, he provided a new perspective on human consciousness and its limitless possibilities. He was someone who channeled information about the universe, along with being a writer. But as Mirtala shared in one of our meetings, he was revealing too much about the workings of the universe. She believed that unfriendly powers took his life in a plane crash.

Like her husband, Mirtala was interesting. She was a sculptor and artist. Many of her works, created in bronze, were inspired and guided by a deeply intuitive and natural spirit. These works of art brought numerous spiritual and esoteric knowings into physical forms and touched many people around the world in powerful ways.

As a child in Ukraine, she had fled communist rule. Her childhood stories were insightful and painful, adding an array of depth and color to our conversations. Her latest multi-sculptured installation had recently been erected at one of Ukraine's newly built universities. Her friendship was such a blessing because she helped me, at this time and in future events, to understand some of my experiences that kept me seemingly perplexed.

THE MAN FROM RHODE ISLAND

The few months in Sedona came and went. I now knew, through nightly visions, I had to return to Bali. I had received several profound visions where I was told that I had to go back to Ubud to meet my family once more. These, I knew, were people I had met in other lifetimes. In one of the visions, I was shown myself and an arrangement of 22 people in the Moon Pyramid, seated in a circle facing toward the center. Each person, sitting in lotus position, was receiving the white "Shafts of Light" through our crown chakras. I was even given a mantra and a melody to be sung. In the vision, I heard the words, "You must go now to meet your family once more." The next day, without hesitation, I made arrangements to fly back and booked accommodations with Agung.

After my return to Ubud, many hopeful and insightful events began occurring, just when I was in need. I remember with great clarity a hot morning when I was sitting at a long wooden table at Yoga Barn. This is a place known for its yoga classes and related classes, as well as workshops and teacher training.

I remember that warm summer morning very clearly. The sun came over the thatched roofline of the Balinese-style roof and pavilion. I was enjoying my breakfast when a young man who looked to be in his mid thirties sat next to me at the large, wooden community table. Across from us were a number of women from around the world. I assumed that they were there to learn yoga or do some sort of training. When the young man sat next to me, he began conversing very quickly and quite abruptly.

"Where are you from?" he asked. "Why are you here?"

In an agitated tone, he told me that he was from Rhode Island in the United States, and that his wife had dragged him to Bali, "...to a frickin' yoga training course." Clearly, he wasn't too happy about traveling across the world to attend this workshop.

Then he said something that shocked me. He quipped, "Man, you got it made here!"

"What do you mean?" I asked.

He pointed at the many women on the patio, as well as three women sitting at the other end of our table. "It's like a kid in a candy store, all of these young women you get to choose from," he said.

I took a deep breath. His comments caught me off guard. I regarded this way of thinking and how it objectified women as very negative. I sensed he meant that I could do what I wanted with them. For him, they would represent nothing more than another "notch on the bedpost."

Shocked by what he'd said, completely affected by his comment, I couldn't articulate what I wanted to say to him at that moment. So I excused myself and moved to another part of the patio.

I looked around the patio, feeling a deep sense of gratitude for the women sitting there—but not for the same reason as the young man. Rather, I was grateful that they had the courage to follow their hearts and desires, to come here to develop their skills as teachers and practitioners. I felt, in that moment, that these women were leading the way into a New World.

From my visions, I realized there would be a New World coming and it was one that needed these women—and more like them. The world didn't need the wounded masculine, nor the destructive side of the Patriarchal world. The objectification of women needed to come to an end. I felt a deep knowing that we would need more storytellers, healers, teachers, and the like to help us through the upcoming world's transition.

A clear response to the young man from Rhode Island came to mind. What I wished I'd been able to say to him is, "Be grateful your wife brought you to Bali. You have the opportunity to dispel your dysfunctional male beliefs about women." I wanted to tell him that if he were to open his mind and heart, he would see the truth of this knowing. A deep gratitude washed over me as I felt these words.

I needed to reflect about what had happened and see if this point of view, this objectification of women, was in my own psyche. Oftentimes, we are given situations in order to see if there is anything that *we* need to take a look at. So I began to scan my memory banks, thinking about how I grew up with women in my life. I had three sisters that I grew very close to. Each of them held a particular period of time in my life, where each of us valued one another's friendship. My older sister showed me the mother that I never had. Her care and love was touching. My younger sisters gave me the opportunity to be a mentor and a soulful friend, often guiding them in their encounters with boys.

But upon reflection, I realized how I, too, had objectified girls during my adolescence. I remembered how my mother's absence and the dysfunction in the family dynamic left me struggling with the idea of how to care and love for a young woman outside of my immediate family. I remembered that when my younger sister's friends would come to the house and spend the night, I would try so hard to conquer them. They often slept outside of my bedroom, on the living room couch, and I would sit up with them during the wee hours of the night after my sister went to bed, trying to hug and kiss them. I didn't really know what to do, so it usually became awkward for the girl and me. The lack of love and attention from my mother caused me to internalize this need. It stemmed from my subconscious worry about abandonment and my need to be loved.

As I reflected upon the situation with the young man at the Yoga Barn, I realized that I, too, had a subtle pattern of wanting to dominate women. It was so subtle and deep within my own subconscious, but in that moment, I came to the realization that from that day forward, I would be more aware if such subtleties arose when I engaged women.

A poem was wanting to be born as a result of the experience:

Only in time
Where it will be rewoven
Our hearts will mend
When boys become men
Understanding our place with in the whole
Heart to Heart
Cheek to Cheek
We were always meant to meet
She is not to be conquered, censored or scorned
but held in a place where she's adorned
Holding life's gentle mystery's breath (secrets) in return
simply waiting to be revealed (reborn)

CHRISTABEL'S TWO-YEAR REALIZATION

Several times during this period, I listened to a few more of Christabel's YouTube podcasts, following her growth and maturing nature, interested in what she was learning. During those months on the beaches in New South Wales, Australia, I was moved many times to tears, even to the point of writing her several letters of Love, filled with the desires and understandings that deepened within me. But it wasn't until two years later (to the date) from our initial meeting on that little grassy knoll that I truly understood why Christabel and I had to meet.

In her podcast that day, she began by saying, "I became celibate two years ago on this date. I needed to learn how I manipulated men using my appearance and other factors of my womanhood."

As Christabel continued to speak, it became clear to me why we had to meet, and why Lorraine had said of our first contact, "The two of you have a soul contract with one another and with the east coast of Australia." It was that day, two years earlier, when I first met her and realized my karmic and soul connection to her. My mere presence and the truths that I shared with her that day about Love had sent her on this path of celibacy, a path to find her inner, authentic and Loving self. The words I was guided to speak were a catalyst for her, the beginning of the trajectory she was now on.

I knew she was also teaching me that I could truly love another from a distance with great profundity. In that moment of truth and understanding, I let go of any preconceived ideas I had around the Love that I'd thought we were to share. It was bigger than anything I could have imagined.

That day—a day of liberation for me as well—I felt a deep gratitude that I'd been able to participate in such an experience. I let go of her and the thoughts that we would be together physically in this world. I was overwhelmed with the warmth of Love in my heart.

Ironically, I ran into Christabel in Ubud when she made a return trip to the island. We bumped into one another at Bali Budda, the local health food store.

I smiled at her. "Hi Christabel."

She looked at me as though she didn't remember who I was. Once more, I was given an understanding that no matter how powerfully I viewed an important event, it could fall on deaf ears by another. But all in all, I was quite happy, knowing that Spirit directing me to her was a gift given and received, regardless of the outcome.

COLLABORATION AT THE PYRAMIDS OF CHI

During this time, I began collaborating at the Pyramids of Chi, learning the art of sound healing and frequencies. I watched others play gongs and other musical instruments, and I took a couple of workshops. I became a proficient sound healer/practitioner, something I enjoyed. During this time, Peter's wife, Lynne, was having life-threatening challenges involving the muscles in her jaw and face. To help out, I took on many of Peter and Lynne's responsibilities. Visits to the Pyramids had started slowly, then began to grow considerably as tourists heard about events being held there. Six or seven of us were doing sound healing. It seemed to click, and it felt so right for me to be there.

During the next twelve to fourteen months, I guided many private and group sessions, cacao ceremonies, full moon ceremonies, and new moon ceremonies. Life was full on. I had the privilege of working with people from around the world, and I soon found that much of my week was consumed with the work. During this busy time, I had to remind myself to take care of my body. So often when I learned a new technique or experienced another deeply profound heart opening experience, I got caught up in the enthusiasm and forgot about my health. I lost fifteen pounds and became very thin, resulting in doctor visits and tests to determine what was going on.

The initial physician suggested cancer or HIV. Knowing that I'd never put myself at such risk, I went to a specialist in Denpasar at Bros Hospital to find out the results of the cancer screening and HIV results. They didn't put the results in the computer; the attending nurse had to retrieve an official sealed envelope. When the doctor opened the letter, she gave me a funny look, then quipped, "All the tests were negative. I can't understand your predicament."

"I know the reason this happened," I replied. "Spirit wanted to know if I wanted to stay on planet earth. I view this as another test."

As a result of this incident, self care became very important to me.

SHAFTS OF LIGHT

I was working hard, but what I was shown wasn't happening as quickly as I'd hoped. When my level of frustration reached an all time high, a young Hawaiian woman named Leimomi, her husband, and their young son arrived. When she introduced herself and told me where she'd spent the prior ten years, I was stunned.

"For the last decade, I've been in Sedona, Arizona," Leimomi said.

I was surprised, because in Sedona, I'd known most everyone working in any kind of retail establishment or healing modality. My cigar shop had been the central gathering place for fun and festivities.

Leimomi explained that she'd been mostly working at Sedona's Mago Retreat Center, and occasionally in their uptown Sedona healing store. The retreat center, founded by Iichi Lee, was located miles outside of town, on a long, winding gravel road. Not many people drove out there, due to the distance and the bumpy road. In my twenty-plus years living in Sedona, I made only one trip to the Mago Retreat Center. It was a self-contained center that caused a bit of controversy over the years. Leimomi confirmed much of what I'd heard. She said those factors contributed to her leaving the center.

"Why did you come to Bali?" I asked.

Leimomi told me that her and her family's travels took them to many different parts of the world. While visiting various countries, they activated, opened, and aligned the "Shafts of Light." This was not at all unusual to me. I had been shown visions prior to coming to Bali (and several after) which were in alignment with what she was sharing. As a matter of fact, I was relieved that there would be others here who would open and align what I refer to as portals.

These are areas on the surface of Mother Earth that allow higher level frequencies of Light and vibrations to occur. Some people can see such colors and shafts, while others, such as myself, feel them.

"I never know exactly where the places of Light will be," Leimomi said. "But I follow my guidance and intuition." She said that the three of them were near the Pyramids of Chi, and she saw this as the next place of alignment.

Leimomi gathered several of us to do the energy opening of the Shafts of Light. She gathered plants and leaves from the property, as well as various crystals that she'd brought with her. I was relieved that someone else was confirming part of the vision I'd had. Some years ago, all of this would have sounded to me like something out of a science fiction movie, but now it was as real as could be. I received the confirmation that I needed to carry on my work at the Pyramids.

Some years later, Leimomi and I met up once again, when I traveled to Sedona. She showed me the crisscross pattern of continents and countries that was created as a result of her U.S. and international travels activating shafts of light with her husband and son. She then asked me to look at my travels, both in the U.S. and internationally. When I did, we saw that our patterns of crisscrossing were next to one another's on the globe, but mine were directly east of her travels, creating a similar pattern in Southeast Asia that only overlapped in Bali. We were both surprised to see this similarity in our patterning.

RELEASED FROM PAST KARMA

At the Pyramids, other events occurred that connected several of us who had understandings and beliefs about past lives. The first past life remembrance had been with Sarah, some years earlier, when I lived in Sedona, but there were more experiences to come over the next twelve to twenty-four months at the Pyramids.

One of these experiences involved both Sarah and myself, but from a different perspective of our relationship. When Sarah and I were together, I was always saying both to myself and to her, "I wanted to know what you were like as a young woman." It was something that continually entered my mind, but I didn't know how it could happen in this lifetime.

At that time, I started having visions and dreams of my little boy—my inner child. It was shortly after my near-death experience that these dreams started flooding my mind. They were so vivid. I saw myself as a young boy, screaming in train stations throughout France. I regarded this experience to be the understanding of what I call a "Soul Retrieval." Somewhere in my psyche, I realized that I'd been abandoned in a train station in a previous life. I couldn't fathom any other reason why this circumstance would happen. It was one of the most powerful experiences I had while in relationship with Sarah.

Fast forward to the Pyramids one afternoon. A young woman walked into the reservations area, and my attention was immediately drawn to her. I began to have a feeling of knowing her. I knew something was going to happen.

When she met my gaze, she became fixated. I could see it in her eyes as she looked my way. It was like when you see a long-lost friend of many years. We moved directly to each other.

"I know you somehow," she said.

I immediately knew who she represented to me. It was Sarah in her late twenties or early thirties.

The young woman introduced herself as Anna Paoula. I shared with her a little about my understanding about past lives. She told me she just happened to be going to Sedona a few weeks on the next leg of her journey.

I was more than excited! Excited enough to email Sarah to tell her that I wanted her to meet this young woman when she arrived in Sedona. I did not tell Sarah anything about Anna Paoula or my experience with her. I wanted it to be a complete surprise. I wanted to see if my intuition was correct.

Anna Paoula and I decided to have lunch together to further explore what we had in common and see where this synchronicity might lead us. A few days later, we met at Zest, a health food restaurant in Ubud. We shared our life's stories and how they led us both to Bali. In my sharing, for some reason, I began to share the story about my little boy screaming from a train station in the heart of France.

Anna Paoula's facial expression changed dramatically. Tears began to flow down her cheeks.

"There is only one thing in this life that has haunted me and I never resolved," she said. "In a previous life, I left my son in a train station in France." With a deep breath, she said, "It was you, and I was your mother."

My tears began to flow, knowing in the deepest depths of my being that these were words of truth. Anna Paoula asked, "Will you forgive me?"

Immediately, as a son to his mother would, I said, "Yes, I love you and I forgive you."

Her deepest darkest secret had been released. We ended up spending the rest of the afternoon holding one another.

Days later, she left for Sedona. I'd made the connection for Sarah and Anna Paoula to meet. I knew that Anna Paoula meeting Sarah would be a monumental moment.

When Sarah texted me, she said how blown away she was. "She is my daughter," Sarah said in her text.

This had never happened before in either mine or Sarah's lives—to exclaim and see such truth. All three of us knew without a shadow of a doubt that this was the truth of our existence, and it needed to be released.

I remembered something Lorraine had said during one of her recent readings. Her exact words were, "You are going to meet your soul family once more, and you will release each other from all past karma and the twenty-two major arcana of the Tarot and the twelve Jungian Archetypes. They aren't needed anymore for some of you." She went on to say, "There are those of you who no longer need them. You will now begin to create as creator. And in order for you to enter the New World, you must release one another from all past karma and return to a place of innocence."

TARA AND THE LITTLE BOY

I was not the only one to experience a release of past karma. It also happened for clients of mine, such as a woman named Tara.

It was a typical tropical day—a little rain, then sunshine and a good dose of humidity. I was preparing for a client session. In addition to sound healing sessions and therapy, I also do private sessions where I will work one-on-one with a client, using techniques from Native American ceremonies to reiki and hands-on therapy. Most of what I do has a foundation in formal psychology, but I have learned many other techniques that have been extremely helpful for clients.

I was sitting outside of my guest bedroom overlooking the swimming pool, in meditation and visualizing my connection to my upcoming client's energy field. As I work through this process, I first ask permission from the client, and then I go into a deep meditation, visualizing them and what their needs might be—or, more importantly, I ask to be shown my role is as a guide. What do I need to see or feel regarding the upcoming client? Often, I receive information that can be quite helpful to the client.

This afternoon was no different. As I sat in the lotus position, I began to feel the sharp jab of a knife into my right hand. I envisioned my hand over the right side of the person's belly. The pain was so extreme, and the blood I saw was so intense, the vision caused me to fling my hand in the air. For the next few minutes, I rubbed my hand to release the physical pain. Then I got a glass of water to ground me in my body.

When my client, Tara, arrived, I asked her a number of questions. "Why do you want this sound healing? What is your intention for this session?" This is how I usually start off a session.

I had Himalayan metal singing bowls prepared, as well as several crystal bowls that I intuited prior to the session. Before each session I would light and burn White Sage or Palo Santos (sacred wood) to clear the energy of the room and the area around the client. As the session started, I selected the instruments that intuitively felt correct and started playing.

This went on for about twenty minutes. Then I was guided, by intuition, to place my hands on her body. Whenever I place physical pressure, whether light or a stronger pressure, it's done with great care and respect for the individual. During my sessions, there is never a set pattern as to how I move my hands but generally I either start at the head and move down the body or I start at the feet and go upward toward the head.

I checked to see if the client had any emotional reactions to the placements of my hands. Often while working with a client, I feel something unusual or a surge of energy in my body, and I make inquiries as I go along.

What was about to happen made all the sense in the world to me. As I moved my hand over Tara's lower right abdomen, I received that same sharp, stabbing sensation. Simultaneously, Tara cringed in severe pain and began to cry, almost in terror.

"What's going on for you?" I asked her.

She revealed something she had never before told anyone. "I have a recurring dream that haunts me," she said. "I can't get rid of it." Tara told me that when I placed my hands over her abdomen, she saw a vision of being stabbed in a past life, while she was pregnant. "I was stabbed by a man who was violently jealous and didn't want me to have the child," she said. "It was the little boy I've seen many times in my dreams."

As her catharsis occurred and her tears began to lessen, she said, "I don't feel the little boy around me anymore."

For the next few minutes, as I sat with her, she appeared to enter a state of deep rest and peace. I observed her state of being and determined that this event was finally cleared karmically, releasing the little boy. I then once again cleared the room with white sage and asked her to rest as long as she needed. She nodded and I left the room.

Thirty minutes later, I went back to check on her. She smiled and told me how grateful she was for the session. She no longer felt the little boy's presence with her. She felt he had moved on.

THE SWAMI'S MEDITATION

The morning had a different light to it, clearer and brighter. I had been invited to a meditation with a guru from India, along with his devotees. He felt it was important that I come into the Sun Pyramid as one of twenty-two people for his guided meditation. I was feeling a bit off, particularly in how he had asked me to attend. I couldn't put my finger on the exact feeling; I just felt off.

Just prior to entering the Pyramid, I was talking with two friends. They were both from Australia ("Oz"). One, named Karin, was a radio talk show host whom I'd met a few months earlier when she interviewed me about my book *Trust Patience Surrender*. In our conversation, I was telling Karin and my other friend what had happened to me before leaving Sedona, and about the visions in the Moon Pyramid. I even sang for them the mantra and melody that I was shown, and they seemed intrigued and delighted.

The swami approached us, invited all of us into his meditation. As the swami began chanting mantras and singing, the feelings I had earlier became exaggerated, almost to the point that I felt embarrassed laughter rising within me. I had to use all my will to get control of myself so I wouldn't burst out laughing. As the swami continued, opening his eyes to see what everyone was doing, I sensed a strong ego presence coming from him. I sat as patiently as I could.

When the meditation was over, he strode to me. "I'm glad I was able to present my method of meditation to you," he said. "You need to take this meditation out into the world."

Holding back laughter, trying to be polite, I thanked him for his work, then excused myself. I didn't have the heart to tell him I had been doing meditations for well over twenty-five years.

As I turned to go to the restroom, I heard voices singing in the Moon Pyramid a few steps away. It was Karin and her girlfriend singing the words of the mantra and the melody I'd shared with them before entering the meditation. Tearfully, I turned toward the Moon Pyramid, only to be met by a force that I couldn't push through. I tried several times to move forward, but some force, like a wall, was holding me back.

I knew that what I was shown through a vision, while in Sedona on my last trip, was now beginning to happen. But I couldn't move. Some energy or force held me locked in my position. In sheer desperation, I turned in the opposite direction, fleeing toward home. I had no idea that this was happening because the sheer idea of me not doing what I was shown to do weighed heavily on me, to the point I felt an overwhelming disappointment pervade my very being and thoughts.

"You didn't do what you were asked to do!"

Over and over, it repeated. I was pleading for Creation's forgiveness for not doing my work. It was so devastating that I couldn't rationalize it away, no matter how hard I tried.

A DECISION TO LEAVE

The feelings of disappointment were so strong, I decided to go back to Sedona to leave this world as a result of not doing my part. The grief simply overwhelmed me. I was determined to follow through with the intention. I booked my flight the next day.

In Sedona, I met with Grandfather. I had arranged to stay with him. The next morning I gathered my tent and a few things that I would need for my transition. I wrote Grandfather a letter to let him know that I wasn't coming back and what to do with my belongings. Placing the note on my bed, I took my backpack and headed out, journeying to the highest point among the cliffs that I could find.

My designated spot was nestled underneath a massive boulder that could fall at any moment. I imagined it falling on me, taking my life quickly. In my mind, I envisioned being squashed like a bug. I set up my tent and sat until dark, saying prayers and asking for forgiveness for not doing the work that I was shown I was to do.

Having no supplies or water, I crawled into my cocoon and continued the mental struggle of asking for forgiveness and asking to be received. As the evening went on, it grew colder and colder. I'd only brought a light jacket, and I began shaking. Eventually, my whole body was almost convulsing to keep warm.

As the hours passed and the temperature dropped below freezing, I relinquished any thought of trying to survive this. I pleaded to be taken from my body. Several hours more passed. I grew agitated and angry. Before dawn broke, I shoved my fist and arm in air, yelling at Creation, "Fuck you! I'm not going to die this way. This sucks."

Suddenly, I had the will to live another day. At first light, I climbed several hundred feet down the cliff face and found the roadway. Still shaking from the cold, I sensed I received a new lease on life, but I wasn't sure why.

A PLACE OF INNOCENCE

The next day when Grandfather woke from his sleep, he suggested I meet with Mirtala. He didn't have any clue about what happened. At that point, I wasn't going to try to figure anything out. I decided to just allow life and its circumstances to flow through me. It wasn't for me to try to figure out anything.

Just flow, I thought. It was enough.

I called Mirtala to see if I could meet with her. Delighted to hear from me, she invited me to sit with her in a few hours. When I arrived, she sensed something had just happened with me. "What's going on?" she asked.

I told her about the swami, the two women singing the mantra, and the force that wouldn't allow me into the Moon Pyramid. Her expression was knowing and affirmative, and I sensed she understood what was going on. But I felt she chose to not reveal what she understood in that moment.

She began asking me a series of questions about the incident.

"Why do you think the energy held you back from going into the Pyramid?"

Blankly, I responded, "I don't have a clue."

"Who were the ladies in the Pyramid? Tell me about them."

I told her about Karin and a little about her friend. Mirtala smiled and asked a final question. "When you are doing your work in the world, what is one of the most important things that I must remember?"

I responded, "Everything should come from a place of innocence. It must not be ego based."

Her smile widened. All of the sudden, I got it! I realized that the mantra and melody, the Shafts of Light, and all that was to transpire needed to come from a place of innocence of all involved. *That* was why the feelings about the swami were so prominent. I was laughing underneath because of his ego and how he was so excited to have devotees. It was his ego, I felt, that made me want to laugh.

I began to understand that Karin, if she were to really be included in something that was so other worldly, would want to exploit it and place it on the airwaves. Again, this would be from a place of ego.

Mirtala shared something that had happened to her many years earlier when a similar force field of energy held her back from something she felt was really important. When she finished speaking, it all made perfect sense to me. What I do—and what anyone else does, for that matter—is to be done from the heart, without fanfare and without the ego. It is to be done simply, with a deep level of reverence and innocence. I was so grateful for Mirtala's wisdom and clarity that day.

I returned to Bali with a new understanding and a new lease on life. I resumed my counseling and sound healing sessions. These and other experiences that opened me began to flow with great frequency.

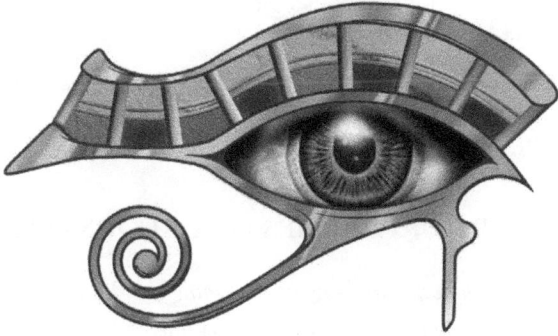

CHAPTER 10

CHAPTER 10: A SERIES OF ENCOUNTERS

"I promise you if you keep searching for everything beautiful in this world, you will eventually become it." ~*Tyler Kent White*

THE HANDS AND REPRESENTATION OF QUAN YIN

When I returned to Bali, I also returned to the Pyramids. There, I met a woman who captured my attention. It began after one of my sound healing sessions. I was strolling through the main restaurant area when a young woman of Southeast Asian descent and I nearly ran into one another. Something about her caught me off guard, but I couldn't figure out what it was. I excused myself, proceeding to the restroom.

This young woman caught my attention several more times. At the Pyramids, I was careful not to get involved with women who came to one of my sound healing sessions or ceremonies. I felt I had a responsibility to hold a loving space, rather than trying to look for a relationship. I realized the perception some women had regarding my role; they viewed me as having a position of authority. I did not want to overstep such a boundary. The young woman and I exchanged pleasantries, then I headed home.

However, the encounters between us happened several more times at the Pyramids. We would meet briefly, and again I'd excuse myself and attend to whatever I was doing. It was difficult to walk away, because I wanted to get to know her.

One evening after the Full Moon ceremony, she approached me. I remember the beautiful red dress she was wearing and her glowing smile. It was the end of the evening, and she said to me, "I'm rather hungry. I'm going to get something to eat."

I stood there for a couple of seconds, then decided, why not ask if she'd like company? She said she would. We went off in search of a nice place to have something to eat and a little privacy to talk. She introduced herself as Mookmai.

From the moment I met Mookmai, one thought continually arose: I wanted her to come home with me. It felt as if I should ask her exactly that. This was quite unusual for me. I hadn't had such strong feelings toward a woman for a number of years. My last serious relationship had been many years earlier. But each time Mookmai was in my presence, I thought again how I wanted her to come home with me. It was so strong, I began to think that I wanted her to stay with me and never leave. This overwhelmed me—but in a good way.

We went to a restaurant in central Ubud and were escorted to an area off to the side, where we had some privacy and a jungle view— as much of a view as we could get in the dark. Our eyes locked and our conversation became interactive, intense, and playful. Not only was Mookmai attractive, she was also funny. Her slender, taut body and Asian features were intoxicating. Her eyes sparkled. There was an elegance in the way she presented herself.

Toward the end of our dinner, the thought that I'd continued to have came out as a question. "Would you come home with me?" A second passed, then I blurted out, "This is the first time I've asked a woman to come home with me."

She nodded. "I have never gone home with someone I just met."

I took her hand. We went out to the parking lot, jumped on my scooter, and headed home.

We didn't become physical that evening; we both had a bit of innocent reservation. But we lay beside one another, and eventually I asked if she would like a massage.

"That would be nice."

I grabbed some towels and coconut oil and spent the next hour massaging her body. Briskly, she shared what kind of pressure she wanted, then she began to relax into the massage. Two-thirds of the way through, she fell asleep, but that didn't matter. I wrapped her in the towels and lay on my side of the bed, watching as she slept. I was taken by the way that she folded her hands over her heart. In the silence, she looked angelic to me, as I watched her breath gently rising and lowering her chest. Her hands and fingers were long, slender, and delicate. But I also knew that she could speak her truth whenever she found it necessary. There was a strength about her.

In the morning, Mookmai made herself right at home which I appreciated. I made French toast with walnuts, bananas, and figs sauteed in butter. After we ate, we held one another for a few minutes. Then I dashed off to the Pyramids to the sound sessions that were scheduled for me.

Around 3:30 p.m. in the afternoon, I returned home, excited to see her and to share more conversation and dinner. As I walked through the front door and into the living room, I was stunned! She had rearranged things. She had placed a tablecloth on the dining table and purchased new flower pots with arrangements throughout the house.

For the past few weeks I had imagined exactly these modifications, made by her. It blew me away. I thought, *How did she know what I wanted?* She'd placed individual, freshly cut flowers into the moist green foam blocks in the pots. It must have taken her most of the day to do all this.

Tears welled up as I considered this beautiful gesture. I was overwhelmed, but in a wonderful way. My heart and mind were blown open like a barn door by her kindness and thoughtfulness.

We ended up spending most of the day together, enjoying each other's company and conversations. But she appeared to be troubled by the fact that she would be leaving soon to return to Thailand. She, too, seemed to have a desire to stay with me. We both felt it. Wow, it had been such a long time for me—and for her, too, I sensed.

"I need to go into town to be with myself," she said. "I need to digest all of what is happening." So I drove her into the center of Ubud.

A few hours later, she phoned, sounding upset. She took subtle, short breaths, as though she'd been crying. "Would you meet me for dinner?"

"I would love to," I said.

I sensed there was a part of her that wanted to stay and another that wanted to leave. I hung up the phone and left to meet her at the restaurant. I sat next to her, attempting to comfort her.

Then words came from my mouth with beautiful intention. "I want you to stay with me," I said. "I will take care of you."

It seemed so right to me. No shock value, merely a heartfelt request. She seemed pleased by my request. She said, "I need a little time to think about it. I'll let you know in the morning."

We enjoyed a savory French dinner and a glass of wine. We were both exhausted by all that had occurred in such a short time. We went home and ended up curling into bed, falling asleep.

The next morning came much too soon for me. I stayed in bed a little longer. Mookmai went downstairs, and I followed shortly after. She'd been staying with me for a couple of days and had brought all her things. As I came down the staircase, I saw that she was packing on the sofa.

With a heavy heart, I said, "You're going back home."

Her smile was sad. "I need to go home," she said, "I need to take care of things there."

My heart felt shattered. I sank onto the couch next to her, breaking into tears and asking why she wouldn't stay a little longer. I literally dropped to my knees, kissing her feet with great reverence. "Why?" I asked. "Why won't you stay?"

Then I realized something profound. Suddenly, I knew who she represented to me: the sacred Quan Yin. I flashed back to watching her sleep, her hands and fingers delicately folded on her heart. I knew they were the hands and representation of Quan Yin.

It made perfect sense to me. For weeks, I had been praying to Quan Yin to bring me comfort. In a flash, my mind flew back in time to my altar. I visualized the slender, delicate, cream-colored porcelain figurine of Quan Yin. And here she was, her energy, in human form.

Knowing this didn't make Mookmai's departure any easier for me.

My heart broke open. For a long time, I hadn't allowed anyone into my heart at this level of opening. I composed myself and watched her pack her things. Shortly thereafter, a driver arrived to take her to the airport.

I was left with a big hole in my heart. But as I allowed my mind and heart to recount our short time together and its intense nature, I realized that it was also an enormous gift given. As I allowed my thoughts and emotions to merge into the experience, I realized, with great clarity, how my prayers to Quan Yin had been answered. It was a painful experience, yet transcendent.

Over the next several months, we stayed in contact. Once, when I felt overwhelmed with a desire to be with her I told her I wanted to visit her and make love. She said she would make love to me anytime, just come. But she ended by saying, "This is not what you're really looking for." In my heart I knew she was speaking the truth.

Two and a half years later, when Mookmai returned to Bali, I came to a greater understanding about our connection. She called to say she would love to meet up. I thought how wonderful it would be to catch up with her. We made plans to meet at a resort in the Champuan area.

At the appointed time, I waited for thirty minutes, then forty. I began to wonder whether I wanted to keep waiting, but I decided to stay a bit longer. Then she messaged that she was on her way.

She arrived cheerful and excited to see me. We sat down and she immediately ordered a bottle of wine. I didn't wish to drink that evening but told her I was appreciative of her gesture.

One of the first things she said was, "My boyfriend just went back to Thailand. I'm free to have fun."

Prior to this comment, I'd had the thought of spending a little time together before she left, to see if an intimate connection was there. But then she went on to talk mostly about drinking, partying, and having a great time. She seemed to revel in recklessness. She said she was living the life of Ji Gong, a Chan Buddhist monk who lived in the Southern Song. He possessed supernatural powers, had wild and eccentric powers, ate meat, and consumed significant amounts of alcohol.

To me, it felt like abandonment on her part. "Do you remember what transpired between us just a few short years ago?" I asked. "Do you remember the intimacy and connection we had with each other?"

She looked at me and said, "I don't remember." She changed the subject, saying she has to leave in the morning, but she would love to party with me tonight. I politely declined.

In that moment, I saw with crystal clarity the lesson and experience for me. I understood that this was the closure I needed to release myself from any notion that there was something between us. A more expansive knowing and gratefulness came from this. It was a knowing that Spirit had brought me another lesson: To live in the moment and let all the rest that is to occur happen on its own accord.

Simply live in the moment, and see the gift of Grace given to me, without expectation.

Where I am Supposed to Be

The next woman I met was from Morocco. Her name was Kenza, and she was accompanied by a friend from France named Patricia. They had come to the Pyramids for a sound healing, but they weren't really sure until they heard about it from several people.

When I met them, I welcomed them to the Pyramids. There seemed to be a strong attraction between Kenza and me. She said, "I lived in the Kuta area years ago."

Kuta is a touristy area in the southwest coastal region of Bali. Kenza told me that Patricia did powerful healing work. The three of us seemed to click. Our conversations flowed, then I needed to play the sound healing session.

"This is my last night in Bali," Kenza said. "I leave tomorrow to return to Morocco." She added, "And I'm not all that happy about it."

We entered the Sun Pyramid, the larger of the two Pyramids. I did my usual presentation about the Pyramids, sharing facts about them and other information that was relevant, including sound frequencies and energies. The introduction and session ran its usual length of ninety minutes. Afterward, Kenza, Patricia, and I resumed our conversation, with Kenza sharing what had happened to her in the Pyramids and the visions she had.

We then discussed going to a Balinese water temple and decided to go to the Sebatu Holy Water Temple in the village of Tegallalang. I had visited this water temple on several auspicious occasions with Agung. I liked the warung (restaurant) at the top of the stairwell. The real challenge was traversing the one hundred steps down to the water temple, so the warung was a nice place to change clothes and get something to eat after coming back up.

While asking them to accompany me, I also had a nagging thought: I wanted Patricia to act as our chaperon. Once again, I didn't want to use my perceived authority to take advantage of the situation.

At Sebatu Holy Water Temple, we changed into our sarongs for the trek down the steps to the waterfalls. We stayed for some time, placing offerings we had purchased in the appropriate places along the journey down to the waterfalls. The water was icy cold, and we had to walk through the stream to reach the cascading water where we placed our last flower offering under a colorful umbrella. We took turns immersing our bodies in the icy waters. Then we climbed the many stairs back to the warung. As soon as we arrived, we changed out of the wet sarongs and put our warm, dry street clothes back on. It was a welcome relief from the chilling waters.

We sat down to eat, and Kenza and I engaged in deep conversation, with Patricia listening. It was obvious to all three of us that there was something happening between Kenza and me.

When Patricia excused herself to go to the bathroom, Kenza revealed to me that she was attracted to me. "It's as though it's something that had happened before," she said.

I reached out my hand, inviting her to sit closer to me. She accepted, and as I wrapped my arms fully around her, she began to shake. She told me she'd had difficulties with her libido for the prior two years— but, she said, this was no longer a problem as I held her. Kenza also shared that she had been to a seer, and the woman told her she would meet a man who plays music, and that the two of us would come together. "I asked her, 'Will we sleep together?'" Kenza told me.

"What did she say?" I inquired.

"That she didn't know," Kenza replied. "And that it would be up to us."

By now, Patricia had returned and was listening to our conversation. "I have done this once before for the two of you," she said. "You are like children."

When she made that statement, it somehow sounded and felt vaguely familiar to me. It *was* as though this wasn't the first time Kenza and I had come together.

We ended up holding one another for several more hours, while Patricia dozed in and out, until the owner came to our table and said the restaurant was closing. The three of us went to my house to drop me off, and along the way my thoughts covered the full gamut: *Should I ask her to come into the house? I'm really glad that Patricia came to be our chaperone.* I felt confused by these thoughts bouncing around my head.

In the end, I did not invite her in. At my home, Kenza and I held one another, then shared our goodbyes.

In the midst of these encounters, there were many months when the sound healing sessions, private clients, and my other activities seemed to find their own flow. But there were also periods of time when I would once again become frustrated, thinking that the visions I'd seen were once again put on hold. I had to remind myself of the beautiful moments that had occurred. I was simply a human desiring something other than what I was doing. And always something—someone or an event—would remind me that I was exactly where I was supposed to be.

Woman in the Fifth Dimension

One of these events happened when I was setting up for a cacao ceremony in the Moon Pyramid. One of the other gong practitioners was walking around me in circles. I looked up from the mandala that I was constructing because I felt something was wrong. So I asked Sky, "What is going on?"

His voice was magnified. "Someone is having an episode. I don't know how to help them."

I got to my feet and the two of us exited the Moon Pyramid. Outside, I saw a woman sitting on the bench outside of the Sun Pyramid. Her body was shaking, her face appeared fearful, and her partner was sitting next to her, completely baffled. I knelt in front of her, looked into her eyes, and I asked her to describe what she was feeling in her physical body as well as what emotions and energy she was feeling.

"Something is happening to me," she said. "It's never happened before. I'm frightened."

"Where do you feel this energy in your body?" I asked.

"My heart feels like it is going to explode!" she exclaimed.

I asked medical questions to ensure she wasn't having a heart attack. She made it very clear that it was not a heart attack. I asked her to take deep breaths in and out, in order to allow the energies to move through her body. She complied each time I requested this.

Based on my own experiences, I felt strongly that she was having a kundalini awakening. This is where the body receives a lot of energies flowing through the body. It's quite frightening the first time and can make you feel unsure whether you are going to live or die. Drawing from my own experiences with this energy, I continued to guide her through the experience. It was important that I kept direct but soft eye contact with her, so she would feel supported. As I guided her through the experience I asked more questions and made statements. "Is the energy moving through your body? If so, where is it now? Continue to focus on your breath, because it is the key element to help you move through this."

At the same time, I was reassuring her partner that she would be okay and not to worry. I explained to him what was occurring and advised that he, too, should continue to focus on his breath. He looked relieved, but I could tell he was still worried.

"She is in a heightened state of awareness," I said. "For several hours, she will have a hyper awareness of the people and things around her." The woman gave me a look of acknowledgment, agreeing with what I was sharing with her partner. I continued to check in on the woman as her emotions and feelings changed.

After some time of fear, she began to move into the next stage, where the Heart begins to open. Often, it is frightful for the individual, but some time later, tears flow as the Heart opens because of the hyperawareness that is unfolding. The tears are not of sadness or fear any longer; they are tears of Joy!

When her tears began flowing, I asked her to allow them, not stop them. Crying is part of the Heart opening process. Again, she looked at me with great gratitude.

Through this process of the Heart opening and the kundalini energies flowing, the endocrine system is in heightened awareness, leaving the head, hands, fingers, feet, and/or toes feeling a sense of exaggerated size. I call it "crab claw" or "crab feet." The energies are so exaggerated, these extremities feel three times their normal size. This is all part of the process.

Eventually, the woman came into a quiet place within herself. She began to smile, and I could tell she felt an overwhelming sense of joy. Let's just say it is when we began to understand our connection to all that is in the universe. That is why I refer to it as the Fifth Dimension and the Feeling State of God—or simply 5D.

I asked the woman to continue to allow this state of being to anchor in her body. I said she would return to her normal self in several hours or by the next day.

"Be very gentle with one another," I instructed her and her partner. "Do things that will nourish and nurture you."

Once I saw she was in a stable physical and emotional space, I thanked both of them for allowing the experience to occur. "Do not be afraid of what just happened to her," I said to her partner. "It is her heart opening." I assured him she would still love him, but in a more profound way. Tearfully, they both thanked me for helping them.

One of the things I know, based on my own experiences and what I've been shown through visions and dreams, is that this will begin to occur for more and more with people when they first open their mind to such a possibility, and then their hearts to this expansive process. It is what I call the "Awakening." It is the process in which we begin to understand, through experience, that we are much more than the sum of our daily lives.

In the scriptures, it is believed that Jesus said, "Do not try and take Heaven by storm, it can kill you." My interpretation of that is about the kundalini energies that move through the body.

I also believe that if you try to make kundalini awakening happen through force, it can cause irreversible damage or even death. The key is a natural state of surrender. At times while in the experience we might not believe it, but we are never given more than we can receive. The experience of the woman at the Sun Pyramid was a perfect example.

A BUFFALO CALF WOMAN VISION

Like the woman at the Sun Pyramid, I, too, sometimes entered experiences unknowingly, often without anyone's help. I believe that if the experience is to happen, it is meant to happen. Surrender is the key.

One afternoon, I finished a sound healing session that appeared to be no different than many others. As I finished the sound healing, I slowly opened the doors of the Pyramid, allowing sunlight to enter. Then I stepped outside into the sunlight. Many participants followed me out with smiles on their faces. Others exited slowly, looking disoriented. Then a middle aged woman approached me, asking if I would allow her to share what had just happened to her while she was lying on the mattress, receiving the sounds.

It was not the best of days for me. I'd been feeling overwhelmed and wasn't too excited about what was going on in my life. I'd begun to have thoughts of travel. I needed a break from all the sessions. Nonetheless, I said to the woman, "Yes, please share."

"I don't understand the vision or dream I had," she told me. "In my mind's eye, or maybe my imagination, there was a dark skinned woman in the Pyramid wearing a white buckskin dress. She was placing white feathers on the heart of each participant in the session." Her eyes welled with tears. "It was so moving, knowing that such a benevolent figure was in the Pyramids."

I found myself tearful, too. "I think I know who that woman was," I said. "It was White Buffalo Calf Woman. Placing white feathers on the heart was White Buffalo Calf Woman's way of aligning and opening their hearts. I also feel she was laying a white feather of the Divine Feminine of Love on each of them."

White Buffalo Calf Woman is a powerful figure to the Lakota Native American peoples. It is their belief and mine that she came to them many generations ago to present the Lakota with the Seven Sacred Rights, the Chanupa (sacred pipe), the sacred blanket that connects us all, and the many teachings of the Seven Sacred Rights about how the people should live.

Given my love and understanding for White Buffalo Calf Woman, I was grateful for her presence at the Pyramids in Bali. She was also known to me as a female form of Creator; I believe she reveals herself in other traditions, as Quan Yin in the Buddhist faith, Mother Mary in the Catholic tradition, Saraswati within the Hindu faith and the White Tara to the Tibetans, just to name a few. I believe this energy of the Divine Feminine shows herself to people in ways in which they will understand. She is the Divine Feminine aspect of Creation, or a presence of God.

I explained all this to the woman, who grinned, wiping her tears as we hugged. I thanked her for sharing what she had witnessed. As on other occasions, I felt that the world of Spirit was with me. This knowing made my frustrations dissipate from my body and mind.

THE AVATAR AND COUNCIL

Another episode of understanding and confirmation that I was doing the work I was called to do occurred, once again, after one of my sound journeys. Again, a woman approached me. A look of bewilderment on her face, she shared that she had seen something during the sound journey session. "There was a tall man in a formal military uniform, aqua in color, with gold epaulets on his shoulders. He had blond hair. There were several people gathered in a semicircle; they appeared to be a council. They told the man to tell you, Kevin, that you're doing a wonderful job and they're proud of you."

As soon as I heard those words, I knew exactly who the man and council were. I explained to her the first experience I had with the man (known as the Avatar) and council. In that episode, which had occurred ten years prior, I was shown what was going to happen in the future to humanity. "Much of it will be viewed unfavorably by people," I said. "Because of the devastating events that will occur." That was not the only time the Avatar and council appeared to me in vivid dreams and visions. Over the years, it has happened many times.

When the woman mentioned the Avatar and council to me after one of my sessions, it was, again, a time when I was feeling defeated by the work I'd been doing for the previous three years. It felt as if I was doing all of this work alone. But in that moment, I understood what the Avatar and council were saying, and I felt it was for my benefit. I began to believe I had the strength and fortitude to continue the work that I was asked to do.

My current and future work is tied to helping people see that there is something more going on, here and that this is a time of awakening for humanity. It is another opportunity. Many indigenous nations believe that we have entered the beginning of a new world. It is often referred to as the Fifth World of Existence. The four other worlds have been destroyed, due to Man's floundering, poor stewardship, and ego.

"BLACKBIRD" — AGAIN

Mike was the third person to come into my life when I felt frustrated. I was trying to learn the Indonesian language, Bahasa Indonesia. I was struggling to make sense of its structure. Not only Bahasa Indonesia, but also the Balinese language and the formal (or royal) language were used on the island. As is the case with most non-native-speakers on the island, I focused on learning Bahasa Indonesia, the most widely accepted and used language.

I began by taking a group class, but it overwhelmed me. Expats and tourists would continually blurt out questions, which I found disconcerting and disruptive. I decided to use a private tutor instead. My tutor, a young Indonesian woman who had lived in Australia, was a welcomed relief. She knew many English language colloquialisms, giving her a wonderful ability to pronounce words in a manner that felt familiar to me.

One day, she was unavailable and had to send a substitute, a man named Mike. Due to Mike's heavy Indonesian pronunciations, I became frustrated. Halfway through the class, as I continued trying to hear and grasp the words and sentence structures he was trying to teach me, I felt exhausted.

"Let's take a break," Mike suggested. When I agreed, he asked, "Do you mind if I tune and play my guitar a bit?"

All too happy for the fifteen-minute break, I went into the cafeteria for water. *Will I even pass the class?* I wondered. I teetered on the decision of whether to quit the classes altogether.

As I returned to the meeting room, I heard Mike tuning his guitar. Just as I was about to announce I was quitting, he began playing. I was shocked by what I heard. The song was my old favorite: "Blackbird" by the Beatles!

The synchronicity of the moment and my facial expression of joy caused Mike to stop playing. "What's going on?" he asked. I told him that on many occasions when I was ready to give up on something I was working on or toward, the song "Blackbird" would be played.

Smiling, Mike suggested we get started again. I agreed, and when I resumed learning the Indonesian language, things went much better.

ANNA BEL LAURA AND MOTHER NATURE

Another experience at this time helped me through a rough patch of wondering if, when, and where I would ever have another long lasting relationship. Most of my experiences gave me glimpses of understanding for which I was grateful, but the powerful connections to the women I'd encountered were all so fleeting. I once more became frustrated. I was doing everything on my own and living my daily life without a significant other.

From time to time, I would search the internet or go into Ubud to see what event might be happening to take me out of my mood of longing for a significant other. One day as I perused the local Facebook page for things to do in Ubud, I saw that a band was going to play that Saturday night at BetelNut Bali, a noodle, satay bar, cocktail lounge, and creative space.

On Saturday night, I got a little dressed up, since I was taking myself out for a date. I arrived at the venue only to be told to wait. They wouldn't allow anyone inside until show time. I decided to stay, and eventually all of us who were waiting were invited in.

The band was from Norway (I believe). An Indonesian woman

sitting in with the band introduced herself as Anna Bel Laura. The name alone was beautiful, and she was quite attractive. She also reminded me of a woman I'd dated in Sedona. I wanted to see where this might lead.

As the band played, Anna Bel Laura was the central focus, strumming her guitar. Her songs were melodic and her voice was soothing. Many of the songs she sang that evening were from her compact disc *Ibu Pertiwi.* Many were about Mother Nature.

Her style of playing and her voice were magical to me. The songs took me on an emotional roller coaster ride of longing for a lover and a knowing that it all happens at the right time. I fantasized about going on a date with her, but it was simply a fantasy.

As the evening wound down, I debated whether or not I should talk to her. Finally, when the music was over, I mustered up the courage to speak with her. I complimented her lyrics and melodies, especially the song *"Hujon,"* which translates to "rain" in English. I then told her a little about what was going on in my life, including my desire for a loving relationship.

"I completely understand," she said. "I, too, have just come out of a long term relationship that ended." She went on, "I have something I would love to give you." She stepped over to a table where her CDs were for sale. Beside them was a large satchel. She began digging through the contents.

She pulled out a 3 x 5 black and white card that bore a picture of a kneeling, nude woman who had flowers emerging from her head and feet. I was so taken by the symbology of Mother Nature that tears began to fall. I turned the card over and read the inscription: "We Are Nature."

"May I give you a hug?" Anna Bel Laura asked. I was all too happy to oblige. She looked me squarely in the eye and said, "We can't give up."

I smiled in agreement. For a few moments, we stood there, feeling each other's sadness and hope. Then we said our final goodbyes and I headed toward the door.

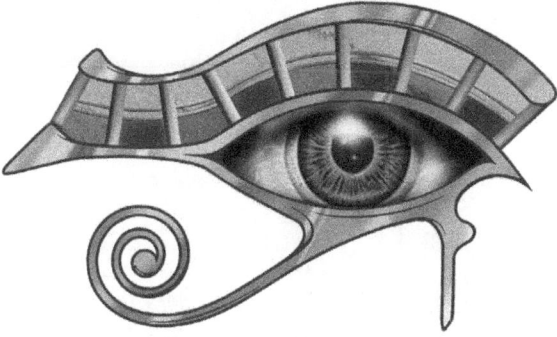

CHAPTER 11

CHAPTER 11: PEACE AND VISIONS

"When you reach your edge, soften. Soften until you slip through the constraints and can create a new rhythm, a new route, a new release. Water is soft yet powerful. Reach your edge, and soften."
  ~Victoria Erickson

AT PEACE WITH MOTHER

Within the next eighteen months, I met a couple named Elizabeth and Dennis from Almaty, Kazakhstan, as well as some of their friends. The three of us spent considerable time together traveling around Bali. In the beginning of our coming together as friends, Elizabeth had a strong feeling that she and I were meant to be together. She even stopped being with Dennis in a physical and intimate way. I felt it, too, but I would not reciprocate because I didn't want to come between them and their six-year relationship. We enjoyed each other's company for the next three months, going to beaches and traveling the island.

One trip we took was to Amed, a small coastal fishing village on the northeastern coast. Weeks before, I'd met a woman who owned several small villas on the beach in Amed, so we jumped on our scooters and headed north. Upon arriving, I noticed that the little town wasn't as clean and exciting as I'd expected. I kept getting this feeling of nature's imbalance in the area. There was plastic and debris on the side of the road, and I saw the disparity of local villagers compared to the foreigners' homes, which seemed out of place. It was so out of balance, it felt like a deep chasm. These thoughts would grow more the longer we stayed. I could feel how the land in Amed was out of balance, and in turmoil and pain.

The young man who was managing the property hadn't expected us until the next day. I showed him the text with the owner's agreement of our arrival time. After a few minutes, things got straightened out and we entered our rooms.

After we settled in, I lay down in a comfortable lounge chair on the beach only a few steps from our villas, while Dennis and Elizabeth took a stroll along the sand. As I sat on the beach, a young girl came by, selling trinkets and beaded items. I was the only one on the beach, and I didn't want to buy anything. But as she passed, I heard an inner nudge to call her over. I pushed the thought out of my mind as I watched her head down the beach.

Some time later, she returned. This time, my inner voice was loud. *Call her over here!*

So I did. She was about ten years old, with beads hanging from a bundle on top of her head. She held several knick-knacks in her hands. "Did you make the beads?" I asked her. When she said no, I asked, "Did you make anything yourself?"

With a big smile, she said, "Oh yes, I made these." She held out a couple of 3×5 cards with paintings on them.

"Which one is your favorite?" I asked.

She thumbed through to a card with a forest green and navy blue background and beautiful white flowers in the center. "This one!" she exclaimed.

I asked, "May I buy that one?"

With a big smile, she said, "Yes." I handed her some money.

"Salamat Pagi, Terimah kasih." I said—which means, "Good morning, thank you."

She replied, "Mawali." You're welcome.

When she handed me the beautiful card with her favorite hand-painted flowers, I was struck by the form and shape of her hands. They were so delicate and refined, I was taken aback. As she walked away, I looked at her picture, enjoying that she had sold me such a beautiful card.

As I sat there after she'd continued down the beach, I envisioned a man diving into the water and scraping his right leg. I decided I didn't want to get into the water, due to the rocks beneath the surface of the water. But after thirty minutes of lying there in the sun's blaring heat, I decided to wade into the water to cool off. As I entered the coolness of the ocean, looking around for coral and not seeing any, I thought, *Why not just lean forward and dive in?*

So I did. As soon as I broke the surface of the water, I felt a jagged coral tear into my right leg. Man, did that hurt! Why didn't I listen to the premonition that I had received only minutes earlier? With blood running down my leg, I hobbled up to my room on the second floor, opened my first aid kit, and took care of the long gashes. After cleaning and bandaging the wounds, I went back to the beach and sat under the shade of a nearby coconut tree. I knew my time in the water had come to an end, but that was fine by me.

About forty-five minutes later, Dennis and Elizabeth returned, asking if I'd like to join them for lunch at Blue Earth, the health food restaurant up the street. We headed up the hill and pulled into the parking lot. As we climbed the staircase to the second floor I was overtaken by dizziness and shaking. I was experiencing some type of vertigo, and as they watched me wobble back and forth and turn a pale shade of white, I exclaimed, "Please catch me. Help me down the stairs. I need to ground myself in Mother."

Downstairs, Dennis and Elizabeth placed me on the ground amidst a few small tables and cushions. Something like this had happened to me years earlier in the Unity center while I was in Sedona, so it felt as though I was repeating a similar experience. I placed my hands as deeply into the earth as possible.

Suddenly, an overwhelming sense of grief filled me. I didn't understand, at first, where this was coming from, but I knew I couldn't stop it even if I wanted to. I felt emotions from deep within me and a strong sense of connection to Mother Earth. I felt her pain of neglect, rape, and even abandonment. I sat there with my body folded forward and my head almost resting on the ground. Then I placed my hands into the soil and grass. I was unable to speak, so I just nodded to Elizabeth.

She looked deep into my eyes, saying in a soft voice, "You are with Mother, aren't you?"

Between tears and gasping for breath, I nodded. I simply couldn't speak. This went on for fifteen to twenty minutes. I knew that these painful feelings were not mine alone. I felt the presence of Gaia. The presence of the land and Mother. So I simply allowed it to happen.

As quickly as it started, it subsided. I returned to a place of internal peace. I guess my face showed that, because Elizabeth said, "Mother is at peace now, isn't she?"

I was amazed at her ability to see into what was going on within the experience. No one else had ever had this ability of knowing where I was and what I was going through. Elizabeth was the first. When most people observed these states of being within me, they either tried to share the moment by trying to hold me in hopes of receiving the energies (or even literally sitting on me), or else they verbally discounted the experience altogether.

This was entirely different. Elizabeth acknowledged what had just happened and allowed me to rest my head on her shoulder while she held me in a loving space of openness. I knew at that moment that there was a special connection between the two of us. She allowed me to rest upon her shoulder as I gathered my breath and awareness. I was so moved that I wrote this poem to Mother Nature.

> And there will come a time when she's complete
> Entering into the wholeness we shall meet
> No more pain no more wandering into suffering
> Truly a knowing that comes a sundering
> Through the forests and the rain
> We will no longer feel her pain
> Holding her in our Hearts and a place of Grace
> Will we know and remember once more
> That all was known and not a race
> But a gentle return to Grace

AN EXPRESSION OF LOVE

Elizabeth and Dennis insisted that two things would occur between us, and there was also something they needed to share with me that was important. The first occurred after we had spent the day in Nusa Dua in the south of Bali, at a private beach sandwiched between the Regency Hotel and the Hilton Resort. We spent the day frolicking in the water, enjoying each other's company. When I was walking down the shoreline, an octopus kept following me at the water's edge. I found it very playful. At one point, it literally washed itself up on the beach next to my feet while opening one of its eyes to look at me. I was shocked and delighted, and I had to take a photo.

Later, we went to a seafood restaurant to have a bite to eat. Dennis had once said that he knew Elizabeth and I were meant to be together, and that afternoon at lunch he said it once more. As soon as he made the statement, Elizabeth reached out and wrapped her arms around me, declaring her love for me right in front of Dennis. He nodded that this was the truth and that I should receive her. For the next several moments, she and I held one another. It felt a bit awkward at first, but something inside of me opened to her expression of love.

From that point on, things began to change, as I allowed Elizabeth's affection and Dennis accepted it. He even remarked, "I had been waiting for six years to receive what she is feeling and lovingly giving you. You must open to her. You are meant to be together."

The next day, Dennis called to let me know that he was bringing Elizabeth to my house. "She is to stay with you," he said. It was flattering and exciting, but I still felt discomfort, because I sensed the pain that he was in and his lack of acknowledgment of that pain. Or so I thought.

That evening it was pouring rain. I heard them saying hello as they entered my front gate. Dennis only stayed a few minutes. He hugged us both and said, "This is so right and beautiful. You are meant to be together." He then said goodbye to us both.

Thirty minutes later, he returned with a couple dozen roses in his hands. He extended them to me. "I bought them for you," he said. His gesture left me speechless.

Something else occurred prior to this expression of love. For days, both Dennis and Elizabeth said they had gotten something for me and that they had something important to tell me about who I was. This had me intrigued, to say the least. The next day, they came to my house bearing a gift of two keys, one painted gold and the other painted silver. They were so excited to tell me how they had painted the old skeleton-styled keys themselves and that the keys came with an important message. They both looked at me with all earnestness, saying, "You don't know who you are yet. We are giving you keys of remembrance." I was shocked by their gift and the efforts they went through to create them.

They told me the significance of the keys to them, and that it would help me to understand more about myself and who I am. "These two keys represent the keys of Heaven, which were given to Saint Peter by Christ, and we are presenting them to you." Once more, they exclaimed, "You don't know who you are yet."

This all overwhelmed me, and I felt shyness and embarrassment at their gift of keys and words. But I accepted them with an open heart, thanking them for their kindness.

LORRAINE'S THREE KEYS, AGAIN

Dennis and Elizabeth's gift of the key reminded me of what Lorraine had said a year or so earlier, when she claimed she saw in my future that I would receive a total of three keys presented to me, and this would occur at a time when I would then be able to create whatever I wanted to in the world, as long as it was for the good of Humanity. Lorraine also made reference to the matrix and explained the part I would play in all of it. During that initial reading, I didn't feel as though I could fully grasp the totality of what she meant, but now I was beginning to see the vision she described unfolding. I had been given the first two keys, and I wondered what would be the outcome when I received the third and final key.

All of this seemed like it was of another world, and I found it equally exciting and unsettling. It would be a few more years until I reviewed my Astro Cartography map, combined with a recurring thought, and it all began to make sense.

Prior to meeting Dennis and Elizabeth that summer, a recurring thought had floated around in my brain: The desire to meet a young woman and young man whom I wished to care for. Remembering this thought after I met Dennis and Elizabeth caused me to look further into our connections. When I dug out my AstroCartography map, our friendships and connections made a lot more sense. One of the ideas suggested by the map and the connection it showed for me to Kazakhstan indicated that I would meet a man and woman with whom to explore a more Bohemian lifestyle.

ASTROCARTOGRAPHY

AstroCartography involves comparing your natal information to the location of the sun, moon, and other planets relative to the Earth when you were born. It's a map of how and where the planetary energies in your astrological chart have an influence on you across the world. It also indicates what you will experience in this life, based on the geographic location and your birth chart from astrology. On the map of the world, vertical lines running from top to bottom indicate if the planets, at your birth, were ascending, in a mid-heaven position, or descending. Astro-charts go on to say:

"While your ascendant, or rising sign, shows the mask you wear for the world, or how others first perceive you, your mid-heaven relates more directly to your career, public life, and reputation. It points the outward expression of your individuality."

[https://www.allure.com/story/what-is-your-midheaven-sign]

I've used the AstroCartography map for more than twenty years. You can find it here: www.astrocartography.co.uk.

When considering when these kinds of events were happening in my life, my question was always, "Is this experience a result of my desire and my ability to manifest, or is it more that I received it as a premonition about some future event that is coming into my life?" My answer, even today, is still "blowing in the wind." The belief it could be a combination of both.

This spark of questioning is a good opportunity to bring forth another concept about AstroCartography for me: What it said about me living on the islands of Bali or Borneo. Some thirty years ago, I purchased my first AstroCartography map after arriving in Sedona. As I studied the map, one of things the chart seemed to indicate was that Bali and Borneo were two of the most powerful places in the world where I could live, and that I would experience great expansion and profound love in either one, since both my Jupiter and Venus lines lay vertically over both of the islands. It also further indicated that each of the lines had what is called a zenith directly over these two islands. With the zenith, symbols are represented by small rectangular shapes on each of the lines, suggesting with their presence an amplified, powerful effect of the two planets and their astrological meanings, as much as tenfold.

DONNA, THE WATER TEMPLES, AND THE WEBSITE

Around this time, I met Donna. She was from England and of African descent. When we met, we quickly bonded as friends. While we toured the beautiful Royal family lotus pond in central Ubud, our conversations were fun and somewhat playful.

An August afternoon with Donna is one I will always remember. We visited Tegenungan Waterfall Temple because of my intuition about visiting this temple. After we walked down the long ramp to the lower water pool area, we found several women bathing. We quickly turned, heading to the waterfall itself. Seeing and hearing the water cascading down the cliff face, I began to feel sick, as if energetically something was off.

In shock, we stood at the edge of the sacred temple. There were tourists in bikinis. People were running around like it was a playground.

I asked Donna to pray with me to clear and balance the negative energies in the temple. She was only too happy to hold prayer with me. As my tears began to flow, Donna said, "You are with Mother?"

I was surprised by her words. She was unfamiliar with what had happened prior to this at other temples and areas of Bali. Nodding, I said, "I am."

We sat for several minutes. The negative energies became clear. We sent a brief prayer of gratitude to Mother for her perseverance and for not giving up on humanity.

Soon, Donna would be heading back to India to continue her work as a volunteer at an ashram. While in India, she'd received the call to come to Bali for only a few weeks. During one of our conversations, she talked of the number of websites that she had created for others. She said she was pretty good at creating online content and graphics. I was intrigued, because over the prior couple of years, I'd been asked if I had a website so they could see all the programs and modalities I offered. But I let go of the idea of asking Donna to create my site. I thought she'd be too expensive.

Then she was off to India. Over the next month, we stayed in contact. She considered coming to Bali again for a few weeks, but she wasn't certain she could afford it. When she said that, I had an idea.

"What if I pay for part of your travel expenses to Bali, along with paying for your lodging, food, and motor scooter costs?" I asked. "In exchange, you could design and write the content for my website."

She was all too happy to agree to such terms. A week later, she was in Bali. We met to talk about the site's content, design, layout, and my goals for it. It was important to start soon, since her return flight to India was in thirty days. After our initial meeting, she agreed to get started on the content, but she told me that first she had to complete some work for another client. Somewhat reluctantly, I agreed.

A bit over a week passed. I asked if she had completed any work on my website. She replied, "Nothing yet."

Another week passed. I was becoming agitated that she hadn't called or updated me on her progress, so I texted her again. She again replied, "Nothing yet."

I reminded her as politely as I could that we had an agreement for her to do the work, and that something needed to be done. In response, she asked to meet to review my work. She wanted to know more about experiences of a spiritual nature that I'd had.

During that meeting, we talked for three hours. I shared many of the modalities and processes regarding the work I did with clients, as well as many of the deeply profound experiences that had occurred through me. In the course of that conversation, something very powerful happened for the both of us. About three hours into the interview, a wave of energy, which I call "Divine Grace," brought out a deep emotional response in me. I began feeling enveloped by a benevolent force.

My thoughts came to a profound conclusion. I realized how loved I have been, to have gone through all the experiences I have in my lifetime. It was so overwhelming, Donna began to tear up herself. She said she felt an immense, loving energy.

On a deep level, I understood that all of my experiences were pointing me to this knowing of Love. I realized that each event, whether it was extremely painful to me, someone else, or both, was combined with times of Joy and Forgiveness.

I saw it all from a panoramic view. Love wanted me to see it from many perspectives. It was given to me out of love. It reminded me of the saying, "What doesn't kill you makes you stronger." I was given all of the events to see Creation's Love, which I am a part of.

As it turned out, she never completed the website. At first I was angry, then I realized that this, too, was an experience of acceptance. Still, I concluded that I had to cut ties with her. In doing so, I told her to give me a receipt for all the expenses I'd paid for. Realizing the interview was enough, I said she was released from paying me back.

She was shocked by my response, but after that closure, I didn't need to speak to her anymore. I understood the gift given (the interview), and I didn't need nor want to communicate with her again.

A MYSTERIOUS ILLNESS

It was time to renew my Indonesian visa. Visa runs usually required coordinating travel outside of the country, generally flying to Singapore or Kuala Lumpur, Malaysia for the day and taking a return flight to Bali. During the layover, one had to renew their KITAS (Residence Permit Card) upon arrival, have some fun, and take the next flight out, around 5:30 p.m. On this trip I decided to transit through Singapore and visit the Marina Bay Sands. The resort is described thus:

Marina Bay Sands, owned by Las Vegas Sands, is an integrated resort fronting Marina Bay in Singapore and landmark of the city. At its opening in 2010, it was deemed the world's most expensive standalone casino property at S$8 billion (US $6.88 billion). The resort includes a 2,561 -room hotel, a 120,000 square-meter (1,300,000 sq ft) convention-exhibition center. The complex includes three towers topped by the Sands Skypark, A skyway connecting 340-meter-long (1,120 ft) with a capacity of 3,902 people and a 150 m (490 ft) infinity swimming pool, set on top of the world's largest public cantilevered platform.

[https://en.wikipedia.org/wiki/Marina_Bay_Sands]

After submitting my passport and all the necessary paperwork and payment with the visa agent, I went out to the street to hail a cab. Upon arrival at the Marina Bay Sands I was told it would be a few hours before they let anyone else enter the elevator due to its full capacity. I browsed the retail shops and chilled. When it was time to head up to the reception area, I felt anxious and excited because I have acrophobia, fear of heights. As the lift rose the 57 stories at breakneck speed, I took several deep, relaxing breaths. In the 57th floor reception area, the four-foot high glass retaining walls felt a little protective, but I still had no desire to go to the edge. Instead, I headed to the restaurant for lunch. The service and delicious seafood lunch were a welcomed change from the Nasi Goreng (fried rice) and the Cap Cai (popular vegetable dish in clear broth) that I ate quite regularly in Ubud. I spent the afternoon relaxing and enjoying the first class service and the restaurant's spectacular panoramic view of Singapore Harbor.

After lunch, I took a taxi to the immigration agent to see how things were progressing and to see if I would be leaving on the 5:30 flight back to Denpasar. At the office, I was given the positive response that all was going as planned and I should make the flight in plenty of time.

A few hours passed as I waited patiently for the return of my passport and legal work documents. The documents arrived a bit late but I still had time to make the flight. There were always a number of people from Bali using this Singapore agent, so a few of us gathered and headed for the taxi stand. After waiting about twenty minutes we were on our way to the airport. This is always a good feeling, having completed the process in such a short time.

As we drove to the airport, the driver kept coughing. It sounded deep within his chest, but since I was headed home, I ignored it. It was the day before Christmas Eve 2019, and I just wanted to settle in at home and have a quiet night of rest.

During the night, I awoke with a flu that came on quite suddenly. I'd had plenty of sinus and bronchial infections during the past twenty years; they showed up like clockwork in November or February. Once or twice, they'd progressed into pneumonia. But this didn't follow their same pattern. It came on super fast. On Christmas Eve morning, I couldn't get out of bed. The aches and pains, coughing and sinusitis, were in full bloom. I noticed that the symptoms were vastly accelerated. Rini, a woman I had been seeing for about a month, showed up to nurse me through my sickness.

This virus was so unusual, I thought, because each hour it continued to worsen beyond anything I had ever experienced. I told Rini that when I coughed, it felt as if someone was cutting my lower lungs with razor blades. The pain, sinusitis, and full blown bronchitis was kicking my butt like never before. I remember telling her that if it got any worse, I was checking out of life.

Rini was an aromatherapist. She doused me with every oil she could imagine. She applied them both topically and in an electronic mister to get them into my lungs. But they provided little relief.

This went on for more than two weeks without any signs of getting better. The dry coughing, sore lungs, and aching body seemed too much to bear. It was like nothing I'd ever encountered. I ended up taking antibiotics, many vitamins, and lots of aromatic oils. Eventually, I ended up in the doctor's office to determine what was going on. He prescribed more drugs and an inhaler, and told me to go home and rest.

I rested as much as I could. It went on for another two weeks. Then, just when I began to feel better, it clobbered me again for more than another week. All in all, it took well over a month to feel any sense of normalcy.

Only a few weeks later, the news came out about the COVID-19 virus. I knew instantaneously that was what I'd had. It kept my body in low-level energy for some time after. I remember Rini saying to me one afternoon, "I have paid back my Karmic debt to you. You probably would have died if I didn't use all my oils on you." It struck me that there could be some truth in it, even though she'd laughed while saying it.

VISIONS AT SRI PHALA

After several months of recuperation I began to feel like myself once more. I received a call from Gung de, Agung's son, asking if I would be willing to be an actor in his friend's production company's promotional video. They needed an older man to play a part in a video that was scripted to bring tourists to Bali. I happily agreed, and we set the day and time for the video shoot. I was excited and curious about the adventure. This was during the summer of 2020, and COVID restrictions in Bali were fairly lax.

The shoot was to be held at the Sri Phala Resort in Sanur, Bali, near the ocean. In the days leading up to the shoot, I reminisced about the thirty or so television commercials and promotional ads I'd been involved in as an actor in Sedona. I always found it fun to discover where my limits and faults would show up during the shootings. Often, I laughed hysterically at some of the scenes and blunders.

I arrived early that morning to get briefed on the day's production schedule, where my room for the night would be, and to meet the other actors. During the breaks between shots, we got to chat with one another. On several occasions, I sat with a girl named Nadia, conversing about life and the video we were shooting. It was apparent that this ten-year-old girl had an old soul. The conversations would normally only be comprehended by someone much older. She spoke with a vocabulary that most ten-year-olds couldn't begin to grasp.

At one point, I turned to her mother and asked, "How does she have such a mastery of the English language?"

"She learned it on You Tube," her mother replied.

I shook my head from side to side in disbelief.

Her mother smiled. "We don't understand it either."

Another thing that stood out was when one of the young female Balinese staff said, "You will be staying in room 103 tonight." I found that a bit odd, since I had been given a key to room 127. I just smiled and went to the next location for the production.

It was a hot, sticky tropical day, and when lunch break was called, I was content to go to my air conditioned room to cool off. As soon as I opened the door to room 127, the wave of mold that bellowed from the room was overpowering. The rooms had been closed for some time due to the COVID-19 lockdown. I went to the reservation desk to request a new room. It struck me as funny when the receptionist handed me the key to room 103.

I accepted the key, knowing that something else was afoot. But I headed to the room, turned on the air conditioner, and relaxed until I was called.

The next scene was being shot on the front porch of the villa, right next door off room 105. The shot required me to sit at a desk on the front porch writing a letter with a pensive look on my face. I remember what I was writing and the intention behind it. I'd been given insights and a vision of what was to come in the years from 2020 to 2025, so what I wrote that day on the porch of room 105 was a request that people would wake up to the madness that was about to be thrust upon humanity. I wrote my deepest desires for Love to all of Humanity, the Creator, and Mother Earth. I finished the letter by asking Love and Light to be our guides during the upcoming tribulations. I wrote two letters, one which I left behind the bush off the deck. The other would be placed in a bamboo tube and thrown into the ocean.

The second-to-last scene for the day was where all of the staff, Nadia, and I gathered around the swimming pool to create a family environment. Then Nadia would hand me a simple handwritten note. As we gathered at the pool's edge, the atmosphere was festive. The

171

final shot was me opening and reading Nadia's letter, which said, "Welcome Home."

I was struck by the emotions rising up in me! Even after the years in Bali, I never really felt it as home. But something shifted within me at that moment. I hugged Nadia, with the staff smiling, and the scene ended. The crew gathered up the cameras and lights before heading off to the ocean for the final scene.

With all the camera gear and everyone packed into two vans, we headed for Sanur Beach. It was late afternoon, and the temperature was climbing. We sat in the shade for a bit while the videographer determined the best location and lighting. I gravitated to one of the half-dozen cabanas that extended out into the sea. There, in the shade of the cabana, I watched the crew checking light meters, camera angles, and such. Then they wandered to where I was sitting. Looking into the distance, to the next cabana fifty feet away, I got the feeling we would be shooting the final scene there. Minutes later, the director said, "Lets go over to that cabana. That's where we will get the last footage. The lighting will be better."

I sat in the shade of the tiled roof, wiping my face and neck with a moist towel to cool down. The director asked me to stand up and place the letter I had written in the bamboo tube and close the lid. I did as instructed and the scene ended quickly. He then instructed me to sit down where I was initially and look longingly out to the ocean's edge and the horizon. I assumed the position, embracing the ocean and the horizon with a look of desire and longing as though it was one of the most meaningful things I'd ever done.

I felt a deep peace and gratitude within me. It felt as though I was thanking all that I saw in that moment as a tremendous gift. Tears began to well up. Seconds later, I heard the words, "That's a wrap."

I composed myself, regaining my thoughts about me. And then, there it was! Another 3×5 card showing a scene with the figure of Jesus with others detaining him and the caption, "Jesus being presented to the People." My tears flowed; I didn't understand what was happening. I quietly stayed in position so that no one could see me. This went on for several minutes.

This was so powerful to me because of my belief that Jesus, or at least his presence, would be known to mankind once more. It was a time also where I saw visions of Donald Trump coming back to being president. The Antichrist would appear. John F. Kennedy Jr. was going to reveal himself again; he and his wife had not perished in the plane crash off Nantucket all those years ago.

All of these images flashed before my eyes. It all seemed to be a truth that would be revealed. What was the chance that at eye level on this pavilion's post would be a card with the image of Jesus being presented to the People? I sat for several minutes, then asked the camera man to take a photo of the card. We then packed everything in the vans and headed for Sri Phala.

A MEETING AT THE KUALA LUMPUR AIRPORT

Around this time, I was taking a trip and had a 12-hour layover in Kuala Lumpur for my connecting flight. I had a tendency to purchase cheaper flights for travel, which always involved long layovers that seemed to last forever. This one was no different.

I was sitting in the airport's Starbucks lounge and restaurant area. I wasn't much of a Starbucks fan, but nothing else was open this late at night. I sat there for some time, going down the old rabbit hole berating myself for buying another cheap ticket and having to wait such a long time before my next flight. After a while I began to ease up on myself. A double chocolate muffin and a chai latte helped me pass the time.

An hour or so later, two women appeared to be heading directly toward me. As they approached, the closer one looked at me as though she knew me somehow, or as if she was about to tell me something.

They both stopped at my table, and one of them struck up a conversation with me. Both of their faces seemed familiar. The more outspoken woman and I hadn't exchanged names, but we began talking about a number of things and looking at one another as though we knew each other. It felt very comfortable for me, and I think for her, too.

"You look very familiar to me," I finally said. "Something about you makes me think of the time of Jesus. You remind me of Mary

Magdalene. I have a past life belief that you are of the energy of Mary Magdalene." It shocked me that this came out of my mouth.

Smiling, she said, "I believe you." The other woman didn't speak any English, so she introduced both of them. "My name is Hanah, and this is my sister Myriam." Then she asked, "Would you be kind enough to take Myriam to her gate when the time for her flight comes, since she doesn't speak or read any English?"

"It would be an honor," I said.

The three of us stayed for hours talking, until it was time to go to our respective gates. Hannah told me about her sister's love relationship. Myriam was marrying a man outside their faith, and it was causing a major rift in the family. I suggested that Myriam follow her heart and go through with the marriage, because it was a way to show the family that Love is stronger. The family, I felt, needed to experience the love between Myriam and her husband-to-be.

Hanah and I exchanged social media connections, and she gave me a hug for my kindness. Something felt surreal as I walked with Myriam to her gate. To this day, I'm not certain what this was about, but I felt truly honored to have been a part of it.

SIM ZIMBABWE CURRENCY

Two things rekindled thoughts around the fiat currency that was given to me by Renee and a friend's experience and connection with the Galactic Federation of Light. A couple years earlier, I had started investigating the crypto currency market. Someone my friends and I all knew was pretty savvy about it, so we all opened accounts on the exchanges, and some purchased wallets to store their crypto currency funds. I then got rather busy with my sound baths, counseling, and other work, and I forgot about the monies I put into various funds. I only put in $700 in total, figuring if I lost the funds, I wouldn't be much worse off.

A year later, a friend who had also opened an account asked me, "What has your money increased to?" I had no idea, so I checked my trading account and realized I'd doubled my investment. Wow! Becoming excited, I wanted to get more active in the markets, although I was a novice. I'd recently met a man who had been trading since the beginning of the Bitcoin introduction years earlier. I met with him on several occasions and even brought a few other friends and potential investors to listen to his lecture.

Wow, was this process complicated, learning all the new terminologies, potential scams, and so much more. It made my head spin, but he patiently guided me through the setup and trading process.

One afternoon, a group of us had gathered to hear him speak about what was occurring in the markets and hear about current legislative rules and regulations. The talk was informative, but my head was spinning by the end. I approached him and said that I had received a currency several years earlier and that the story around it connects it to the Galactic Federation of Light and the New World Order currency. He was quite interested in what I had to share.

To this day, I remain perplexed about the whole thing. When he asked me what the currency was I said, "I really don't know. I will have to dig it out of my suitcase where I store it."

He then blurted out, "Is it Zimbabwe currency?"

"I'll take a look when I get home," I replied. "But why Zimbabwe currency?"

"Because it was one of the most hyper inflated currencies," he told me.

Sure enough, when I dug out the envelope, letter, and currency that Renee had given me a few years earlier in Sedona, I remembered what she'd said that afternoon: "I am giving you this 500 million Zimbabwe fiat currency with this letter, because someone in the future will give you any amount of money you want, as long as the money is used in service for the good of humanity."

To this day, I'm still in the dark about this whole thing, other than knowing it triggered something for me—or it was confirmation that all of this is still in process and will come to fruition in the future. Either way, it gives me hope.

AMARA AND THE GALACTIC FEDERATION OF LIGHT

The other event came when I had an urge to see Amara. But before visiting her, I was prompted to visit a young Balinese healer, suggested through a friend, who ran a clinic. She and I talked at great length about healing and what was going on in the world. I became curious about her clinic's vitamin drips. I decided to go in and receive a vitamin drip to boost my immune system. The was one of those clinics where you customize different vitamin drips and health care products based on tests that the clinic administered on you. I thought, *what the heck, I'll get an immune booster drip.*

As I sat in the comfortable, cushioned chair receiving my drip, I recognized I was sitting next to Amara's son. He had his headphones on, and I didn't want to disturb him (or myself, for that matter) so I remained quiet for the duration of the drip.

Afterward, I headed to Amara's house to catch up. As we began our chat, her son came out of his room. We both smiled and said hello. Amara was surprised when we said we were sitting next to one another in the clinic getting drips.

Then Amara said, "I remember you telling me about the Galactic Federation of Light. At the time, I was a bit skeptical but I have someone living in my spare bedroom who claims he is one of them. I'm not really sure how to digest all of this."

I told her the things I'd learned from them about my visions and of others who have had contact with them as well. She said she was writing full-on, under the direction of the man living in her spare room, to create a curriculum around the work she does in the Healing Arts. She shared some of her concerns about the situation, but I asked her, "Do you feel safe with him, knowing what you know?"

She replied, "Yes, I do, but I am working so hard on all this."

I responded, "Years ago, when it all happened to me with the Galactic Federation, I was put to the test as well."

The evening ended with dinner and a knowing that many others are being contacted by them for the New World—the one I refer to as "Heaven on Earth" order, and not the "New World Order," which I believe is all about loss of sovereignty and our free will.

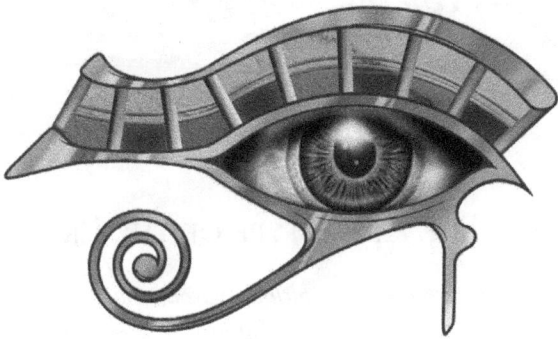

CHAPTER 12

CHAPTER 12: THE ARCHETYPE OF THE PROSTITUTE

"The turnaround is the process by which the unconscious becomes conscious, often in a flash of deep emotional insight." ~Richard Hidalgo

A powerful period of learning came when I was confronted with some bizarre events while I was learning from the Female/ Feminine's dark side. This also coincided with Lorraine's sessions in which she told me that I was now learning about the archetypes of the prostitute.

A DARK ENERGY

The first event happened after I had moved to the coastal village of Amed in the northeast of Bali to get a little rest and relaxation from the Pyramids and my work. It had been full-on for some time, and I thought a period of rest would give me an opportunity to start my next book.

One day, I received a phone call from what sounded like a young woman. She wanted to see me right away for a session. My normal policy was to do a preliminary interview to determine if it would be a fit for both of us and if the client truly understood the work I did. She was adamant that she needed to see me, so I agreed, wondering what this was all about.

The woman, whose name was Carla, rode her scooter for three and a half hours to Amed. As she walked in my front door, I thought she had some familiarity about her. She went to her room on the lower floor to relax a bit before we started the workshop. Later, she came upstairs, and I ushered her into the large, open air living room that gave us a spectacular, 220-degree view of the sea. Since it was getting late in the afternoon, I asked only a few introductory questions and asked her to think of an intention for the session.

The following morning, I formally started the workshop, asking her numerous questions about her life, childhood, family members, and so on, to get a better idea of her history and what she wanted to work on. It struck me that she bore an uncanny resemblance to my ex-wife. As the morning went on, she shared many experiences she'd had that I viewed as dangerous and extremely sexually promiscuous. Once, she'd even been told by her therapist that she could be a prostitute, given her relaxed and comfortable nature around these experiences. Carla said, straight-out, "I like to fuck."

Then came a point when I delved deeply into one of her traumas. She had a complete meltdown, refusing to go on. She ended up going down to her room in a hysterical fit.

After some time passed, I went down to check on her. She was still upset, so I simply reminded her that I was upstairs if I could be of help. Thirty minutes later, she returned, emphatically ending the workshop. She decided to ride back (again, three and a half hours) to the village of Prererenan in the southwest of Bali. Rain threatened, and it appeared she had no rain protection. I brought her a rain poncho to wear for her ride, and I gave her a few other items in case of an emergency. She was appreciative, and off she went.

Several days passed. Then Carla called to tell me that she felt something for me. "I wondered if you felt it as well," she said.

I admitted to her that she intrigued me. I told her how she resembled my ex-wife. "In all honesty, your promiscuity interests me," I said. "I had never known anyone like you." After hearing her stories around sexuality and her many sexual partners, I had a sense about something that she didn't appear to have. I flat-out said, "You know how to fuck but you do not know how to make love."

"Show me," she replied. "I want to learn." And I knew there was something I would learn as well.

179

We scheduled a day and time to meet at her apartment, which was in a compound called Win Win, which consisted of a number of small one-bedroom villas in the village of Canggu. When I arrived, I was shocked; her unit was the one I'd stayed in only a year ago, upon their grand opening. What were the chances of her staying in the exact same place? This, too, piqued my interest.

We continued to spend time together, and once I stayed in her villa for about five days while waiting for my new villa to be prepared. Our time together opened doors to many things that both of us had been curious about.

However, she was prone to angry outbursts. She told me she'd visited her ex-boyfriend and they got in a physical fight. She constantly wanted me to help her with what felt like unreasonable requests. Even she admitted this to be true. It got so bad that I felt she might do something dangerous. One or both of us could be hurt physically.

One morning in bed, she shared that she had fallen in love, and it was the first time. But I felt a knowing that I couldn't take her any further. With pain in my heart, I realized I had to let her go. During our time, she'd shared things she wanted that I could not give her. We both knew it was best to move on. When I said our relationship had to end, she claimed she understood why.

I moved to a new home, but for my own protection, I didn't disclose its location to Carla. All the while, I felt a dark energy coming from her, as well as emotions that were purely evil. I remembered the day I'd had the reading with Lorraine and she said I was learning about the archetype of the prostitute. Lorraine had said she was dangerous and I needed to protect myself.

I prayed for guidance on how to deal with this situation. I knew I was safe in a new place, but something felt energetically wrong. It felt as though someone was doing black magic at my expense. Lorraine had confirmed this even before I shared with her all that was happening. I asked for divine guidance to release Carla from my field of energy, with love and strength.

I determined a bike ride was what I just needed. As I rode, I prayed for Carla's release from her demons and anger. Then, out of nowhere, a Catholic church appeared, with its doors wide open and its interior brightly lit. Bali is primarily Hindu, so seeing a Catholic church is extremely rare on the island.

I stopped my bike and headed into the front area of the church. I felt a cool breeze wash over me, as though my prayers had been answered. I experienced a calmness I hadn't felt in months.

LEARNING FROM OUR DARK SIDES

The second event involved a woman of Ethiopian descent whom I met at a friend's retail shop. In the thirty minutes of chatting and laughing with her and my friend, I thought, *this woman is quite funny but also haughty toward certain people.* But I kind of blew it off, enjoying the humor flying around the table.

About a year later, out of the blue, she sent me a message on the social media platform Whats app (WA). She told me she wanted to be dominated by an older, mature white man. Initially, I enjoyed the topic of conversation, which is considered taboo by many social standards. I found it exciting to talk so openly and freely about what she desired. Some things she suggested challenged my way of thinking; they were simply beyond what I could have conjured in my own mind. It was a time for me to explore parts of my own psyche.

Then she said she wanted me to rape her. Two things immediately came to mind. One, this was so out of my scope acceptable behavior, it was just wrong. Two, someone cannot technically be raped if the act is mutually agreed upon. I said as much, and we concluded the conversation.

Later, I wrote her a long, heartfelt text describing my feelings about her suggestions and saying I wasn't interested in such a relationship. I thanked her for her openness and honesty around her desires but said I was ending it with this text.

Or so I thought. Over the next year, she continually found me through various social media avenues, and at times using different phone numbers to activate new dialogue with me. As each message arrived, I blocked it.

Finally, the messaging stopped. What I learned from this was that each of us has a dark side, and if we are not afraid to look at it and see what it is really asking us to see, it can be a tool for learning both about ourselves and the limits of human nature.

A WISDOM FIGURE...OR SOMETHING ELSE?

The third event in this series involved the manager of the health clinic where I received my vitamin IV drip. On several occasions, she would come to my house to ask me questions about life, boyfriends, and other topics. I was happy to share my understanding of the topics she wanted to talk about. It seemed like she was looking for a wisdom figure in her life. But it eventually came down to the fact that she wanted affection from a man. She shared stories of the young men whom she had been with and how they treated her with total disrespect. All they wanted was sex, she said. I pointed out her destructive pattern of behavior when it came to her partners. I suggested she change her group of friends.

I began to sense that she was directing her affections toward me. I told her we were friends and that I would be happy to listen from time to time. Things began to get strange when she showed up where I worked, saying, "I just wanted to see you and be near you."

This was my first experience being stalked, and I wasn't happy about it. She also tried to connect through different social media platforms, and I continually blocked each one as they occurred. Eventually, I moved into a new place and never allowed her to know its whereabouts. At one point, she texted me to say that as a result of my caring and conversations, she was now accepting only good suitors. But I knew she still wanted to connect when some time later, she showed up at my work, had a meal, and then told me to pay for it. She said she just wanted to be near me. I then blocked her from all forms of communications.

THE CONCUBINE

The next incident, as with others, seemed innocent at first. But it would help me further hone my skills in seeing darkness and dysfunction. Like Carla, Renata was Brazilian. I met her at the Pyramids on one of my days off. I usually didn't show up there when I wasn't working, but for some reason I went in that day. Renata was tanned and vivacious, and there seemed to be a mutual attraction between us. During our first meeting, she wanted to know how she could become employed at the Pyramids. She said she didn't have lots of money and that she was listening to Spirit's directions about where she should travel and live. She told stories of great strengths, disasters, and courage. I was quite impressed by them.

I suggested someone I knew who could shoot a promotional video to assist her in promoting herself. She seemed excited about the idea.

"Do you want to see the Earth Pyramid, to see if it would be a suitable place for the video?" I asked.

We went into the space, and I connected my phone to the in-house stereo. For some reason, I started playing pieces of music that generally only I would listen to, no one else. It just seemed right. Renata began to dance.

As she danced her heart out in the Earth Pyramid, I was mesmerized by the way her body flowed upon the teak flooring. She came over to where I was sitting on the floor near the stereo, selecting songs that moved me deeply. As we sat there, I began to tear up. As a tear rolled down my cheek, she placed her lips on the teardrop and sucked it in with a slurping sound. Then she seated herself behind me, holding me from behind. It all happened so quickly. It reminded me of a movie in which a siren came out of the water to take a man's teardrop in order to be able to come onto land. To me, sirens are sea women creatures that trick sailors, to the sailors' demise. All in all, I felt very taken aback by the abrupt and insensitive nature of the situation. But given the emotions of the moment, I disregarded what I intuitively felt.

I asked if she would like to get lunch next door at Bintang Japanese/Indonesian restaurant. We ordered a wonderful meal and continued talking. Suddenly, her whole demeanor changed. In that transitional moment, her facial expression changed to a grimacing look. Even her persona seemed to change, and I felt a dark presence around her.

Then, as quickly as it appeared, it vanished. I again found myself asking internally what was going on here, but we resumed our dinner. Afterward, she lay next to me and we both took a brief, five-minute nap. It felt both comfortable and unusual at the same time. I observed how quickly I had opened to this woman and the emotional moment. Almost too quickly.

Over the next couple of days, we kept in touch to set up the video shoot. On the day of the shoot, I instructed the man shooting the video footage that he had ninety minutes, and no more, to get the necessary footage. I also made it clear that he would only talk to me about the payment for the shoot and final promotional video. He agreed, and I left to go into town.

Three hours later, I got a call from Renata saying the shoot had ended and that he wanted full payment, or he wasn't leaving. When I got back to the Pyramids, he began yelling at me about full payment.

"Karma is going to get you!" he screamed.

I tried to calm him down by reminding him that I had, just a few months earlier, sent him money because he'd pleaded to me that he was starving. Some months earlier, during COVID times, he had reached out to me pleading for food. I think it was because he could tell I was friendly and caring. I didn't know how he knew me, but he later admitted he had done a shoot before, and I was the one he videoed for his client. I demanded that he finish the product and told him I'd pay him the final half upon completion of our agreement. He left, screaming, "I'm going to immigration!"

He ended up destroying all of the video and photos. He tried to stir up a hornet's nest with immigration—to no avail, since I had honored my part of the deal.

From there it began to level out. Renata and I spent time together, getting to know one another more. I remember the next event well. We were sitting on my bed, having a deep conversation, and all of the sudden her face and energy completely changed. I once again saw and felt that dark energy appear, but this time I wasn't going to remain silent.

"What do you want here?" I demanded.

Again, it ended as quickly as it had started. She returned to her normal self and began to share her perspective of what happened.

She said she'd left her body and she wasn't sure where she went, but she wasn't present. This all began to weird me out. I wasn't sure when or if it would happen again. But over the next few weeks, things began to feel normal until.

Then the final episode happened. We were lying together, caressing each other's bodies, and then suddenly, with all of her force, she tried to climb on top of me to have penetration. But the real shocker came when I heard a blood curdling scream leave her mouth.

"I have to have your baby! I want you to give me a baby!" she cried.

I was mortified. I pushed her body away from mine. She'd told me that up to that point, she had been celibate for the previous six years and had wanted to remain so. She was angry at me for activating her sexual energies—her yoni, as she referred to her vagina.

She was staying downstairs temporarily, in the lower level of my house until her apartment was ready in a few days. From this point on, I began locking my front door.

Over the next couple of days, I started to get very ill. I found out I had dengue fever, but this didn't seem to matter to her. The evil presence became so apparent from this point forward, I went downstairs and demanded she leave. Luckily, she had a girlfriend she could stay with, so she packed up the few things she had and left.

Lucifer's Bride

The final episode involved a woman named Anna. She was from Romania. We spent a few nights talking into the wee hours, and during one of our final conversations she brought up the topic of Lucifer. I sensed she had some kind of connection to that energy—or it to her. It was our third and final evening together when she looked at me and said, "It is only through you that Lucifer can find me."

I didn't even try to comprehend what she had just said. Feeling my energy being depleted, I left her villa in a rush.

Light and Dark Energies

Through all of these situations, I believe I have experienced the Divine Feminine's presence in both of her aspects—those of Light and Dark energies. This was presumably so I would be able to see the wholeness, the two aspects, of the Divine Feminine.

As I stood up after typing the above words, I realized how much I have been pushing, trying to comprehend this concept of the Divine Feminine and to understand the feminine energy, both the Light and Dark, within myself. Simultaneously, I was allowing this concept of reaching or grasping to dissolve into the ether.

I was realizing that both the Light and Dark had their own forms of wisdom and teachings. The young beautiful Ethiopian woman wanted my company sexually, and as an older man, I began to see it take on a new light from within a larger framework. I realized that sexuality wasn't what I wanted—not more carnal knowledge, but a deeper connection. I wanted something more than the physical. I did not want a distraction, but rather a connection of innocence beyond the physical. I often refer to it as "sharing."

I understood now why I'd sent the message thanking her for her openness and honesty with me about her desires, ending the message with gratitude and wishing her a beautiful journey. I wasn't looking for that kind of a physical encounter, even though it was initially tantalizing. It gave me the opportunity to explore my own current level of desires and then began asking more expansive questions. Without this experience, I might not have asked those questions. I was gaining clarity about my role in all that transpired.

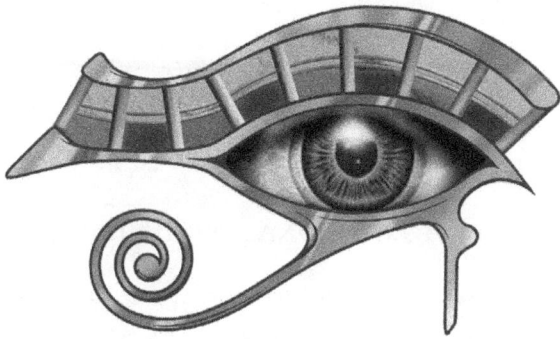

CHAPTER 13

CHAPTER 13: SEDONA AND SATONDA

"The universe is orchestrating the fulfillment of all your dreams and desires. Are you ready?" ~www.secretstomanifesting.com

GRANDFATHER, JAMES, AND THE THIRD KEY

Early one morning, I received a phone call from Soren, a friend from Germany who also knew Grandfather Morning Owl. "Grandfather is going to die!" he blurted. "You need to call him right away! He needs to talk with you." He shared what little he understood about the situation, then exclaimed again, "You need to call Grandfather!"

I quickly got off the phone with Soren and dialed Grandfather's number. When he answered, he sounded very coherent and steady in his voice, not like someone who was in the process of dying.

I asked him what was going on. He said he'd had enough of being in his body, and it was time for him to leave this world. He had spoken to Neptune Society, a cremation service company, setting up his cremation and all the necessary details of delivering the urn to his brother in San Francisco. He'd even had all of his automatic expenses canceled, since he assumed he would be going in the next few days.

"I'm just tired," he said. "I've had enough. I'm ready to leave this body."

I told him I would come back to take care of things for him, since in many previous conversations, he'd always said his family wouldn't want to be bothered by the details. I agreed to catch a flight as soon as all the COVID protocol testing was completed.

Confident that Grandfather really was ready to go, I did all I could to get back to Sedona. It took several days to complete everything, and once I knew I could fly, I purchased the airline ticket.

At Phoenix Sky Harbor Airport, I grabbed the two and a half hour shuttle to the Village of Oak Creek, the southern part of Sedona's city limits, where he lived. When I knocked on the door, he greeted me and invited me in. We sat in the living room, and I inquired about his knowledge of his upcoming death.

"It is similar to the Native American Indian tradition when an Elder foresaw his death," Grandfather said. "He simply prepared for the eventual event." He quickly spoke about all of the bank accounts, phone numbers of relatives, and the order in which I was to tell them of his demise. He even wrote a script for me to use when informing them.

I listened to this, but something just didn't feel right to me. But I let him go on. He showed me the box with the urn and explained the details associated with the process of his burial. He gave me the phone number to call to retrieve his body. He then went to his desk and opened a tin box that held all of his papers, including his apartment lease, the title to his car, and other various documents that would need attention upon his departure.

More than once, he told me that his prepaid, ten-year lease was coming to an end in the next thirty days. He said the monies in his bank account would be divided among his niece and her children.

As I took out a manila folder out of the tin box he was holding, a date flashed before my eyes: May 26, 2024. Why this date? *It is his time of departure*, I heard in my inner ear.

Quickly, I closed the folder and put it back into the box. I knew that I was not to tell Grandfather of this date—at least, not yet. This wasn't the first time I was instructed by an inner knowing not to speak information I had received. So I remained quiet.

I excused myself to shower, lie down, and rest from the long trip. Grandfather said he was going into a deep meditation to meet Brahma.

189

"Brahma is a Hindu god, referred to as "the Creator" within the Trimurti, the trinity of supreme divinity that includes Vishnu and Shiva. He is associated with creation, knowledge, and the Vedas. Brahma is prominently mentioned in creation legends. In some Puranas, he created himself in a golden embryo known as the Hiranyagarbha".
[https://en.wikipedia.org/wiki/Brahma]

Over the next few weeks, Grandfather would go into 12-hour meditations, both in the daytime and at night. I spent many sleepless nights wondering if he had passed on; I often went to check if he was still breathing. This close proximity to death was new to me, but I reminded myself that he was going to be around for a couple more years. Sometimes after a long meditation, he would come out of the mediation with what he believed to be the truth. Once, he said, "I clearly need to help you transcend this world and usher you into your enlightenment."

"Nope," I responded. "It's not about me."

This went on for several weeks. Finally, in frustration, he looked at me and exclaimed, "I'm not dying yet, am I? You've known all along."

I smiled. "Yes, I was shown the date when you are leaving the planet."

"Why didn't you tell me?" he asked.

I retorted, "Because Spirit asked me not to. Spirit said it was for you to come to this understanding on your own."

That changed everything. With this new lease on life, Grandfather began preparing beautiful dinners. He took on a new student, James, in the teachings of the "Red Way"(Native American path). He realized he needed to acquire a Chanupa (peace pipe), so he could initiate James in the way of the Chanupa ceremony. It required training, ending with a ceremony. Grandfather asked Joseph Grey Wolf and myself to participate in the ceremony. I agreed wholeheartedly.

The search for the sacred pipe began. I drove into Sedona's uptown retail area to look at some pipes for sale. The least expensive one was well over $600. When I called Grandfather with the news, he said that it was too expensive. "The pipe will show up somehow," he said.

I asked that he go into meditation to see if he could tap into an inner knowing of where and from whom it would come. It didn't take long before he was shown that he was to call out to Sun Bear, the person to whom he gave his initial Chanupa twenty-five years ago. He left a message for Sun Bear with his request. When she called back, she was pleasantly shocked that it would be him asking for it back. Sun Bear said, "I just cleaned it and placed it in a shipping box to be mailed out. But I didn't know to whom I was to send it." They had a good laugh at the synchronicity of it all. But they both knew very well that this was how Spirit has always worked, providing what is needed when it is needed.

The next morning, Sun Bear shipped out the pipe. While waiting for its arrival, Grandfather asked me more than once if I would do the Chanupa ceremony. I always responded that this was his initiate, and he had to complete the ceremony, not me.

The third time he made the same query, I sensed something was off. "What's going on?" I asked him.

"I can't remember how to do the ceremony," he admitted.

I quickly responded, "In that case, I would be honored."

Something else had been going on between Grandfather Morning Owl and myself. I insisted that he write a book about his memories and his deeply moving experiences. For fifteen years, I had been telling him that people needed to read about his life. Others needed to understand that there is so much more to life than a 9-to-5 job; there is also a spiritual journey. A book by Grandfather would be a good reference to help people along their journeys. He always said he would not write such a book, since it came through him from Brahman, and he worried about not having any so-called credentials or degrees of higher education, as so many others who have written books about this topic do. I assured him that his experiences and wisdom would be well received.

That evening at dinner, I once again urged him to write his book. To my surprise, he agreed. Then he said, "You have my permission to do so."

"It wouldn't be me who writes it," I said. "But we will see how things go."

Minutes later, the phone rang. It was James, his new initiate, suggesting that the three of us meet the following morning.

The next morning at 11:00, James knocked on the door. Excitedly, he shared that both he and his wife had dreamt about helping Grandfather write his book. I looked at Grandfather and said, "He is your writer."

Grandfather was over-the-top with joy. He had a new lease on life and a new purpose to be fulfilled.

A few days later, the sacred pipe arrived. I called James to set up our date and time for the ceremony of his initiation as a "Pipe Carrier." We chose one of my sacred mesas in the Village of Oak Creek as the location to take him through the holy process of his initiation. It's one of my favorite power spots, a place where I would do many ceremonies and hours of meditation.

I laid my yellow prayer blanket upon the red rocks, then carefully placed each of my sacred items, as my teacher had taught me. I shared the importance of the "Red Way"' and what it meant, and that a man's word is all he has and must be spoken in Truth. I continued honoring them by placing the tobacco into the Chanupa as I gave thanks to the Creator-Tonkashila, to Mother Earth-Ititsi Elohi, and to the Four Directions (to the East, to the South, to the West, and finally to the North). After I placed the fire into the bowl, I followed this same sequence, Above and Below, as I drew a breath from the stem, with reverence, took a couple of deep inhalations, and began the same movements, blowing the smoke with deep gratitude toward each of the Four Directions.

When someone is being initiated in some way, it is customary to give the guide leading the ceremony a gift for their participation. I had no idea what was about to happen when James pulled a chocolate brown deerskin pouch from his backpack and said these words, "I never thought I would let this sacred item leave my altar, because it has been with me for many years. But as I was coming here, Spirit told me to give you this and a message." He then prefaced it with, "I don't know the meaning of what I am about to tell you, but I sense you will."

I simply smiled and nodded. As James slowly opened the leather pouch, his words flowed like water. "This is your third and final key."

Upon hearing these words I felt tears well up. My heart pounding in my chest, I responded, "Yes, I do know what this means, and I am most grateful to you and Tonkashila."

I lifted the flap of the deerskin pouch and found a Selenite Crystal Stone in the form of a key.

The Selenite stone was named after the moon by J.G. "Selene" was the name of the Greek goddess of the moon and so, naming this beautifully pale blue crystal in honor of her seemed a fitting tribute. While having roots in Greek mythology, the word "selenite" has profound spiritual implications too. It evokes the energy of the divine feminine and her deep rejuvenation associated with this ancient archetype."

[https://trulyexperiences.com/blog/selenite-crystal/]

Feeling like my heart was going to explode from my chest, I told him of the other two keys that I had received and how they had been part of a prophecy I'd been told of a few years earlier—a prophecy that was now fulfilled.

We stood, shook hands, and embraced, with thanks for the gifts both given and received. We filled out backpacks with our sacred items and headed down the cliff face to Grandfather's house for a celebratory lunch.

THE ENDING OF A KARMIC CONNECTION

A few months after I saw Grandfather through his experience trying to will himself to death, I returned once more to Sedona. This time, I headed back to search for land for a new project in Sedona. Since my arrival at the Pyramids in Bali eight years prior, the owners, knowing I was from Sedona, would often say to me, "You will build the Pyramids of Chi there." During the first five or six years of hearing this, I always rejected any such idea. I simply didn't feel this was my journey. But something changed at this time. As I'll discuss later in this book, a well-respected international sound healer approached me, telling me that I must leave the Pyramids. Also, over the course of two years, my friend Agung (of Balinese royal heritage) had been emphatically urging me

193

to start the project in Sedona, because he wanted to live in the United States. These requests finally began to take hold, and I thought, *why not take this project and expand it twofold?* My idea was to incorporate a number of healing modalities, indigenous cultures, and a children's school for light and sound.

It is also important to note that Agung had been working for a number of years with international royal families of tremendous fortunes who had been voraciously buying land throughout Bali. He told me on numerous occasions that they wanted to invest in my project, because they had the funds available and they wanted to move money into the U.S. market.

I called Grandfather to let him know my arrival date, since he was always kind enough to host my stays. But right before my departure from Bali, I received a phone call from a longtime friend, asking if I would house sit while she was away visiting family. I was delighted to fulfill her request for those two weeks. I let Grandfather know of my change in plans and said I would see him afterwards.

For the first week, I rested from the forty hours of travel and the effects of the dengue fever that I'd experienced. It had left me weak and tired, but after seven days, I felt re-energized, and I started searching for property for the project. I found it interesting that a friend and her real estate associate told me there was no property available in the Sedona area, due to aggressive buyer activity. I wasn't at all bothered by such nonsense. I believed my project was driven by Spirit and that I would find a property in no time. After less than three days of searching and reconnecting with friends, I found two potential properties. Neither were listed on the market yet. One of them was perfect for the project, but it was sixty acres and had a price tag of $15 million. I met with the owner and we walked the property, discussing many things. It seemed that he'd had many spiritual experiences similar to mine, and our conversations were a natural fit. My challenge was to wrap my head around how I could present such a large asking price to the investor.

It was time to go to Grandfather's house for the next several weeks. For the days since I arrived, I made connections with architects, designers, and others I might work with on the project. But something felt off as I traveled to Grandfather's house. On several occasions, I heard that little voice inside my head: "Why are you going to his house? Your time with him is complete."

I recalled three separate instances when he didn't follow through with my wishes and our agreements. It had to do with my prayer blanket, an important pendant, the sacred items he had worn much of his life while conducting ceremonies, and a Cadillac Brougham DeVille classic car.

As I entered his carport, I felt a wave of nausea. Once more, I heard, "Your time here is done. Why are you here?" Immediately as I entered his apartment, he emphatically began to tell me that I didn't need to take care of his classic Caddy and its repair. He said he was selling the car to his mechanic. His agreement was that he couldn't drive any more and that I would receive it. He told me that he was forever grateful for my assisting him when I'd been there last. He also mentioned that he'd torn up the paperwork for the car, he seemed quite pleased with himself.

Still feeling the effects of dengue, combined with his emphatic gestures, I felt overwhelmed. At that moment, I became animated and disturbed, recalling the three occasions when he didn't follow through with our agreement. It left me stunned and furious.

I composed myself, taking a deep breath. "It was hurtful to me," I said, "That you gave away those three important items." And I listed them one by one.

Needless to say, his reaction was not pleasant. In the most loving way possible, I looked at him. With all the love I could muster, I said, "I can't do this anymore. I love you as my friend and teacher, from the bottom of my heart, but this must end."

As I collected my luggage from my room that I dropped off minutes earlier, I knew that our friendship had come to an end. I left listening to him hurl insulting words my way. I again thanked him for all of his wisdom and the friendship he'd shared. I was eternally grateful to him, but it was over.

Later, sitting with all of this, I realized what my lesson was. I had honored a friendship long beyond a healthy boundary. I also realized how I allowed men whom I perceived as wise and powerful to remain in my life and in their dysfunctional patterns of behavior. I gave my own power to them. This was crystal clear when I cross-referenced this situation against other similar experiences throughout my life. In that moment, I took my power back, in the most loving way.

These thoughts also took me back in time to a dinner that Sarah, my ex-partner, and I had with Grandfather. Afterwards, Sarah said to me, "Why are you spending your time here? All he's doing is taking your energy." I knew her words were true then but due to my perception of the wisdom he carried, as well as respect for the fifteen years he and I shared, I decided to continue. In the end, though, I realized how I allowed my perception of wisdom figures to give them my attention and energy far longer than I should have. As this sank in, I sighed with relief.

A day or so later, I ran into Robert, a friend of many years who worked at Crystal Castle in West Sedona. I found him to be quite informed when it came to the occult and esoteric wisdom. He lived a life quite unusual to the mainstream. He invited me to sit with him in a local park in Cottonwood, twenty minutes south of Sedona. As we sat on picnic table benches, he shared a number of things. He also tested my psychic abilities to read cards, determining their images prior to turning them over. I began to tell him about the episode with Grandfather, and within seconds, he said it was about Samskaras.

In Indian philosophy, Samskaras are mental impressions, recollections, or even psychological impressions, and they have a basis for the development of karma. Robert said, "Your karma is complete with him."

He must have read inquisitiveness on my face. He went on to say that my time with Grandfather was finished, and that I had learned all I could. "It's time to move on," he said. I felt the truth of what he was saying.

After looking at two properties and meeting with the owners and all of the appropriate players (designer, architect and builder), my time in Sedona was coming to an end. I needed to return to Bali to put together the business plan and financial information to present to Agung's investor.

CAPTIVE IN A COVID COMPOUND

Before I was allowed to travel from the United States back to Denpasar, Bali, I had to get a PCR test for the COVID plandemic (as I believe it to be). I trotted off to the local Walgreens to get the swab and waited the 24 hours necessary for the results to come back. Not only did I have to get the test in order to travel, at this point Indonesia also required travelers to select and pay for a ten-day quarantine at the cost of $1,000 U.S. for the ten-day stay. The lax COVID restrictions in Bali that had been in place when I was in the commercial in late 2020 were a thing of the past.

In the Los Angeles Airport, I had to run through three terminals to the international terminal to catch my flight to Kuala Lumpur, Malaysia, where I had a twelve-hour layover. At the gate, the Qatar Airlines representative looked at my passports, the PCR results, and my various travel documents. Upon reviewing my PCR document that displayed my results, the gate attendant said I was not allowed to board the plane. "This document isn't the appropriate test, per Qatar Airlines requirements," he said.

"But it's the only test given in all of northern Arizona," I protested.

After several minutes of a heated conversation, I asked to see his manager, since my flight was boarding in twenty minutes. The manager confirmed that I wasn't allowed on the flight with the test that had been administered. He told me I had to go out into one of the parking areas where they had set up a PCR testing facility and get another test that cost $125 U.S. It would mean rebooking my flight to Kuala Lumpur. I was furious, but there was nothing I could do except follow the requirements.

I got my flight rescheduled for the following morning, then stood in the parking lot in the chilled, drizzling November rain. I eventually took my turn at the makeshift wooden building that housed four nurses sitting behind windows administering PCR tests.

"Lean forward," my nurse barked. "So I can insert the swab in your nostrils."

I told her that I would not allow her to jam it all the way up my nostril, as many of them were instructed to do. My resistance had to do with the fact that when the swab was placed all the way up into the nostril, it would reach the blood brain barrier. I wanted no part of that!

After she made several attempts, with me jerking my head backwards, she said my test probably wouldn't result in a proper reading.

"It will be fine," I stated.

Then I waited for my results. The damp and chilly night in the expansive LAX parking lot finally came to an end, and I made my way to my boarding gate.

Forty hours of flights and layovers exhausted me. When my plane arrived at the Jakarta airport, I headed for immigration. Of course, everyone had to stop first at a checkpoint to get another PCR test from the airport military and health staff. The process began with government staff reviewing all of my documents to determine which testing cubicle I went to. When it was my turn for the test, the young military personnel looked at the test tubes and swabs, making what felt to me like a methodical choice. He didn't take the next one in order, instead choosing one further into the rack. It all felt a bit weird and contrived.

Before I traveled, I'd spoken with Lorraine, my friend in Torquay. She said, "Your luggage will get lost on this trip. Don't let it upset you. Just go with the flow." Sure enough, my luggage didn't appear. Frustrated, I went to the Lost and Found office to fill out the forms. Due to Lorraine's prediction, I had taken photos prior to handing over my luggage at the airport. After spending about 45 minutes filling out the necessary paperwork, I headed for the airport exit to greet my assigned hotel staff for the ten-day quarantine. This was not how I wanted to spend my time after arrival, and at a cost that was so much money in a city I didn't desire to be in, but this was the mandate at the time.

My hotel staff asked if I had my PCR results. I looked at him in confusion, not knowing the test results would arrive so quickly. He said he would go back inside to check on my results. Exhausted by trying to be patient, I waited for his return. Thirty minutes later he approached me and said I'd tested positive for the Covid virus, and I was not allowed to go anywhere. I would be placed in an isolation facility for ten days. Within an hour, a superior from the hotel and a nurse, both wearing masks on with hazmat clothing neatly tucked under their arms, presented me with a document that indicated I waived all of my rights when it came to protocol for the virus.

"You're crazy," I said. "I will not waive my medical rights for them to do anything they deem fit."

I began making phone calls to the U.S. Embassy in Jakarta and even to the United States, but I got no answer because it was New Years' Eve. After numerous failed attempts, I phoned Agung in Denpasar. When I explained to him the seemingly unfair practices, his advice was to just sign the document and follow procedures. I tried the U.S. embassy once more and ended up speaking with someone, but their suggestion was the same.

For three hours, the hospital staff and nurse prompted me to sign the document. Finally, in sheer exhaustion, I agreed to sign it. But I wanted recorded evidence that I was signing under duress.

It seemed odd that the two of them, knowing I tested positive for the virus, still toted their Hazmat bodysuits under their arms, rather than wearing them. But I just wanted to take a warm shower and go to sleep. I decided that being friendly would get me closer to that goal, so I struck up a conversation. After about twenty minutes, they invited me to lunch.

Lunch? I thought. Was I not in quarantine?

In any case, I agreed, But as we began to leave the holding area, the manager of the hotel where I would eventually stay, as well as a military personnel, said I was going nowhere but to an isolation hotel. Another 45 minutes passed before an ambulance arrived. Fully suited personnel drove me an hour to the quarantine hotel.

At the hotel, I was given a room above a carport. The shower didn't work, and I tried to call for service on the hotel phone, but it was dead. I unscrewed the shower head, and the trickle that flowed allowed me to cleanse fifty-plus hours of travel and fatigue from my body. As I looked around the room, I observed that there was mold everywhere

SEE THE GOLDEN THREADS

and the sheets were heavily stained. But in exhaustion, I fell onto the bed and slept.

The next morning, I was awakened by someone outside my room screaming at the top of their lungs. I ran down the stairs and out into the roadway, and there stood a man and a nurse. I asked the man to calm down and said I would help if I could. He said his name was DeMonte. He was from Detroit, Michigan and was in Jakarta for a basketball tournament.

"Screaming doesn't help in this country," I told him. "It could get you in quite a bit of trouble." Then I asked the nurse what was going on, and she handed me the same form they'd forced me to sign at the airport. She said the man had the Omicron variant of Covid and that he would be taken to the hospital. I told her in my best Bahasa Indonesian language that he would only sign it under duress, but he even declined that.

"Then he will be taken to the hospital against his will," the nurse said.

That was just the beginning of what occurred there in that compound. About fifteen or twenty of us gathered and began sharing our stories of how we got here. All but two of the people were expats or tourists. The other two women were of Indonesian heritage and were returning to visit their families, but they divulged they were married to foreigners.

I decided to go to the front office to tell them about my broken shower, the stained sheets, and the mold issue. All they said was that I should go back to my room. None of those issues were ever addressed.

One of the expats, a Russian, said he'd had a party in his room with prostitutes and alcohol purchased from the restaurant on the property. The story was getting even better!

As a result of DeMonte's screaming, I met another American who said he was a crypto currency fund manager with $80 million U.S. under management. He tried to convince me to leave with him in the middle of the night by jumping the barbed wire fence. But I'd learned that on separate nights (in the middle of the night), DeMonte and a pregnant woman had been taken to the hospital. Given this, I declined his offer. I told him I must stay to help the others, and that I was a permanent resident.

"You're crazy," he replied. "Our lives are in danger here."

"I agreed," I told him. "But I can't leave. I'm sorry."

That evening, he escaped the compound by jumping the barbed wire fence. I later learned that in the morning, he went to a doctor to get a new PCR test. Low and behold, it was negative. He created a Facebook post, revealing my full name and what had transpired. I was shocked when I received phone calls from friends in Bali, Singapore, Australia, and other countries checking in to see if I was still alive and okay.

This all happened quickly, and what followed was even more challenging. The staff started giving me miniscule portions of food, most of it rotten and moldy. They even denied me drinking water for a day. At the reservation desk, I told them about my lack of water.

"Go back to your room," the clerk said.

Serious human rights violations continued to occur. Everyone in the compound was there for at least seven to fourteen days, at a cost of $1,000 U.S. per week. Everyone got a positive result on their PCR test, yet no one showed any signs of Covid symptoms.

I finally called pretty much everyone I knew in Bali, asking them to call anyone they knew in the government to assist. I made several calls to the U.S. embassies in the Indonesian cities of Jakarta, Singaraja, and Denpasar. I stirred the pot with my calls explaining the human rights violations. Eventually, the Indonesian government got involved. Even the Indonesian president's office and the General of Military internal affairs took interest in the situation. Naturally, this didn't make the hotel staff happy.

On my fifth day in the compound, I was contacted by an investigative reporter and a public figure known for her human rights efforts. "Would you be willing to do an interview?" the reporter asked. "We would like to publish your story."

"Yes," I replied. "As long as you don't use my name and the story is not released until I leave the hotel and Jakarta." When they both agreed, I went on to ask, "If anyone were to find out that I was the one behind the article, would I be in danger?"

The reporter and the human rights activist admitted that yes, I might be. Nonetheless, I was determined to move forward with it. They told me that the isolation center I was in was a transient hotel where people could rent a room "*by the hour,*" and that it normally rented for $15 per night—not the $143 per night each of us was paying.

At this point, I contacted an attorney through one of my friends The attorney later became my friend. Her help in my case certainly helped move my case along. The combined efforts of my attorney, my friends, expatriates, and high ranking government officials finally got me released on the ninth day—one less than the prescribed ten days. We were also able to get all the other detainees out of the compound. All received a negative result on their PCR tests. Most of the people that were in the facility had been in there for at least two weeks and counting.

This all took place within twenty-four hours, on my ninth day of captivity. Once everyone was released (including the pregnant woman and DeMonte from the hospital), I was ready to leave the facility.

As a result of everyone's efforts and the news article being published, the hotel was forced to close its operations and facilities. I was never happier than I was the moment I was released from that place.

A Visit to Satonda

The attorney who had helped me get out of the COVID compound was named Day. She and I became good friends; she often referred to me as her "bestie." Over the next twelve months, we traveled together to two Eastern tropical islands within the Archipelagos of Indonesia. First, we visited Sumbawa Island, where Day had spent much of her childhood and where her father was the police chief for many years. The second was an island just north of Sumbawa called Moyo Island. We made a couple of these trips to look at her properties that she had owned for several years and a new development she was trying to get off the ground, consisting of ten teak wooden villas on the coast line on the sea of Flores.

A couple of months into our friendship, I received a call from Day. Her voice filled with excitement, she told me about a man she had met and an island property he owned. Day also said the man, who was named Adi, spoke about many spiritual things. "He sounds just like you," she exclaimed. "You need to meet him."

Intrigued, I listened to all she had to say. She asked, "Do you have a photo of yourself? Adi wants to see a picture of you before he decides whether or not he will have a conversation." Then she said, "Wait, we found one."

As a result, Adi asked Day to set up a date to meet me. This all sounded a bit like something out of a spy novel, but again, I was curious. Day scheduled the meeting for a few days later.

The thing that really blew me away during that initial phone conversation was when she said the name of the island was Satonda. I just about fell off my chair. Tears began to well up, and I blurted out, "She's Sedona's sister."

I went on to tell Day about a rock formation in Sedona referred to as the "Two Sisters," which is located in the Chapel area off SR179, near the Chapel of the Holy Cross. "During my twenty-two years of living in Sedona, I knew Sedona was one of the sisters, but I didn't know who her sister was," I said. "But now that you've said that name, I'm certain it's Satonda." I was elated by what had transpired, and I was excited to see where this journey would take me next.

Satonda is an island in West Nusa Tenggara province of Indonesia. It is off the north coast of Sumbawa island. The Island is located in Dompu Regency, 3 km from Sanggar Strait in the Flores Sea and is administratively part of the Nangamiro Village area of Pekat District. [1] Satonda island was formed from the eruption of Mount Satonda thousands of years ago. Satonda volcano is said to be older than Mount Tambora, which is about 30 kilometers from the island.[2] Satonda island has a vast natural coral reefs in the surrounding waters and was designated a Marine Nature Park (TWAL) in 1999 by the Ministry of Forestry of Indonesia.

[https://en.wikipedia.org/wiki/Satonda_Island]

The day of the meeting came. Adi and his son, along with Day and myself, sat in their living room learning about this magical island. We spoke about many things, and one of the things that struck me was that Adi said, "I was the custodian of this land for the past twenty-one years. Now I believe it is you who will be the next custodian of the land."

I was mesmerized by his statement. We spread the island's maps out in front of us on the wood-and-glass coffee table. Adi said he owned 40 hectares (98 acres) of beachfront properties on the island. He told us the island was the result of volcanic activity a thousand years ago, and that it had a heart-shaped lake in the center. The lake water was 9.5 pH, which is very alkaline. It's also a wonderful match for the human body's pH level. "There are only five other lakes in the world like it," Adi said. "It has a fresh underground well on one of its inner walls." It sounded magical.

The meeting came to an end, but before we departed Adi's son asked to get a photograph of us for the occasion. We gathered in front of a beautiful painting of a lotus flower surrounded by triangular shapes, colored gray, light gray, and cream.

A few days later, with land maps and land certification in hand, Day and I scheduled our next travel excursion to the island of Satonda. We flew from Denpasar, Bali to Lombok Island for a short layover. Then we headed to Sumbawa, a flight that took only about twenty-five minutes. We checked into the hotel and headed to our rooms to freshen up.

The next morning came bright and early as we prepared for the six-hour drive to the Nangamiro Village. From there we would take a ten-minute boat ride to the island. Before we went across, we had lunch at a warung (little restaurant) nearby. Then we jumped onto the long fiberglass boat referred to as the "clack-it y clack clack boat," since that was the sound the motor made as we slowly traversed the calm inter coastal waters of the Flores Sea.

As we approached Satonda Island, we were greeted by a long, golden colored beach and crystal clear waters that transitioned from blue, turquoise, green, and then crystal clear as we reached the dock. There we met up with Tuk Tuk, who would be our guide for the next few hours.

It was a magical, exotic place. I enjoyed trekking up the steep edge of the volcano's rim for well over forty minutes to get a glimpse of the lake. As we crested the rim's edge, I thought, wow, what an amazing natural wonder for my eyes to behold. The water was so tranquil, and I noticed that I couldn't even hear the sound of the ocean as I stood inside the crater.

Adi had instructed Tuk Tuk to cut back the overgrown vegetation from the path on the east rim so I would be able to climb all the way to the top. The view of the heart shaped lake and the ocean in the distance was simply amazing. I stood there for some time soaking up the scenery. Then I climbed down the steep rim to the edge of the lake from where I had started two hours ago. I sat at the lake's edge as the sun was beginning to set. As I soaked in all the natural beauty, I began to see many figures emerge from the shadows of the south rim. I knew somehow that they were the Elders of this land, and in my mind I heard them speak.

"You must protect this land, It is Mother's womb."

Tears began to well up as I took in this message. It seemed all too familiar to me, yet I didn't exactly know what all of this meant. And as time went on, more was to be revealed.

WHAT COMES NEXT?

Over the following several months, both Day and I took several more treks to the Sumbawa and Satonda. On my next trip, I stayed for three days and camped for two nights while Day went on to Dompu to check with the land department regarding Satonda's land certificates of title.

My couple of days on the island felt otherworldly as I explored more of its beauty. I also had forgotten what it was like to camp without a mattress. The first night, I didn't sleep much, and in the morning my body was sore and stiff from the previous day's hike. I spent the day with Tuk Tuk on his little speed boat, touring the island and stopping at several locations to explore the topography of the land and check locations on the topography map.

As the day progressed, I received another message, from the Elders: an instruction to not build on the island further. They said it was to remain a peaceful and calm place. Only a year earlier, before the COVID lock-down, hundreds of people had overfilled its sandy beaches. The Elders stressed that this was not to happen in the future. "This is Mother's womb," they said.

I took this to mean that the land did not need another glitzy resort—and I wholeheartedly agreed. Any retreat center that I planned would be peaceful and calm, the same as I planned for the Pyramids of Chi project in Sedona.

During the next several weeks, the owner, Day, and I came to a negotiated price for the 40 hectares of leasehold land. Now I was in search of funding. Several times, Day and I traveled to Moyo Island, looking for land to purchase for a holistic center. On one of our trips, we spent several hours chatting with her local representative and touring beachfront properties. It was getting late on a hot summer afternoon when her local friend and another young man from the area approached us.

"We have a beautiful piece of land on the beach!" they said. "It had golden sand."

We all climbed on our scooters to check it out. Twenty minutes later, we pulled up to the area. The land offered was 4.2 hectares (roughly 10.378 acres). There was a little wooden joglo (a Javanese house with a distinctive roof shape) placed on stilts, surrounded by beautiful green grass, coconut trees, 60 cashew trees and tropical foliage near the water's edge. It had a perfect view of Satonda Island. It seemed magical.

Day instructed me to stay by the beach, as she and her friend were going to chat with the owners. She implied that if I went with them, the price would dramatically increase because I was an ex-patriot living in Indonesia. After their meeting, we drove thirty minutes along the coastline, bouncing up and down through the potholes in the concrete pathway. It was exciting and tiring at the same time.

Weeks turned to months as I looked for funding while working on a business plan for the site. I also attempted to get drone footage of the topography. I was unsuccessful in this after two attempts, but I wasn't willing to give up.

I was running into roadblocks regarding the monies, not to mention my hours of work at the Pyramids. I started to fizzle out. I knew I was in need of a small break. Not really knowing what that might be, I island-hopped for a bit. But it was disappointing, since many of the islands near Bali are overpopulated with villas and tourism, to the point that some of the once-pristine coves are often filled with party barges toting playground slides and lots of alcohol.

As I sat in bewilderment, wondering what was to come next, I began having thoughts of traveling to places I'd wanted to visit for twenty years or more. In the back of my mind, I'd had a desire to travel to Morocco, to sit with the Bedouins in the Sahara Desert while riding a camel, and to visit the islands of Malta and Gozo, just south of the southern tip of Italy on the Mediterranean Sea.

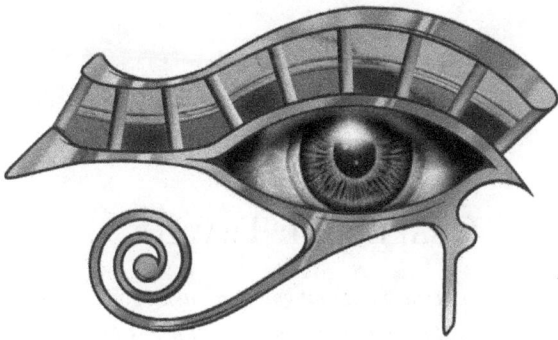

CHAPTER 14

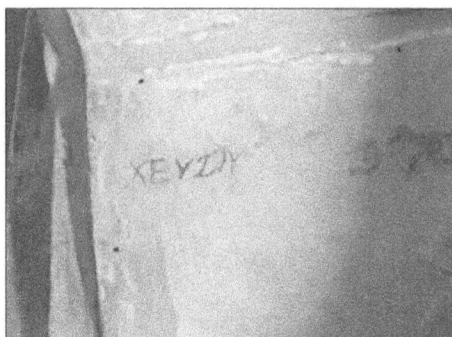

Chapter 14: Travels

"But you cannot have ecstasy without going through agony. If the gold wants to be purified, it has to pass through fire. Love is fire." ~Osho Gita

A Few Days in Barcelona

The strong urge to travel quickly turned into a reality, and I was on my way. Barcelona was my first stop. The cabby who took me from the airport to my accommodations was very friendly, sharing a lot about the small village he'd grown up in, as well as suggestions for eateries near my accommodations. I settled in, then went for a walk, ending up on La Rambla, an avenue lined with restaurants and shops. I enjoyed browsing the shops, but soon realized I'd worked up an appetite. It was getting late, so I decided to find somewhere close to where I was staying. Several people, including the taxi driver, had warned me of pickpockets and other shady characters hanging out on La Rambla. I was even told of an incident in which a thief grabbed someone's suitcase and fled on foot, never to be caught.

Near my home base, I saw an Italian restaurant. Many people were entering and exiting the establishment, so I figured it had to be pretty good. I crossed the busy street, walked in, and saw a packed house. The hostess took me to the back of the restaurant where one small, cozy table was nestled in a little alcove. I perused the menu and ordered a pizza. As I sat there, I thought how ironic it was that I was sitting in an Italian restaurant in the middle of Barcelona. But the place was packed with locals laughing and talking loudly while enjoying their cuisine and friends. When my pizza arrived, it was spectacular looking, with fresh ingredients, a subtle crème sauce, and freshly shaved ham in the center. It was a thin crust pizza, and the extreme heat bubbled the crust in just the right way. I enjoyed my pizza, as well as a tiramisu dessert that simply melted in my mouth.

Over the next few days I explored the city. I snapped a few photos of the infamous Basilica La Sagrada Familia by Antoni Gaudi, as well as the Arc de Triomf, Cascada Monumental, Mirador de Colom, and Font de Santa Anna, where I spent considerable time. I saw several of Barcelona's famous sculptures, such as Roy Lichtenstein's *El cap de Barcelona*. Then it was time to travel to my next stop, the Island of Malta.

EXHILARATION AND DISAPPOINTMENT IN MALTA

Malta is an archipelago in the central Mediterranean between Sicily and the North African coast. It's a nation known for historic sites related to a succession of rulers including the Romans, Moors, Knights of Saint John, French and British. Its capital Valletta, a lively, bustling city with many buildings dating back to the 16th century teems with cathedrals, palaces and forts. The impressive Grand Harbor offers a dramatic arrival. The top archaeological attraction is the UNESCO-Designated underground prehistoric temple the Hal Saflieni Hypogeum temple ruins, with 5400 square feet of subterranean complex of halls and burial chambers dating to circa 4000 B.C.[12]
    [https://shorturl.at/kuEGR]

One of the reasons I wanted to travel to Malta was to visit the complex halls and burial chambers of the Hypogeum. Nineteen years earlier, when Sarah and I were together, she had given me a CD that was recorded and produced in the chambers. The vocals and chanting of the female voices were mesmerizing, giving me a sense of another era. I, too, wanted to sing and chant in the complex halls. It is said that at the right tones and octaves, one could be healed of maladies, and I wanted to experience this for myself. I also wanted to meet with Radha, a woman in Malta who had been doing healing work for over twenty-five years and had been knighted with the Maltese cross. Leanne, a friend of mine, highly recommended that Rhada and I meet, believing that we had more to explore regarding future connections and work opportunities.

In the late afternoon, I arrived at the Airbnb where I would be staying, in the capital city of Valletta. It is a city in which cathedrals, palazzos, farmhouses, villas, and even city walls were erected of Maltese limestone. I contacted Radha and we made plans to meet later for a stroll and dinner. As we walked arm-in-arm the few blocks to the center of the palazzo, we felt like old friends. She told me about Malta's history: the Knights (Templars) and so much more. We enjoyed ourselves thoroughly as we walked the streets filled with the sound of ringing bells.

Radha suggested we have dinner at her friend's restaurant, but it turned out to be closed. She suggested another one, but we found that it, too, was closed for the evening. We spent the next twenty minutes scouting out a place for evening dining. We were in the center of the main palazzo, and we ended up ducking into a restaurant as rain began to fall. We found comfortable seating towards the back of the restaurant. During the course of our meal, we shared many of our life's experiences and beliefs, but it wasn't until we were sipping chamomile tea that she revealed her deepest secret. Tears began to well up as she told me, "I am dying of colon cancer. It's in advanced stages."

As the words left her lips, I blurted, "You are not going to die yet. You have things to do."

Upon hearing my words, her tears began to flow. Shocked by what had just come out of my mouth, I heard a little voice inside me flashing, "Is what you just said true?"

Radha excused herself to go to the restroom and compose herself. When she returned, that little voice in my head said, "Go to the restroom." I thought that was odd, since I didn't feel I had the need to go, but I have listened enough to that little voice to know I should excuse myself from the table and go to the men's room. I traversed what seemed like more catacombs, only to find the restroom deep underneath the restaurant.

Just as I entered the restroom, I heard that little voice again. My doubting Thomas said, "Did you speak the truth about her condition?"

I looked to my right, peering at an old, spiral, ascending staircase. And there it was: an engraving in the Maltese sandstone: KEVIN. My name was deeply engraved, several feet above my head.

I quickly looked to see if anything else might have been cut into the walls but as I scanned the entire restroom, nothing else appeared. I was so taken by the event, I snapped a photo on my cell phone of my name on the wall. Then I headed back to our table to share with Radha what I had just experienced. I showed her the photo, and her tears began to flow again as I told her that was Spirit's way of confirming what I had said.

Yes, I concluded, it *was* the truth.

The next day, we visited a number of sacred temples. As we walked several of the pathways, the wind was blowing hard and several bursts of air pockets blasted us. I thought we might be airlifted off the ground. Radha clutched my arm as the wind blew across our path.

The day after next, I was scheduled to visit the Hypogeum. I'd booked the ticket online twenty days earlier and was never given a confirmation receipt for my purchase. All I had to go by was the date and time that I had memorized. Sometimes, that is iffy at best. I hired a Bolt vehicle, which is similar to the on-demand Gojek in Indonesia, and sped off to the Hypogeum to verify my admittance ticket time and date. The man behind the counter said, "Yes, it is at two o'clock p.m. tomorrow."

The next morning Radha dropped me off at the Hypogeum, and with much excitement I waved goodbye to her. Since I was a bit early, I sat in the small waiting room until the other guests arrived for our tour. The lights in the waiting/retail area were so bright I had to go outside to cool off. When everyone was there, we were instructed to place all our belongings, including cameras, in the little lockers provided. I was disappointed but I understood how the flash of many cameras could potentially harm the interior spaces.

As we descended into the catacombs, something struck my mind. The space in which I was standing was dead energetically. It was as if someone or something had capped the energies of the place. Extreme disappointment began to settle in as I tried to remain open to other possibilities. But I was fairly certain my initial feelings and thoughts were correct. I had waited more than nineteen years to experience such a place, and to be met by disappointment was disheartening. But I ended the tour with gratitude, knowing I had experienced what I'd waited so long to see. Radha and I ended up spending the rest of the afternoon visiting several temple ruins scattered throughout the countryside.

That evening, we bid each other good-bye. The next day, I was to travel to the island of Gozo.

HEALING MODALITIES ON GOZO

The next morning, there were again gale force winds, and I wasn't sure if the ferry to Gozo Island would head out into such rough seas. But the ferry arrived a few hours later, amidst the torrential sea. The massive ferry's journey was tumultuous, the seas rising and falling. Everyone took shelter in the interior of the ship as waves crashed over the bow. As we rounded a small island halfway along our journey, we were protected for a short period of time from the stormy seas. Once we went beyond the tiny island, the sea rose up again. But docking on Gozo was uneventful since the docking area was in a harbor shielded from the sea.

Once I was again on dry land, a sense of relief set in and I took a taxi to my accommodations. The description on the internet booking site had described it as a farmhouse. It was nothing of the sort—more like a house with three floors, five rooms, and a mutual kitchen. But as soon as I met the proprietor, Maximo, I was reassured. His attention to detail and morning breakfast spreads deserved nothing short of a five-star rating. After putting my suitcase and backpack in my room, I headed downstairs and met a couple of young women talking with Maximo about a cave nestled on a cliff. The three of them were getting ready to visit, and I went along. The ride over potholed roads was bumpy and led to a gravel road, then the edge of a cliff. We stayed for some time, sheltered from the high winds, taking photos of the cliff face and the beach below. On my second day, I rented a car to visit a few places of interest, among them the UNESCO World Heritage site Ggantija Temples.

Prior to my departure from Bali, I'd done a little research to see if there was anyone on Gozo that I might want to meet. I found a woman named Karin who had a retreat center that looked interesting, so I reached out. What piqued my interest was her work doing past life regression and other healing modalities.

Later that afternoon, I was scheduled to see Karin at her home, which was only a kilometer away from my Airbnb. She'd asked that I park on the street and walk down her driveway to her home. Upon arrival, I found what would actually be called a farmhouse. I walked down the narrow gravel driveway with fresh green grass lining its edges beneath the sandstone-stacked walls.

The feeling I had as I walked down the driveway to that 900-year-old farmhouse was pretty amazing. The familiarity of the walk and old farmhouse gave me a strong notion that I had been there before. As Karin greeted me, what she said gave me pause.

"I'm glad you made it here," she exclaimed. "I've been waiting for you for quite some time."

I simply smiled and entered her home, not exactly sure what she'd meant. But I had a sense I was about to find out. We spent the next few days traveling to megalithic temples of the Divine Feminine. There were many scattered on hilltops, and we could see numerous cathedrals perched in the distance. From where we stood at a particular megalithic temple, the cathedrals had a symmetry that I found interesting.

Near the end of the day, we walked out to the edge of a cliff with a spectacular view of the ocean and the cliff face, and a glorious setting sun. Karen shared that she had brought many women to this sacred place and conducted ceremonies to the Divine Feminine. She asked if she could do a ceremony on my behalf as we took in the scenery. I felt honored and gave her my consent. She began to dig through the items she'd brought with her and pulled out some sage and a small conch shell. She smudged my body, then went once again to her satchel, pulling out a metal Himalayan bowl and a friction mallet.

She proceeded to walk slowly in circles, rotating the mallet around the rim of the bowl. I lay there relaxing, wondering what might happen.

As she approached my head, she said, "Now I know even more about you and who you are." Once again, my curiosity was piqued but I remained silent until she completed her ritual.

When she was done, I asked, "Who am I?"

"I will reveal it to you in due time," was her response.

We sat for several more minutes photographing the beautiful sunset and the steep cliff faces. She insisted I sit on a huge rock at the edge of the cliff. Due to my fear of heights, I was not too happy with the idea, but I did it, sweating profusely as she snapped photos of me. With each click of the aperture, I felt as though I was going to leap over the edge of the cliff. It is a weird sensation I always have when I'm on a cliff's edge—the need to jump and get it over with.

We returned to her majestic farmhouse, talking into the wee hours of the night. During our conversation, Karin began to use words and phrases that repeated themselves. I could feel an energy I'm familiar with, when something traumatic is about to release. I probed her with several questions and prompted her to place her intention and awareness to her body and the feelings that were present. Several minutes went by, then she began to shake—slowly at first, then more forcefully.

"Stay in the energies," I said. "I feel something very significant is about to release." I was sure that it was not only from her emotional and physical bodies, but also from her energetic body that this release would occur. I had experienced this with numerous clients.

Moments later, she revealed something that rocked her world. She told me about a traumatic event that had occurred with her mother. She said it was something she could not release, no matter how hard she'd tried. As she spoke, tears flowed and she took a deep breath of release. This went on for several minutes. I could see in her facial expression and the energies around her face that this trauma was released and forgiven. She eventually beamed from ear to ear, knowing that what had plagued her for most of her life was resolved and released. I felt grateful to be involved in such an experience.

We sipped tea and nibbled hors d'oeuvres. Then Karin, with pad and pen, took a historical profile of my life, including all the events and memories of my life. Good, bad, and traumatic, I held nothing back. This took several hours, ending somewhere around 3:00 a.m. Both of us had reached a level of exhaustion, and I excused myself and headed back to my accommodations. The plan was that next morning, she would perform her work on my behalf, which she said would take several hours.

At 9:00 a.m., I drove to the farmhouse, parked on the street, and walked along the driveway to the house. Karin greeted me with a newfound happiness in her facial expression. I was excited to see what would come about with her work. She took me to the section of the house where she had her workplace. She handed me a glass of water with cucumbers and flowers in it. Then she sat down at her desk and began her work with me.

First, she rearranged the many crystals and precious stones in white porcelain dishes on her desk. She laid out before me a circle of precious stones, with a clear crystal pointing upward in the center of the circle. "The circle of stones represents all of the events in your life," she said. "The large crystal in the center is you."

She went on to say that many of the outer experiences were meant to take me away from my authentic self. They were forces meant to distract me from my "Light of Being." Looking at it from this perspective made a lot of sense to me at that moment.

Then she instructed me to lie down on her massage table. She placed several blankets over my body. She told me a bit about what was to happen, then the journey began. My mind was alive with thoughts. *What will happen? Is something going to be revealed to me?*

A few deep breaths later, my mind began to quiet as I entered a deep meditative state. Karin began asking questions that she'd formulated from our conversation the night before. I began seeing clear images in my mind. First was a triangular shape, approximately four or five feet high, with another beside it to the right, twice the height of the first. Both had small triangular shapes covering the larger triangular shapes. In the background appeared to be a council of Elders.

As I allowed these thoughts to free-flow in my mind, I began to

217

hear a voice coming from the larger pyramid, directed to the smaller one. I felt confident that I was the smaller of the two, as I heard sounds telepathically. I realized the large triangle was my teacher and wisdom figure. One of the things I heard was, "You will have a difficult time where you are going, but don't give up." I immediately realized the reference to "where I was going" was planet earth. I looked in the near distance, watching the council observing the two of us. Then, as quickly as the vision came, it dissolved leaving me with this impression and understanding.

The rest of the modalities Karin performed seemed to be in some distant place. Then I came fully aware of my body once more. I realized how hot I was with the two heavy blankets on me. As I rose from the bed I asked once more, "Who do you believe I am? You have said this now three times."

"You are Jesus Christ," Karin said. "And I have been waiting four and a half years to marry you."

Stunned, I sat motionless on the massage table. Then I replied, "I am not Jesus Christ the Man, but from time to time, I have been told that I hold the Light of Christ within and through me, and I never know when it might happen. It is often spontaneous when it occurs." I went on to say I was deeply flattered that she wanted to marry me but I hadn't come for marriage. Placing my hands on my heart, I thanked her for such insights and beautiful work. I explained how I understand the concept of Jesus and the Christ Light. I shared with her that Jesus was the man and the Light of Christ is the energy that is connected to the Source of all things.

"Jesus was an avatar," I said. "Several before him were trying to wake up humanity to their Divine Nature. Not the Nature that churches and other religious beliefs hold—that we need to be redeemed and we are somehow flawed through guilt and shame."

We hugged and I thanked her again. Then we headed to the kitchen for something to eat.

CITY OF CONTRASTS: CASABLANCA

I headed onward for the last leg of my trip: visiting the Moroccan cities of Casablanca and Marrakesh, then a three-day journey to a desert camp in the Sahara Desert. Casablanca means "White House." The city is also called Dar al-Bayda, and as the largest city in Morocco (over four million people), it's also Morocco's economic center and is considered a global financial center. The movie *Casablanca*, starring Humphrey Bogart, Ingrid Bergman, and Paul Henreid, was filmed here in 1942.

I was looking forward to my visit to Casablanca. I'd hoped to meet my friend Kenza there, but unfortunately she was in Paris for a jewelry trade show. But she was kind enough to send her driver to pick me up and show me the city. He drove me to the apartment I'd rented for the next couple of days, and we agreed to meet the next morning for a sightseeing tour. The next day, we first headed to see the massive Hassan II Mosque:

This opulent mosque, built at the enormous expense, is set on an outcrop jutting over the ocean with a 210m-tall minaret that's a city landmark. It's a showcase of the finest Moroccan artisan-ship: hand-carved stone and wood, intricate marble flooring and inlay, gilded cedar ceilings and exquisite zelliage (geometric mosaic tile work) abound.
[https://www.lonelyplanet.com/morocco/casablanca/attractions/hassan-ii-mosque/a/poi-sig/1379578/1331580]

I was impressed by the massive size and height of the tower. I marveled that humans can build such structures of architecture and art but still can't figure out how to get along with one another. I was taken in by the geometric mosaic tile work, its sheer size, and the colors. My driver, Tarik, was very helpful and courteous. Whenever a photo op arose, he made sure the snapshot was taken.

I asked Tarik where he enjoyed eating real Moroccan food. One of the things I'd noticed was the Moroccan diet, which consisted of lots of meat and little-to-no vegetables or bread. We made a lunch stop at Cafe Maure, at the harbor, enjoying a traditional dish called tagine. Tagine is a round clay dish with a cone-shaped lid used to lock in heat and flavor, braising meat (usually lamb) and vegetables until tender and super fragrant. Later that evening, we ate another heavy dose of Moroccan meat and bread at Tarik's favorite food stand as we watched the International UEFA soccer tournament. That evening's game was between Morocco and the United States, and the U.S. took the game into overtime to win. Tarik was very polite about the outcome.

Another thing I noticed was the condition of many of the buildings in contrast with the cars the Casablancans were driving. It seemed that many of the buildings were in disrepair while many people were driving BMWs and Mercedes. The imbalance struck me as odd.

I made several more trips to the waterfront. On my last evening, I chatted with a group at a local restaurant. The next morning, Tarik dropped me off at the train station and off I went to Marrakesh. I enjoyed watching the people getting off and on the train during the several-hour trip. At one point, a girl of about ten across the aisle from me was singing a simple tune that was quite charming.

In Marrakesh, I not only wanted to see the city, I also hoped to ride a camel and sleep in the Sahara desert. This was something I had romanticized—sitting with the Bedouins in their camp under the stars. The camel trip and Sahara overnight were still in the making, but I was optimistic.

JEMAA EL-FNA SQUARE IN MARRAKESH

"Marrakesh, a former imperial city in western Morocco, is a major economic center and home to mosques, palaces and gardens. The Medina is a densely packed, walled medieval city dating to the Berber Empire, with maze-like alleys where thriving souks (marketplaces) sell traditional textiles, pottery and jewelry. A symbol of the city, and visible for miles, is the Moorish minaret of 12th century Koutoubia Mosque."

[This content comes from the Knowledge Graph, Google's collection of information about people, places and things.]

At the Marrakesh station, I enthusiastically hopped off the train for my next adventure. The station was jammed packed with people arriving and departing, creating a lot of confusion. I spied a McDonald's. Not what I really wanted; I don't normally eat their food.

But I appreciated the familiarity of the place, so I went in and ordered a fish sandwich. After stopping at an ATM to get a little more local Dirham currency, I went out to hail a taxi. It became somewhat of a brawl between two men fighting over who was going to take me to my destination, and I simply laughed off the discomfort. Before getting in the taxi, I made sure the driver and I agreed on a price for the trip. Then we headed to the Jemaa el-Fna Square where I was to stay in a small hotel. It sat on the southern edge of the Jemaa el-Fna, down a labyrinth of narrow streets. After leaving my taxi, I got somewhat lost. Eventually, I bumped into a young man with a big handlebar mustache who was happy to walk me down the winding, merchant-filled streets. It became evident that even he had a challenging time as he asked for directions from several other locals. But we eventually found our way.

I won't even go into how I was treated by the man at the hotel upon my arrival. It was one of my most disappointing events while traveling. But I tried to shake it off. Tired, excited, and a bit frustrated, I settled into my room, took a quick shower, and headed out to the merchants' square.

The Jemaa el-Fna Square is one of the main cultural spaces in Marrakesh and has been one of the symbols of the city since its foundation in the eleventh century. I spent the day among the merchants. In the evening, it turned into an enormous food market. I was to learn that this massive transition happened daily. During the day, the square was filled with cobra snake charmers and merchants selling their wares. I was shocked by their aggressive nature when I tried to take a picture. As soon as my camera went into a position to shoot, several people demanded money for the opportunity. This happened to other travelers, too, and I noticed many putting their cell phones and cameras away. On one occasion, several people were arguing about the whole thing, and I pulled out some Dirham and gave it to the vendor. He smiled and thanked me.

I have traveled to many locations in the world, and my observation in Marrakesh was that the residents were frustrated with tourists. It felt, to me, that they were only interested in how much money they could extract from visitors. When I called my Moroccan friend, she said, "Be careful, many are rather dishonest and will try to take your money."

There was one positive transaction with a young man selling Moroccan men's apparel and shoes. He was very friendly and we struck up a great conversation. I eventually purchased a pair of shoes and a pair of pants from him, and I was quite pleased by the experience.

Other than that, my time in Morocco began to take on a theme of dissatisfaction around the level of chaos and greed I observed. I kept getting thoughts from Spirit to sit in the center of the market and hold the "Light." I heard thoughts that this place must be leveled to start again. I really wasn't sure what it all meant, but I ended up sitting and standing at the center of the market, in prayer, holding the Light.

SAHARA SURPRISE

After a couple of days in Marrakesh, I was ready to leave. I had paid for additional nights at my lodging, but it was evident I couldn't stay another day. By luck, there was a merchant selling a trip to the Sahara desert, with a two-night stay and a camel ride. After meeting the sales agent and a previous customer who was at the time booking another tour, I was excited by the opportunity.

At 6:00 the next morning, I met a driver who took me to the gathering spot for the trip. We were sorted out and assigned to large vans for the three-day trip. It ended up being ten hours of driving each day. The first day was quite a drive before we stopped at our night's lodging, a Bedouin hotel. The temperature had reached freezing, and as we checked in, we learned there was no heat in the hotel. Many of the travelers were upset. One woman yelled, "I paid extra for heat! "As we were arriving, I'd noticed that two couples departed. They must have gone to another place of lodging.

For the next couple of hours, while dinner was being prepared, many of our group huddled around the one space heater in the lobby to keep warm. Finally, dinner was called, and we gathered in the only room with warmth. It was enjoyable as we all conversed about the day's travel and accommodations. We met others from our home countries, and the dinner was satisfying and nourishing. After dinner, I climbed the stairs to the third floor and curled up, fully clothed, under three heavy, weighted wool blankets. It was a cold night, but the morning finally came, and we were off for another ten-hour drive with a couple of tourist stops.

One of the stops was in a Bedouin village. It was pleasant seeing their gardens and water systems and getting a reprieve from the day's travels. We saw Bedouin rugs being produced in many colors and sizes. Some in our group were a bit unsettled by the small interior of the building where they sold rugs. It seemed to be a pressure sale as each new group of rugs was laid before us. But all in all, it was an experience to remember.

The next site was a small village called Ouarzazate that seemed to be very famous. It's located between Merzouga and Marrakesh. Nearby is Ait Ben Haddou, an almost 1,000-year-old fortified village located on the route to the Sahara Desert. It was previously used as a meeting point for travelers from Sudan on their way to Marrakesh.

As we navigated the small village and across a dry river bed, I was in awe of the mud and straw structures and the village that had been created. But as we entered the walled city, I spied posters of Hollywood movies pasted all over the walls. Ait Ben Haddou is popular among Hollywood producers. They love to shoot films there, since the village provides timeless visuals for period pieces that would otherwise be difficult to replicate. Some of the shows and movies filmed there include *Game of Thrones* and *Gladiator* with Russell Crowe. Talking about this encompassed the majority of the tour guide's repertoire, which I found displeasing. I wanted to hear more about Ouarzazate's deep history. So I separated from the group to visit the small mud homes and grounds on my own.

After another eight hours of driving and a stop at Ait Ben Haddou, we arrived at the parking area for the camel ride and the evening's rest. We adorned our heads with the hijab cloth we'd purchased at our prior stop, to protect us from the blowing Sahara sands. I was separated from my travel group and paired up with three young guys. Unfortunately for me, it turned out to be more of a party for them as we rode our camels across the edge of the Sahara desert. I was hoping for a quiet, contemplative trip. But during most of the trip, all we could see was the parking area. The edge of the sand and the land were to our left the entire time. Our Sahara excursion consisted of many stops for photo ops and selling of gifts and wares. The camel guide was very polite and often stopped to tell jokes.

Eventually, I saw tents off in the distance. I was relieved that the ride would be coming to an end, so I could get some quiet and rest. When we were within a few hundred feet of the campsite, I saw two couples from my original group who were heading off in another direction. I was confused because they'd been headed toward beautiful white tents with wonderful lighting, but then the path veered in the opposite direction, leading to tents made of black canvas cloth. They appeared quite gloomy. One of the guys in my group even quipped, "Those must be the workers' tents." To our surprise, they were not.

It was another evening without water and heat. We huddled around the campfire for several hours for warmth. Three of the women I'd been traveling with ended up around the campfire as well. They, too, were disappointed by the accommodations and lack of heat. I really felt sorry for one of the women, because she was due to give birth in about a month. She was a real trooper.

After another sleepless night under the weight of heavy woolen blankets, we received a 5:30 a.m. wake-up call, inviting us to breakfast. Most of us were out of drinking water, and when we asked for some, our waiter said, "We have no water." He laid a plate of blackened and rotten pomegranate and various other fruits before us. In his best English, he said, "Fruit not rotten. It's good, eat."

We all just started laughing. The laughter was a pent-up release of our frustrations, and it was well needed. We returned to our respective tents, packed what little gear we had, climbed onto the camels in freezing temperatures, and navigated our way in the darkness back to our vehicles, about an hour away.

We made the eight-and-a-half hour drive back to Marrakesh, stopping on a couple of occasions for a restroom and stretching and to watch a soccer tournament. When we made it, I couldn't have been happier for a warm room, a hot shower, and a clean place to lay my head.

The next day was my trek back to Casablanca, where I would spend the evening before returning back to Bali. After two misguided detours in the train station and two cab rides, I finally made it to my hotel. I was grateful that the trip was almost over. In my frustration, I told my final taxi driver that I had never been so happy to leave a country as I was to leave Morocco. I could tell by his embarrassed facial expression that he knew I knew he'd doubled the cost of the cab fare. I told him the driver before him had negotiated the fare on my behalf since I had so much misinformation about when to get off the train.

"I need the money," he said.

"You've given your price," I said. "You should stick to it."

He reached in his pocket and handed me the additional fare he'd added. I looked at him for a moment. Then I gave it back to him, saying, "You need this more than I do."

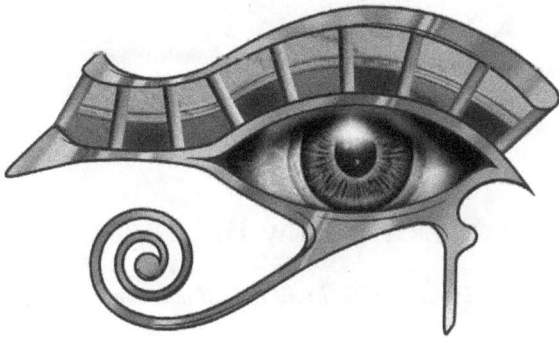

CHAPTER 15

CHAPTER 15: NEW BEGINNINGS

"Your desire to know your own soul will end all other desires." ~Rumi

LEAVING THE PYRAMIDS

It was now a month before Christmas. I was still working with the Pyramids, but I knew that my time there was coming to an end. It was a new chapter change for me, but until then, I hadn't been ready to see it.

After I returned from my trip to Morocco, a friend named Moojka, a gifted sound healer for whom I had the utmost respect for her skills and world travels, showed up at the Pyramids. She was a concert musician and understood the dynamics of sound and vibration, as well as their abilities to heal. She had traveled the globe teaching the art of sound healing, and I was quite honored to be in friendship with her.

We greeted each other with big hugs. Moojka said she'd come to hear me play that morning. I was flattered and very appreciative of her kind words. That morning, everyone attending had entered the Sun Pyramid to my guided sound healing. I'd played as I always did, feeling first my heart's energy and then asking quietly for guidance from Spirit as I played.

Afterward, Moojka made a point of saying, "I need to share something with you but not here." Fifteen minutes later, we met in the restaurant. Her determined beeline to where I was standing told me she had something important to say.

Her expression was stern. "Get out of here now," she said. "Your energy is being taken here."

She went on to say that those who were assisting me during my session were part of the problem. Emphatically, she restated, "Get out of here. Your time here is done."

I was in total agreement with her. I knew she was speaking the truth, because when I'd returned from my trip to Morocco, I remembered the moment I had stepped on the Pyramids property. I'd felt an overwhelming urge to throw up. It wasn't the first time this had happened to me, and I understood its significance.

I also recalled that after one of my Full Moon sessions, a man in the restaurant bee lined directly to me, just as Moojka had. "What the hell are you doing here?" he'd asked. "This place is too small for you. You need to be in the world."

"When Spirit shows me the direction," I'd said, "I will do so." Now, it was Moojka's words that drove the point home. Another compelling reason was that my business plan was completed. Also, I was getting ready to go to Sedona to start the project.

The very next day, I told the Pyramids' owners that I would no longer be participating with them. I handed in my notice with great gratitude for all that I had learned and created while there for the previous eight years.

ANOTHER TRIP, AND A REVELATION

With my newfound freedom and a few months off, I felt another trip coming on. This time, it was to the island of Borneo, where I would visit the sovereign state of Brunei, then Northern Malaysia to see the orangutans, and finally the city of Balikpakpan, the soon-to-be-capital of Indonesia.

After much planning, I took off for Brunei and the other points of interest. Looking back, Brunei was the highlight of my trip. I met a man with seven daughters, and he became my hired driver. It was interesting hearing his stories about his family, the book he had written, and how his life was, on some levels, quite similar to mine. We were the same age, both of us writers sharing our knowledge and spiritual experiences.

My travels to Northern Malaysia turned into another trip from Hades. The points of interest and hotels I stayed in were in the two-star range, and I quite honestly tried to return home, but because of the massive price increase for changing my return ticket, I decided to tough it out. After a few days, I happily returned to Bali. This trip drove the point home that I needed to complete my next book and to finish the business plans for both Sedona and Satonda. I returned and started immediately on all fronts.

The book (which is this book) progressed quite rapidly, but the business plan for Sedona went a little slower, since it had been more than twenty years since I'd written one. But what began to happen during this process opened a whole new world and direction for my life.

LES SOLATIONS

What happens next, I am still trying to wrap my head around. Ever since my first visit to Satonda and the purchase of beachfront property on the island of Moyo, coincidences, synchronicities, downloads, and visions had come to me quite rapidly. I'd known that a holistic center was to be built on the island of Moyo, and also Satonda would play a magical part in the development.

For several weeks, I meditated and prayed for guidance around the design and master plan for the holistic center that I wanted to create on Moyo and Satonda. Then came that Christmas morning, which brought into my conscious awareness how it was to be developed and laid out. In a moment of inspiration, after I opened my eyes from the night's sleep, I received visuals around the center's layout. It was based on sacred geometry, numerology, and frequencies based on particular harmonics. I also knew it had to be built from natural materials that were available, because it had to be in tune with Mother Nature. The raw materials would be made from bamboo, rammed earth, and teak wood.

The master plan, as I sketched everything out that I saw in my mind's eye, resulted in a mandala of a floral pattern. At the center would be a bamboo structure with a roof line resembling the frequency of 111 Hz. This would create the center point where everything would attach, just like the peduncle of a flower. Branching out from that center point would be four rectangular shalas, equally spaced, reaching out to the four directions and each containing various modalities such as sound healing, yoga, watsu, cold plunge tanks, and sauna. Around and interspersed between the shalas would be thirty-six bamboo villas. The first nine would be smaller villas, and flowing outward would be twenty-seven more, expanding in size, thus creating the parts of a flower. As I drew this out in a matter of minutes I was not fully aware of what it was that I was designing.

Within days, I began working with several contractors and bamboo designers on the logistics, design, and costs of such a project. It appeared everything was flowing beautifully. Each person in their field of expertise felt encouraging and inspiring. As I continued working with Jordan, my counterpart in the Moyo/Satonda project, we narrowed down the costs and budget to begin the project, once the funding was in hand.

One afternoon I read on my phone that my storage was at 95% of its capacity. I was instructed to delete some files to open more memory. I started going through the 1,500 or so photos and deleting, until I got to a picture of Day, myself, and Adi in front of the painting with the lotus flower. It was surrounded by the three gray, multicolored triangles I had seen in my past life regression with Karin on the Island of Gozo.

I was blown away. What were the chances that those colors and triangles would show up again, especially relating to Satonda? This really got me buzzing with ideas.

As if that wasn't enough, I received a text from Jordan, saying he had found something that a friend of his in California had built for Burning Man. It was a picture of a large pyramid with the same three repeating colors housed in small triangles.

This simply blew me away. One of the things I have come to understand is that when something shows up in threes, it means, "I am in the Divine flow of Creation."

That evening, I had a session with Lorraine. When I shared what had happened, she asked, "Do you know what all of this means?"

Reluctantly, I responded, "I don't really understand its full meaning."

"You are building a Galactic portal for the advanced beings of Light to enter into the Earth's frequency," she said.

It all made sense. Especially during this crazy period of transitioning on Earth from climate change to Artificial Intelligence and the potential of World War III. Also, this is the time on Earth that I refer to as the "Collective's Dark Night of the Soul." It is referenced by many Indigenous Peoples around the world as a time of the *Clearing* and the *Purification of Mother Earth*. It's believed that this purification, on Earth, has happened four previous times throughout history. These predictions were also connected to what I'd been shown ten years earlier, in a vision, by the avatar with long blonde hair in an aqua-colored uniform and the Council of the Galactic Federation of Light.

A day or two later, Jordan and I had a meeting at the restaurant Melali to discuss more of his findings around the project. As we sat there reviewing the information he had gathered, a man walked in.

Jordan looked surprised but enthusiastic. He said to the man, "Juan, this is Kevin, who I have been talking to you about."

Juan seemed unimpressed by the comment. "I'm going to work on some emails," he said, walking off.

Jordan looked perplexed. We went back to our meeting, discussing more about the project. Thirty minutes passed, then Juan came by the table again. "Juan," Jordan blurted out. "This is Kevin, the guy I was telling you about. I told you about the pyramids of multicolored triangles and his visions."

Juan appeared shocked. Then he apologized, asking if he could sit with us and chat. As I showed him the pyramids and the course of events around the tri-colored triangles, Juan remarked, "Do you know what this is?"

"What do *you* think it is?" I asked.

"You are building an inter-dimensional portal, or gateway," Juan said. "It is designed to open the frequencies and open the portal for 'Light Beings' to enter Earth's lower vibration and frequency. They needed this structure for this purpose."

I'd understood this prior to Juan's sharing, but it was good to hear it from another. Both Jordan and I beamed. "Yes, I have heard this from other sources as well," I said. It was obvious to all of us that something greater was occurring, and we were all too excited to keep working. We decided to explore it more at a later date.

During one of our next meetings, this one with a builder and Canadian contractor who had lived in Bali for twelve years, we discussed much of what Jordan, Juan and I had shared at our last meeting. Then something else happened. I was trying to think of the name of a project that I'd recently visited, in order to help the contractor understand the design and style I wanted to create. For the life of me, I simply couldn't remember the project's name. I kept saying the word *Solation,* over and over. Finally, Jordan looked at me and said, "It's called Solana Villas and Retreat Center."

He was right, but I couldn't get *Solation* out of my head. There is one thing I have learned, and it is this: If I keep repeating a word or phrase over and over, I know that it is a sign to further investigate what's going on. So I did. I asked Jordan if he'd look up the word *Solation* and send it to me, and I would look at it later (since I was deep in conversation with the builder). But Jordan looked it up then and there, telling us that solation is the process of liquid transitioning into a gel. The image that came to my mind was a caterpillar in a cocoon. Eventually, the gelled form of the caterpillar transforms into a beautiful butterfly.

Our meeting ended enthusiastically, just as the one with Juan had. We vowed to stay in touch and further our discussions.

I continued to hear the word "solation" being repeated in my mind, so finally at 2am I got up and did an internet search for the word. What I found was simply mind blowing.

The Solations can appear to be white-skinned humanoids, though their true forms are beings of light. They are able to turn themselves immaterial and through this form are capable of extracting pure Core from asteroids.

History – The Solations were the first beings to appear in the universe in an event they called the First Light or what is commonly called the Big Bang. They coexisted alongside another race called Draykanians, a race of pure darkness. Both dwelled within a dimension outside the confines of the material universe, and though both species were diametric of one another, an eternal stalemate lasted for eons between the races.

When the jump-gates were created by an unknown race they accidentally stumbled onto the realm of the two ancient species. The Draykanians seeing a chance to shift the cosmic balance in their favor, tried to invade the material universe. The builders, sensing their error, closed the gate, but not before one Draykanian escaped. To maintain balance one Solation was sent outside to counter the imbalance cause by the Draykanian. The jump-gate connecting to the celestial realm was lost creating the legend of the Lost Gate.

[ens.fandom.com]

Based on this, I came to the conclusion that the Holistic Center will be called "Les Solations."

NOT THE RIGHT TIME

On Thanksgiving Day 2023, I was invited to a traditional dinner at a friend's house in Kuta, south of Ubud. The turkey and mashed potato dinner was quite pleasant, as was the conversation, since I typically would not observe the holiday, instead carrying on doing what I do on a normal day. The host, my friend Mary, was gracious and hospitable. I was happy to see a number of people I knew. I also enjoyed carving the Thanksgiving turkey. Being an American, I employed my many years of the tradition of carving a turkey.

A man with three young adults caught my attention. He and his children seemed different than most, but I couldn't put my finger on why he came across that way to me. Then, at the end of the dinner, Mary leaned across the table to me. "You need to talk to Eduardo," she said.

"He's also into pyramids."

Moments later, he sat down in the open chair next to me. We began to talk about pyramids and what he had just completed in Mexico City. He shared that he had just completed a construction project of pyramids, domes, and a children's school. He showed me pictures on his phone of the completed project. I was blown away and excited, knowing this was similar to what I was to build in Sedona and that I had, for the first time, seen a version of it in completion.

Talking about the experiences we'd encountered along our journeys, Eduardo and I realized there were numerous parallels in our lives. We talked about many things of an esoteric nature, the pyramids of Giza, and so much else.

Eduardo shared that he'd been told by an old man years earlier that he would complete such a project and that he was not to worry about the money. "The funds will come," the man had told Eduardo. I asked about his budget and learned that his completed project was well within the monies I needed for my project in both Sedona and Satonda.

Sharing his final thoughts, he hesitantly, almost whispering, said "The moment the project was completed, my family and I had an attempted assassination at our home. We came to Bali to lay low for a while."

I walked away from our meeting knowing that things are still in process for my project, but I'd been given a sign. Someone who crossed my path was of a similar mindset, giving me the continued hope that the projects were still a possibility. I believe it was a clear sign from Spirit that this is not yet the right time to build.

A NEW VANTAGE POINT

A friend with whom I've had wonderful conversations over the last year or so sent me a link to a podcast that opened me, once more, to an expanded version of my life and the bigger picture. It gave me a new vantage point into my journey. The podcast was hosted by Robert Edward Grant, a scientist/mathematician, who was in conversation with Richard Rudd, a mystic and the author of *The Gene Keys*; and Alan Green, a celebrated pianist, composer, author, and Shakespeare scholar. These three individuals share their areas of expertise with one another and their interpretations within their fields. Their conversations illuminated my own journey. As the podcast is described, "Prepare for a mind-expanding experience as they unravel Shakespeare's enigmatic identity and decode the veiled symbolism across language. Together, they unveil covert codes concealed within Shakespeare's masterpieces, illuminating a deep understanding of the human experience and tapping into the depths of collective consciousness."

Their conversation gave me a deep sense of clarity about where I am on this life path of awakening—something I hadn't actually been able to put into words. It was important for me to hear Alan Green and Robert Grant speak of the Egyptian pyramids of Giza and their connections mathematically to the Masculine the Feminine, and then of transcendence. Alan further talks about his connections to the pyramids and how Shakespeare's sonnets fit perfectly in them. He discusses how the uppermost part of the pyramid is enlightenment. He says he talked with a man who believed he had attained enlightenment through sex with a prostitute. Alan states that the experience of the Divine prostitute is the final stage before enlightenment. He has further details about this, but I believe they are best listened to in the podcast. For me, this directly correlated with the archetype of the prostitute that I'd experienced some time earlier. Alan further broke that down into the idea that it was an aspect of the Divine Feminine, which Alan believes is the final state before enlightenment.

I highly recommend that those on a path of awakening check out this podcast.

https://robertedwardgrant.com/podcast-episode-015/

TATOU – WE ARE ALL HERE

Just a couple of weeks ago, during the last Full Moon of 2023, one of my closest friends and adopted Lakota brother, Joseph Grey Wolf, walked the Red Road home. He was a friend, mentor, and someone with whom I'd enjoyed many long talks over a good Cuban cigar. I learned of his passing when I received a phone call from his wife Ayanvil (pronounced "yawna lee"), who was of the Cherokee Nation.

I was stunned and tearful. Ayanvil and I reminisced, sharing memories of singing, of the sweat lodge (also known as the purification lodge, ASI in the Cherokee Nation, and referred to by the Lakota/Blackfoot as Inipi, meaning Mother's womb), and so many, many other stories. I had always felt he would be a powerful presence in the project that is to be built in Sedona.

That night, I completed the second night of the Full Moon fire ceremonies and sound healing at the Pyramids. I dedicated the fire ceremony to Joseph Grey Wolf, knowing that he had walked the Red Road home and was now at peace with the Elders. I received confirmation when a man coming out of the Pyramids said to me, "I received a message during your sound healing that I believe it is intended for you. The messenger was named Joseph and his message was, 'I am here but not for you.'" Then he said, "Joseph spelled the word tatou. T-A-T-O-U. He wanted you to know the proper spelling."

Knowing that Joseph was present that evening, my heart warmed, giving me a sense of completion about his death and the reminder that we are all connected, whether on the physical plane or on the other side. That evening, all the participants shared a meal. I sat with the man who had shared the message from Joseph, as well as his two friends from Australia. We all seemed to be kindred spirits (souls).

At home, I looked up the word *tatou.* Two definitions presented themselves. One was that of the armadillo, and the other was the French plural of a word that meant "We are all here."

This took my breath away. A saying entered my state of consciousness. Mitakuye Oyasin is a Lakota term which roughly translates, "I call to all of my ancestors who have come before me and all of those who shall come after me to be present with me in this moment." It is a belief that the wisdom and presence of the ancestors from the other side often culminates in a deep healing and a new wisdom.

The spiritual meaning, armadillo, means *rest.* Time to burrow in.

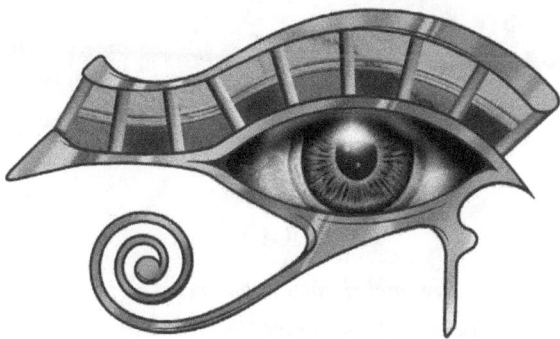

EPILOGUE

EPILOGUE

"One individual who lives and vibrates to the energy of pure love and reverence for all of life will counterbalance the negativity of 750,000 individuals who calibrate at the lower weakening levels."
    ~Dr Wayne Dyer

If you have gotten this far, I appreciate your attentiveness and perseverance. I hope the experiences I've shared have been helpful, insightful, or inspirational. Deep in my heart, I believe we are ultimately walking each other home through this divine process called Life. We are going home to our hearts.

I also thank all who have entered my life, and I theirs, on this beautiful journey called Life. For the ones who are yet to come, I am excited.

I'd like to share where I am with the potential projects. I have completed the business plan and financial statements for Sedona and have put the numbers to paper for Satonda. It took several months to complete the Sedona paperwork due to my accountant's workload. Upon its completion I called Agung.

"How much is the project?" he asked. "And are the documents ready?" I gave him the figure and he replied, "That's exactly what the investor transferred to the account."

What a coincidence, I thought.

Then came the bad news. Agung went on to tell me the investor had just fallen into a coma, and the project was on hold. The coma, as best I could surmise, was brought on by his advanced age of ninety-five years. I was a bit shocked and naturally disappointed, but I remain hopeful. To this day, some six months later, he is still in a coma. But I have been in conversation with a couple of potential investors. We'll see how things unfold. In the meantime, I have returned to the Pyramids, and I am waiting (surrendering) until something presents itself.

All that has been given to us is a gift. All experiences. It's all in how we perceive it.

AFTERWORD

So where am I today?

First, I am going to chill out for a while and allow life to simply flow.

I am scheduling new upcoming international travel to Japan and Cuba. Global travel is the best education.

My potential projects in Sedona and Satonda will be held near and dear to my heart with bated breath of their beginning. While waiting I will once again lean into patience once more. I also hold the idea that all that is to happen will happen in Divine flow and I will do my part.

My healing philosophy and of being of service involves working with those who come to me helping them empower themselves and to uncover their authentic self. This will involve travel, workshops for both individuals and groups and speaking engagements.

For more information, or to schedule a session, please contact me via my website: kevinwestrich.com centerforsoulfulguidance.com or social media at FB: kevin.westrich.96 and sedonasoulscapesretreats or on IG: westrichk.

Trust, Patience, Surrender	kevinwestrich.com	centerforsoulful guidance.com